William Cumming

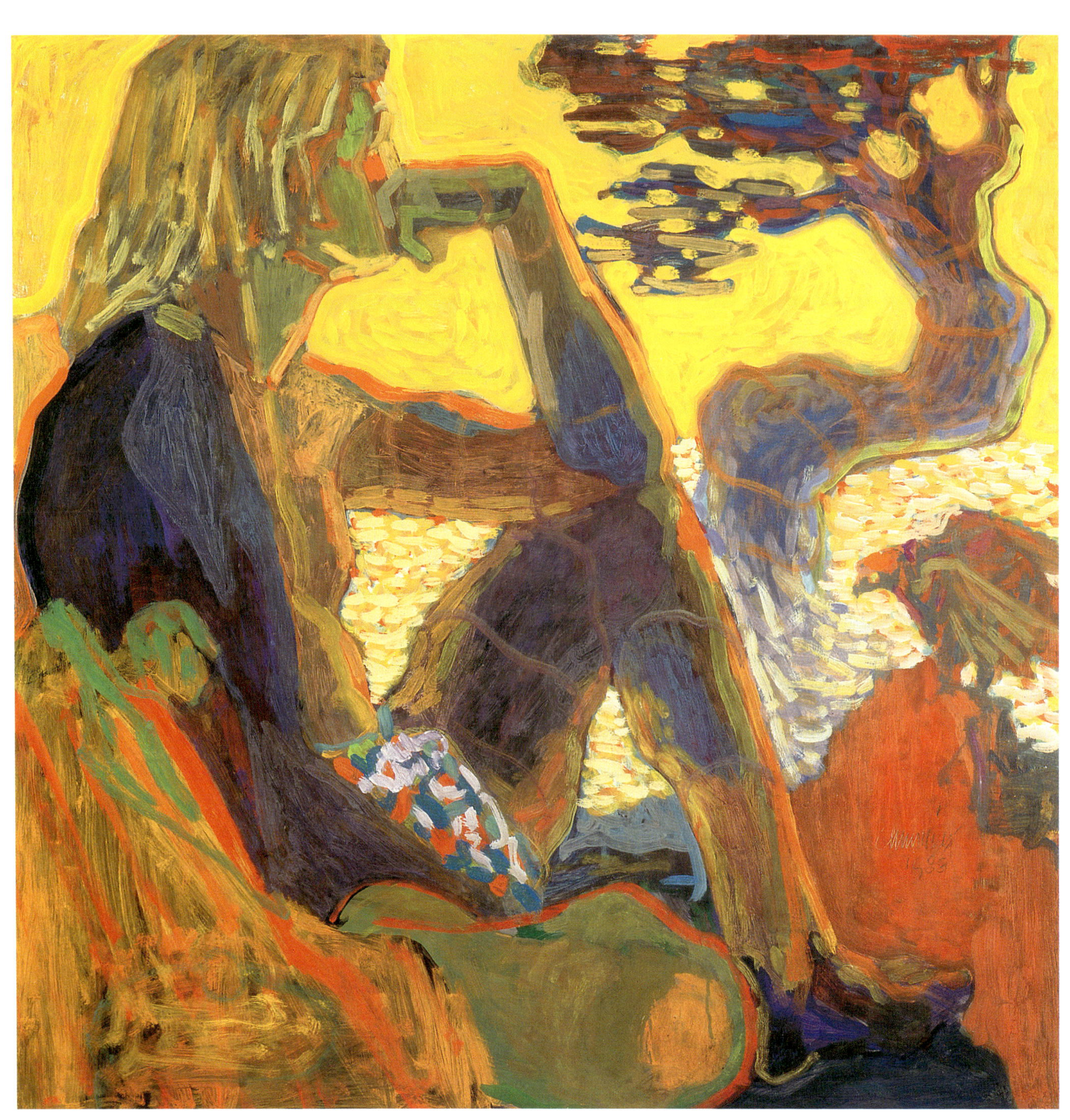

William Cumming

The Image of Consequence

Matthew Kangas

The Charles and Emma Frye Art Museum
Seattle

in association with

University of Washington Press
Seattle and London

Printed in China
Designed by Phil Kovacevich / Kovacevich Design
12 11 10 09 08 07 06 05 5 4 3 2 1

The Charles and Emma Frye Art Museum
www.fryemuseum.org

University of Washington Press
P.O. Box 50096, Seattle, WA 98145
www.washington.edu/uwpress

Library of Congress Cataloging-in-Publication Data

Kangas, Matthew.
William Cumming : the image of consequence / Matthew Kangas.— 1st ed.
p. cm.
Issued in connection with an exhibition to be held Aug. 20, 2005-Jan. 1, 2006, Charles and Emma Frye Art Museum, Seattle.
Includes bibliographical references.
ISBN 0-295-98554-2 (ltd. edition hardcover : alk. paper) — ISBN 0-295-98555-0 (pbk. : alk. paper)
1. Cumming, William--Exhibitions. I. Cumming, William. II. Charles and Emma Frye Art Museum. III. Title.
N6537.C794A4 2005
759.13—dc22
2005012226

The paper used in this publication meets the minimum requirements of American National Standard for Information Sciences—Permanence of Paper for Printed Library Materials, ANSI Z39.48-1984.

This publication was produced in both a limited slipcase edition, with a linocut print signed by the artist, and softcover.

Frontispiece: *Poet at Big Sur (Homage to Robinson Jeffers)*, 1980, Oil and tempera on board, 35 ½ x 35 ½, Charles and Emma Frye Art Museum MA(G)585, Anonymous Gift

page 160: *Untitled* (Hatted Man with Polka-dot Shirt), 1966, Pencil and watercolor on paper, 10 ¾ x 8 ¾, Museum of Northwest Art 2004.039.001, Gift of Simon and Carol Ottenberg

CONTENTS

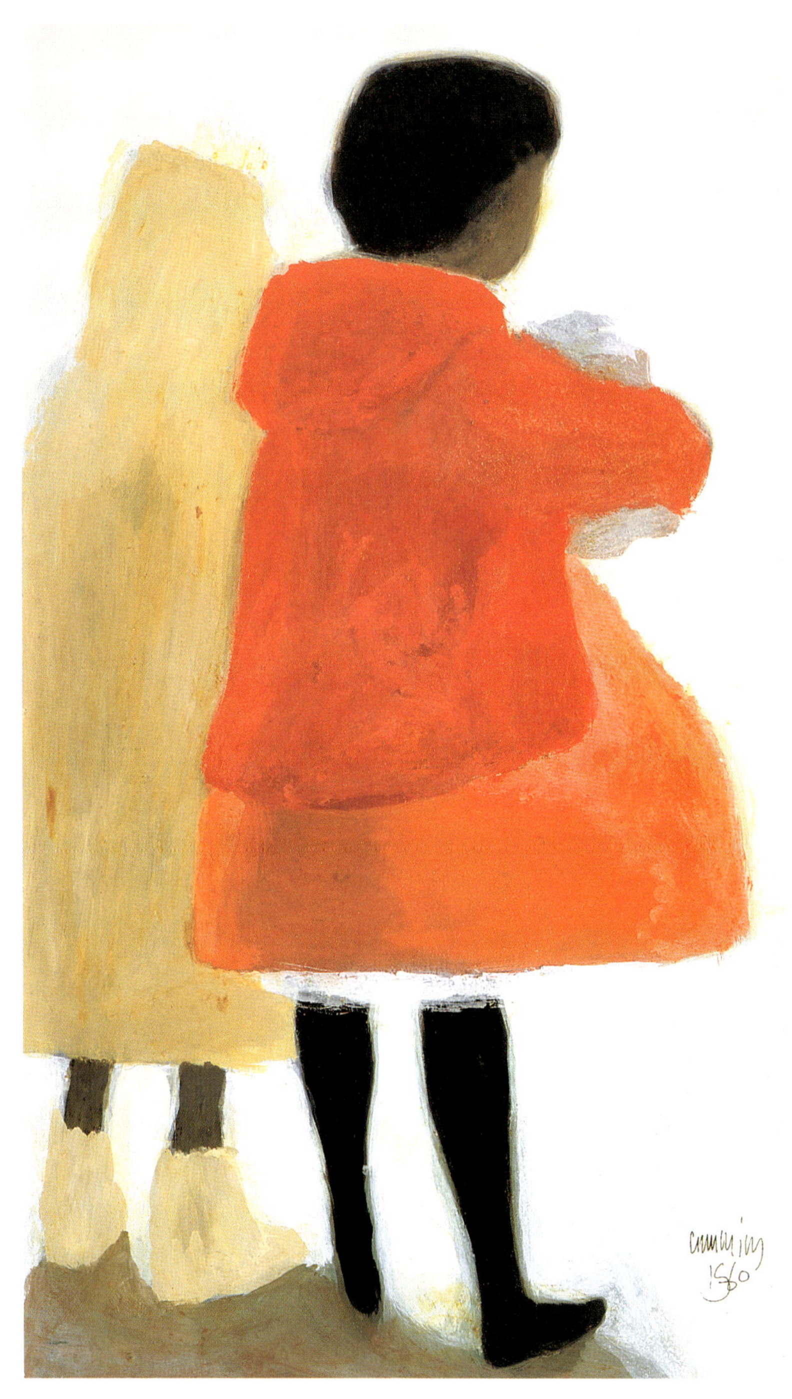

Two Girls, 1960
Oil and tempera on board
34½ x 22¼
Charles and Emma Frye Art Museum 1960.014
Purchase Prize from First Invitational Exhibition
by Puget Sound Artists

FOREWORD

William Cumming: The Image of Consequence, an authoritative survey of the last living artist associated with the Northwest School, offers a seventy-year retrospective of almost a hundred and fifty drawings, prints, works on paper, watercolors, oils, temperas, and sculptures organized for the Frye Museum by independent curator and art historian Matthew Kangas.

For the exhibition and this publication, Kangas charts the evolution of William Cumming's work from socialist realism—a representational art created in service to political ideals—to a socially relevant but less instrumental art that Kangas terms "figurative formalism." As Kangas demonstrates, Cumming remained committed to the figure through the 1940s and 1950s, when many other ambitious Northwest artists, like their colleagues in other parts of the United States and Europe, developed an allergy to this compositional device, turning their interests instead to modernist abstraction. Cumming later merged his passion for populist figuration with an increasing focus on color, shape, and form. This productive mix of representation and abstraction is where Matthew Kangas stakes his claim for Cumming's unique contribution to Northwest art history.

The twentieth century's dichotomy between abstract art and representational art (the avant-garde versus kitsch, to use American art critic Clement Greenberg's politicized and influential phrase) has softened and blurred. As an increasing number of contemporary artists demonstrate an interest in recognizable subject matter, the term "representational art" is losing its negative connotations. This emerging context provides an ideal opportunity for artists, scholars, and audiences to reexamine the work of an artist like William Cumming.

It is particularly gratifying to the staff and trustees of the Charles and Emma Frye Art Museum that this project exemplifies both our long championing of Northwest artists and our commitment to representational art, in all its complexities. Cumming had works shown at the Frye every year from 1959 to 1963. In 1960, he was awarded first prize at the Museum's First Invitational Puget Sound Area Exhibition.

This exhibition catalogue would not have been possible without the strong partnering of the University of Washington Press, under the direction of Pat Soden, and the generosity of those individuals who supported the initial idea as conceived by former Press Director Donald Ellegood, who unfortunately did not live to see his vision fulfilled. We are especially grateful to Diana and Christopher Ackerley,

Diahann and John Braseth, Sharon Lee and Don Hebard, Sharon and Steve Huling, Pete Higgins and Leslie Magid-Higgins, Debra and Peter Rettman, Maki Tamura and Anthony Erwin, Douglas Williams and Ann Haggerty-Williams, Gordon Woodside, and Donald Teichman for their support.

We want to give special acknowledgment to those institutions which so graciously agreed to loan works to the Frye on the occasion of this exhibition, including the Museum of Northwest Art; Whatcom Museum of History and Art; Portland Art Museum; Henry Art Gallery, University of Washington; Tacoma Art Museum; and the City of Seattle, Mayor's Office of Arts & Cultural Affairs Portable Works Collection. Our most heartfelt thanks go to our sister institution, Seattle Art Museum, for its generosity and collegial goodwill during a time of great transition. We also thank the many individuals who were so kind as to agree to share their beloved Cumming works with the public.

Special thanks go to Matthew Kangas whose exhibition and essay give us new insights into and appreciation for the art of William Cumming. Northwest art scholar Laura Landau's close reading of the essay was invaluable. In closing, we acknowledge with deep appreciation the work of Chief Curator Robin Held and other Frye Museum staff involved in all aspects of this project: Sherry Prowda, Mary Coon, Donna Kovalenko, David Anderson, Julie Johnson, Annabelle Larner, Charla Reid, Mark Eddington, Mary Jane Knecht, TJ Johnson, and former curator, Debra Byrne. Their dedication and commitment have been outstanding.

Most of all, we thank the artist, William Cumming. Many years ago, he observed that the success experienced by his colleagues in the Northwest School brought with it such disillusionment that he had himself decided to eschew it. Perhaps more important than fame and success, William Cumming has achieved a full life as an artist, activist, teacher, and thinker. Most certainly he has won our critical admiration, respect, and affection.

MIDGE BOWMAN
Executive Director
Frye Art Museum

ACKNOWLEDGMENTS

Many individuals at many institutions have helped immeasurably to make this exhibition and accompanying book possible. Their prompt and thorough assistance is greatly appreciated. Besides the wonderfully supportive and professional staff at the Charles and Emma Frye Art Museum, two other people deserve special thanks: William Cumming and John Braseth, president of Gordon Woodside/John Braseth Gallery. Without the former and his generous donation of time and loans from his personal collection, the project would not have been as detailed as it has become. Without the latter, the entire project would never have happened. John's generosity and insistence that a Cumming retrospective was overdue proved to be matched only by his enthusiasm and agreement to act as liaison to the many collectors and other supporters of Cumming's art and achievement. I also owe Christine Charters, my curatorial assistant, a great debt of gratitude for her countless hours spent on research and other related details. Phil Kovacevich of Kovacevich Design did a magnificent job on the book and the special hardbound and slipcased limited edition. Thanks also go to the artist for the prints commissioned for each of the special edition copies.

The many others who helped include Kim Baker, Jim McDonald, and the Hon. Gregory Nickels, the Mayor's Office of Arts and Culture, City of Seattle; Julie Breidenbach, principal, Lowell Elementary School, Seattle Public Schools; Marty Dennis, executive director, Northshore Senior Center; Ann Eichelberg, registrar, and Amanda Han, rights and reproductions, Portland Art Museum; Diane Elliott, curator, Swedish Medical Center; Anthony Erwin and Gordon Woodside, Gordon Woodside/John Braseth Gallery; Mimi Gardner Gates, director, Chiyo Ishikawa, chief curator of collections, Lauren Tucker and Nicholas Dorman, conservation, Traci Timmons, research, and Jill Walek and Scott Nacke, rights and reproductions, Seattle Art Museum; Darlene Hamilton, John LaMont, and Steve Kieson of the History, Travel and Maps Department, and Stan Shiebert and Carletta Wilson, Arts, Literature and Recreation Department and the Scandiuzzi Writers Room, Seattle Central Library; Gail Hansen, Art Institute of Seattle; Frederick Hill, Berry-Hill Galleries, New York; Mrs. Violet Kangas; Jackie Kozak, collection curator, SAFECO Insurance Companies; Gary Lundel and Karyl Winn, University of Washington Library Manuscripts Collection; Patricia McDonnell, chief curator, and Emily Shirbroun, exhibitions assistant, Tacoma Art Museum; Janis R. Olson, registrar, and Lisa Van Doren, curator of art, Whatcom Museum of History & Art; Susan Parke, acting director, and Lisa Young, external affairs director, Museum of Northwest Art;

Mark Rosenzweig, research library, *People's Weekly World*; Shannon Shepard, director, Holt Labor Library; Pat Soden, Marilyn Trueblood, and external reader, Laura Landau, University of Washington Press; Elizabeth Brown and Judy Sourakli, curator of collections, Henry Art Gallery, University of Washington; and Laura Thayer, registrar, and Jochen Wierich, curator of art, Northwest Museum of Arts and Culture. Photographs are credited elsewhere but I do want to thank the principal photographers for this enormous project: Jim Ball, Annette Bauman, Eduardo Calderón, Bill Cannon, Christopher Dahl, Dean Davis, Frank DeSantis, Paul Foster, David Howe, Ron Karabaich, Thomas Kelly, Paul Macapia, Bob Mattherson, Richard Nicol, the Estate of Josef Scaylea, and David Scherrer.

M. K.
Seattle, April 2005

(facing page) JOSEF SCAYLEA
(American, 1913–2004)
William Cumming, 1963.
Black and white silver
print photograph
14 x 10.
Collection of William Cumming

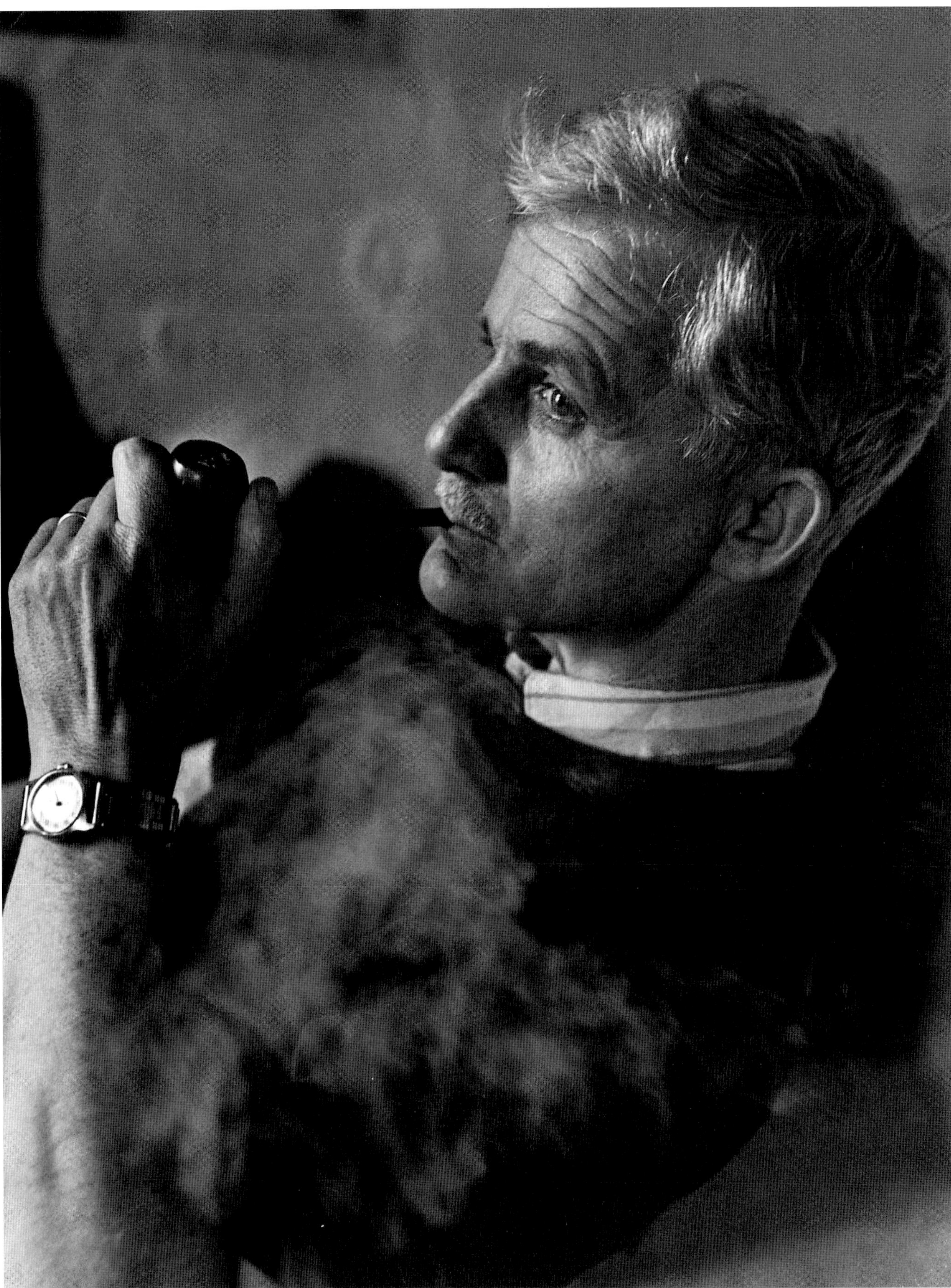

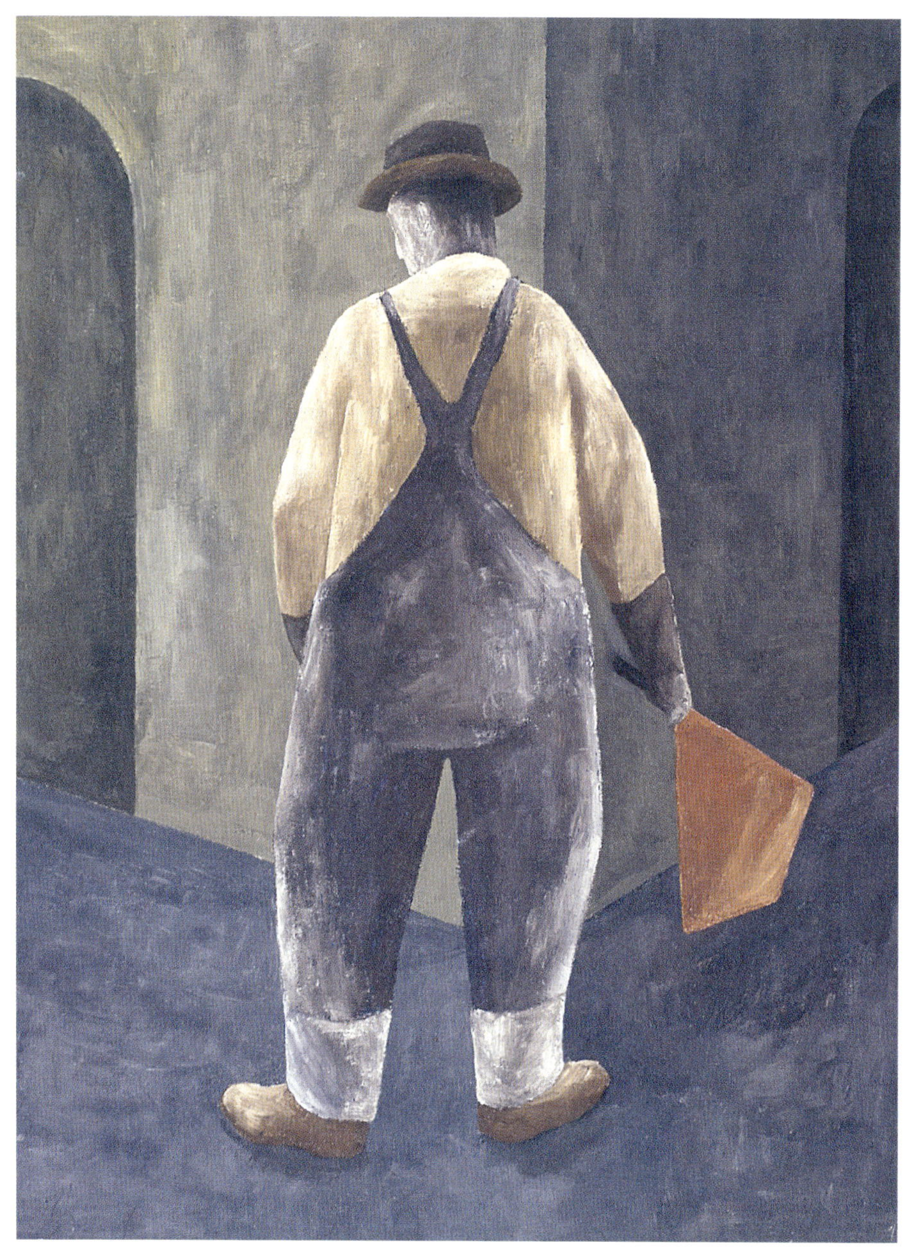

FIG. 1
Workman, 1943
Gouache on board
20 x 15
Collection of B. T. Callahan

INTRODUCTION

American art history of the Pacific Northwest has lagged behind that of other regions of the United States partly because the cultural institutions of the region—museums, galleries, and collections—developed later than those in other geographical areas. Although one of the first parties of settlers in Seattle, the Denny Party, landed at Alki Beach on the SS *Exact* in 1851, the Seattle Art Museum did not open until 1933, six years after the founding of the state's first art museum, the Horace C. Henry Art Gallery on the new campus of the University of Washington.

Culture follows money and population growth. Compared to cities like Portland, Oregon, and Vancouver, British Columbia, Seattle was a late bloomer. The situation of the city's earliest artists followed accordingly. Artists exhibited sporadically in Washington Territory before the arrival of the city's first modern artist, Australian Post-Impressionist Ambrose Patterson (1877–1966) in 1919. He arrived by steamship at the invitation of the president of the University of Washington, Henry Suzzallo, to help co-found the university's School of Painting, Sculpture and Design.

Before that watershed event, visiting artists to the state included itinerant scene painters like Albert Bierstadt (1830–1902) and Sanford Gifford (1823–80), who, interestingly, painted scenes of the region both before and after their sojourns. Folk artists like Harriet Foster Beecher (1854–1915) and Emily Inez Denny (1853–1918), a descendant of the original Denny Party, made crude but earnest expressions of the wilderness and nascent settlement. However, in a conservative environment, without substantial patronage available, many turn-of-the-century Seattle artists followed the example of Imogen Cunningham (1883–1976), a gifted photographer who fled to San Francisco in 1922 after creating a stir by exhibiting nude photographs of her husband taken on Mount Rainier.

The subject of this monograph, William Lee Cumming (b. 1917), did not move to Seattle until May 1938. Before then he had been a resident of the Foster-Tukwila area south of the city, where his family had arrived in 1924 seeking better opportunities.[1]

Unique within the annals of Northwest art history, Cumming has never received the full focus of a study that such a complex figure deserves. Perhaps most widely known as the author of a loose autobiography, Sketchbook: A Memoir of the 1930s and the Northwest School,[2] Cumming's extraordinary range of creativity only begins to make sense this late in his life.

Several factors in his life have combined to make an overall appreciation of his achievement difficult, paramount among them the contradictory and occasionally

FIG. 2
Near Twelfth and Yesler, 1938
Gouache on board
9 x 13
Collection of B. T. Callahan

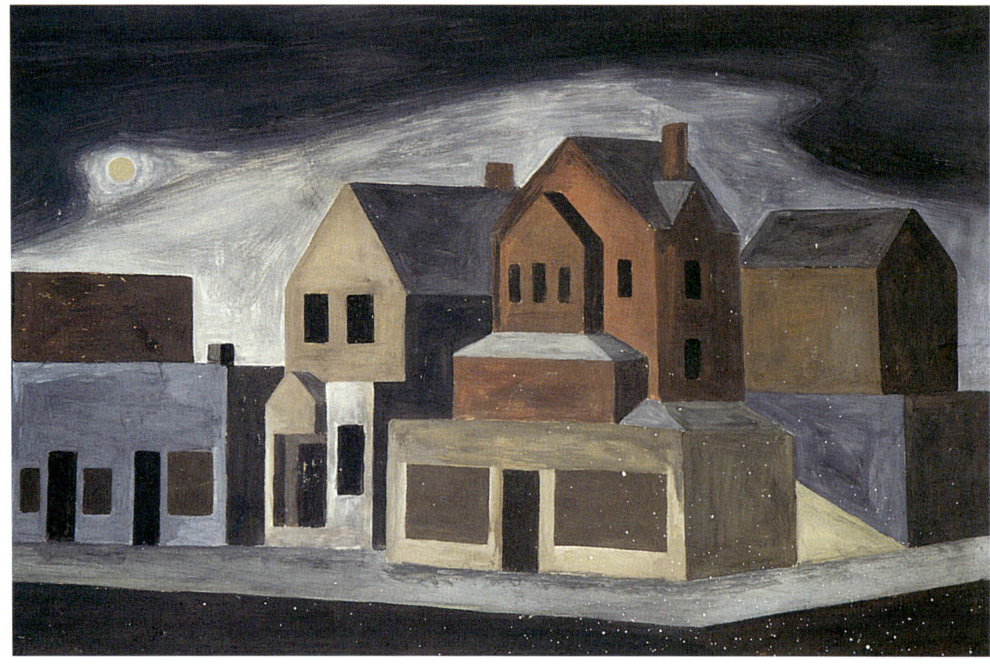

unreliable nature of *Sketchbook*. Transcribed, taped, and sometimes published interviews with the artist[3] are both illuminating and frustrating, though always entertaining to read. Thanks to generous access to the artist through interviews between December 6, 2004, and March 10, 2005, Cumming's story can be somewhat clarified and told through his own voice and occasionally revisionist memories. Autobiographical truth is refractive, dependent upon the remembered point-in-time and the strength and significance of the original events. What was left out of *Sketchbook* proves to be almost as interesting as what was left in. My interviews and research have also helped to correct a misconception about the structure of Cumming's career, normally considered (partly by his own published accounts) to have been divided into two parts. The first period, roughly between 1935 and 1945, encompasses his early years as an acolyte and teenage darling of a circle of artists and writers associated with poet and essayist Margaret Bundy Callahan (1904–61). The second part begins at his return to the art world on the occasion of his second Seattle Art Museum exhibit in 1961, which culminated in his current, highly prolific period. The artist shows no sign of winding down at the age of eighty-eight.

What has been missing, concealed (by no less than Cumming the memoirist), or repressed is the artist's middle period, 1946 through 1960, a sad, dark, and mysterious time when recurrent pulmonary tuberculosis, three marriages, the birth of four children, and prolonged involvement in left-wing politics conspired to cut back on Cumming's production. A disabled welfare recipient during these years, with fitful teaching appointments in a small commercial art school, Cumming nevertheless continued to make art, some of which has been assembled for this retrospective exhibition and accompanying book.

Like many other American artists and critics of the World War II and McCarthy eras, such as Ben Shahn, Dwight MacDonald, and Irving Howe, Cumming's ardent

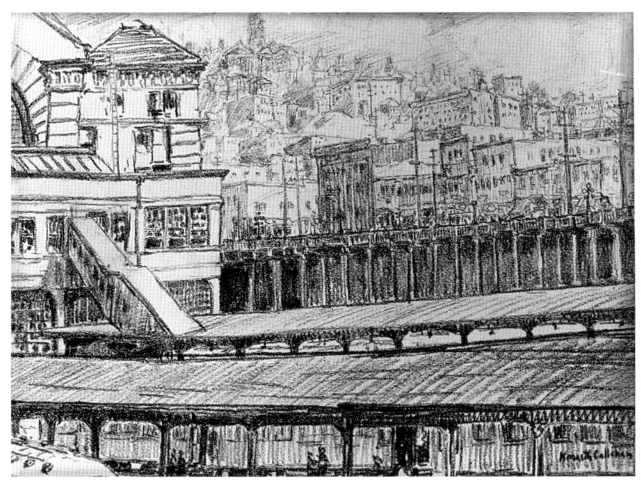

FIG. 3
KENNETH LORIMER CALLAHAN
(American, 1906-1986)
Profanity Hill, 1927
Pencil on paper
10¼ x 13½
Collection of Alan Brandmarker

anti-fascist sympathies hardened into a committed left-wing politics. As we shall see, there were very real personal reasons for this awkward development, long played down or laughed off by the artist with the hindsight of sixty years. What was denigrated and evaded by Cumming the memoirist and interviewee involves the extent to which the artist's membership in the Communist Party of the United States of America (1944–57; CPUSA) affected his art. During his long hospitalization for tuberculosis, Cumming seriously studied the writings of Karl Marx (1818–83), Frederick Engels (1820–95), and V. I. Lenin (1870–1924). Upon his release from the hospital and an abortive move to stay with a writer cousin in San Jose, California, Cumming returned to live with his father and stepmother in Spokane, Washington, whereupon he began his activities as a union organizer, youth worker, and functionary and operative for the CPUSA. He was once even listed in a National Chamber of Commerce publication as one of the "one hundred most dangerous Communists in America."[4] His life in Spokane had a lasting impact on his art, and his political odyssey as an artist is examined in chapter 3. To set the stage for a broader analysis of his art it is necessary, however, to stress at the outset how Cumming's politics touched his art long after his resignation from the CPUSA in 1957.

What remained of such an avid commitment to social justice and economic equality was his dedication to the image of consequence, that is, subjects that ordinary people could relate to in their own lives, images that could resonate without the taint of a moralizing propaganda. The residue of social realism that he witnessed in the art of his friends Mark Tobey (1890–1976) and Kenneth Lorimer Callahan (1906–86) took on far greater ramification in Cumming's art and has stayed with him to the present day. People at work and leisure, minority groups, young people and families, agricultural and cattle ranch workers, street people, and the homeless all became topics for artistic transformation. These subjects were encouraged initially by Margaret Bundy Callahan who, as Cumming remembers it, pointedly asked him, "Why are you painting these sorts of Parisian whores with their cute little bits of lingerie and black lace, like Pascin or some Parisian painter, when in your sketchbooks you're drawing the people around you all the time who don't exist anywhere else?" [5] Cumming recalled to interviewer Bill Hoppe in 1972, "I remember at the time it sort of cast me down because I looked down on these things I drew in my sketchbooks."[6]

Once Cumming took Mrs. Callahan's advice and began to take his real-life observations more seriously, an artist was born. Furthermore, whereas Tobey and Callahan eventually dropped the figure like a hot potato in, respectively, the late 1940s and 1955, in favor of a more fashionable modernist abstraction, Cumming's dark journey underground during the early years of the Cold War kept the image of consequence alive, simmering into something that could outlive the Great Depression, cope with the persecution and vagaries of the McCarthy period, and prove to be a fruitful path to the artist's final paradoxical shift: his own version of figurative formalism.

When the details of Cumming's long encounter with Communism are filled in, his determination to retain the image of consequence is not surprising. What is perhaps more problematic, though not completely inexplicable, is how he ended up at the "Finland Station" of modern art instead of on the crumbling platform of dogmatic social realism. Younger than prominent East Coast left-wing artists Ben Shahn (1898–1969), Philip Evergood (1901–73), and William Gropper (1897–1977), Cumming took a hitherto unexplained detour that they never experienced. At the same time, unlike Shahn, Cumming was never pressured to "name names" or harassed, except for an extended period of surveillance by the Federal Bureau of Investigation that he only learned of many years later.[7]

As art critic Clement Greenberg (who had had his own flirtation with Trotsky and Marx) wrote in his preface to *Art and Culture*, "I would not deny being one of those critics who educate themselves in public,"[8] so Cumming's published and unpublished comments on art delineate clearly his glacial assimilation of modernism's basic precepts: flattened pictorial space and a rejection of Renaissance perspective, close-value colors, abstracted figures, and a unified field of brushstrokes leading, if not always in Cumming's case, to an "all-over" composition. Cumming's image of consequence, however, constructed of detached horizontal brushwork and dazzling chromatic expression, was closer to Édouard Vuillard than to Jackson Pollock.

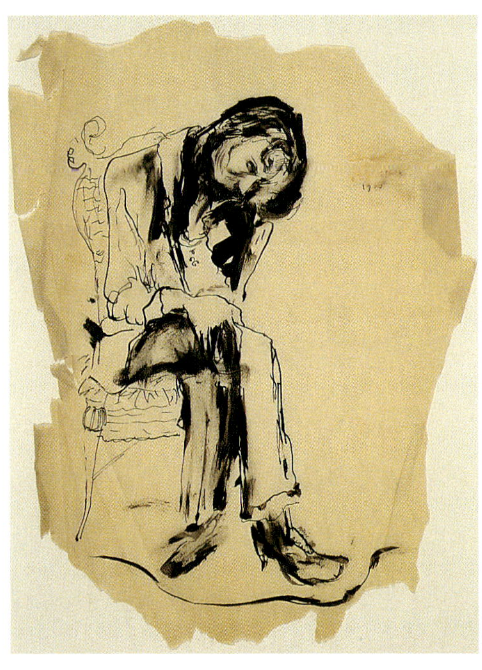

FIG. 4
LUBIN PETRIC
(American)
William Cumming, 1938
Ink on paper
21 ½ x 15
Collection of the artist

Cumming is also unique in that he is one of only a few American artists who began their public careers as art critics rather than as painters; he wrote roughly a half-dozen music and art reviews for *Town Crier* in 1937. Many art critics, such as Peter Plagens, Ron Glowen, and even Clement Greenberg, tried to succeed as painters only to fall back upon art criticism as a safe haven. Cumming, however, did the opposite. In this sense he resembles another Seattle artist, Barbara Noah, who began as an art critic for *Artweek* and *Art in America* before concentrating full time on her photo-based paintings and prints. Cumming's "cultural nexus," which is examined in detail in chapter 2, makes clear his roundabout arrival as a young artist of promise picked up by the Callahan circle: they were attracted to the art critic first.

As a Johnny-come-lately to American literature through his 1984 publication of *Sketchbook*, Cumming's long literary apprenticeship is discussed in chapter 4.

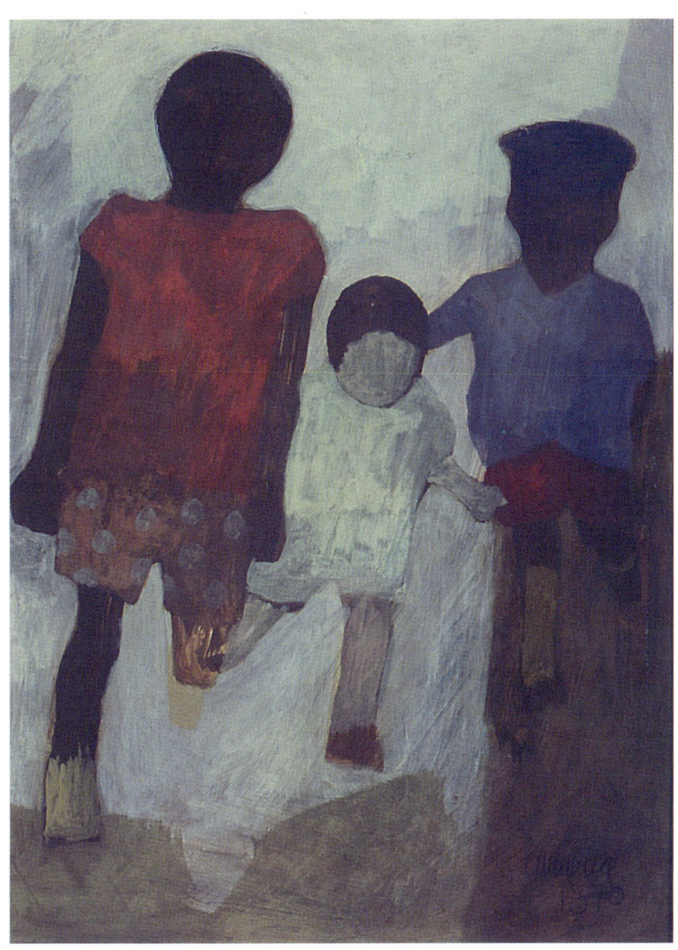

FIG. 5
Three Boys, 1970
Oil and tempera on board
21 x 15¾
City of Seattle, Seattle City Light 1% for Art
CL03.003

Cumming's massive reading program began before his hospitalization in 1942, but while at Firland Sanatorium his reading included Tolstoy, Dostoevsky, Emerson, Thoreau, Twain, D. H. Lawrence, and his beloved Thomas Wolfe—along with the requisite Marx, Engels, and Lenin.[9]

William Cumming's art bridges regional and international modern art currents. In fact, it embodies a fusion of both local-color "human interest" with abstracted figures and chromatic experimentation. As such, Cumming offers a new paradigm for discussing Northwest art in general. By shifting the focus of studies away from fin-de-siècle Orientalism and "iridescent light" as explanations,[10] a far more sophisticated, multicultural set of influences may be accommodated. Cumming was not alone as an artistic intellectual of his generation and "philosophical anarchist," as he explained himself to an interviewer.[11] It is apparent that, compared to the polyglot mix of occult philosophy and Eastern religions embodied in Graves or the shallow enthusiasm for mystery novels of Kenneth Callahan, Cumming was closer to the widely read cosmopolitanism of Tobey. Tobey's 1919 conversion to Baha'i World Faith found its counterpart in Cumming's conversion to Communism in 1942: both were relatively esoteric bodies of thought that promoted human equality and the brotherhood of man.

No one book or exhibition can fill in all the blanks, especially those so artfully left concealed by such a self-conscious memoirist as Cumming. Thanks to a series of interviews and available archival material, we can attempt a better, fuller picture of Cumming's achievement. With the advantage of a long life despite catastrophic personal interruptions, Cumming has accomplished much more than his older one-time mentors. As a commentator on their generation and observer and active participant in his own times, he takes on greater significance as a cultural figure with the passage of time. Socially relevant and artistically refined, his art forms its own pillar of Northwest—and American—art history: modernist realism.

Thus, his long life has led from the artist's early acclaim in the form of a Seattle Art Museum exhibition at the age of twenty-four, through his comeback "rehabilitation" show at the same museum in 1961 (when he was forty-four), to the current

FIG. 6
Cutting Horse II, 1974
Oil and tempera on masonite
14 3/4 x 19 3/4
Courtesy of Mr. and Mrs. Robert M. Sarkis

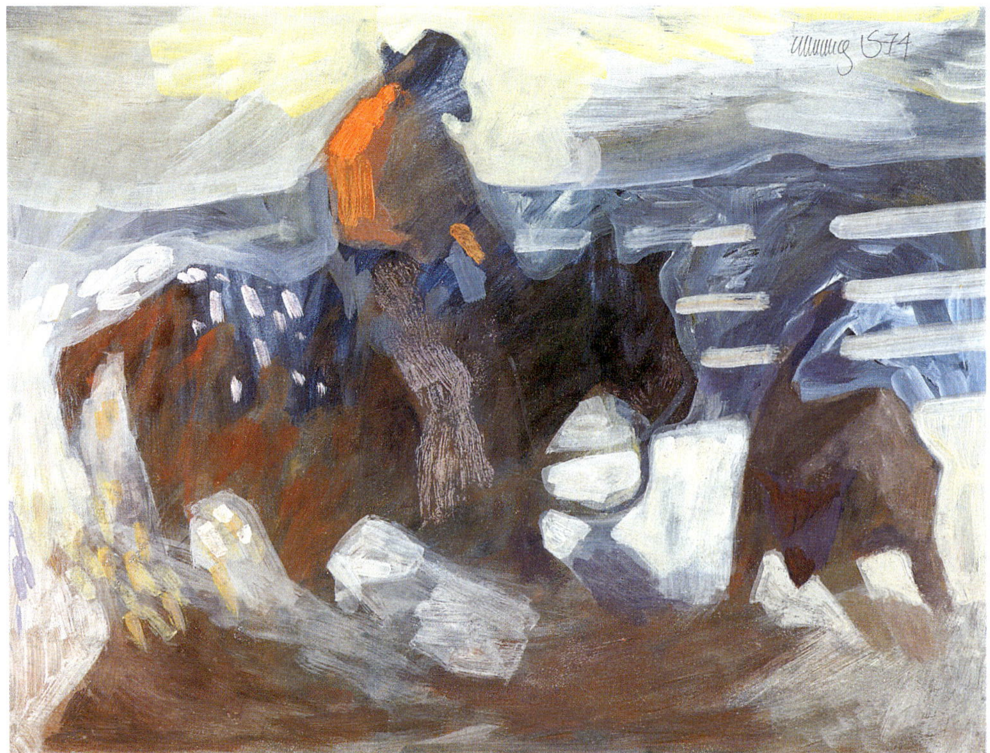

stocktaking survey at the Charles and Emma Frye Art Museum. Conceived and executed far from the centers of artistic and political power, his achievement now seems important and more necessary than ever to examine. With his social-political subject matter—the image of consequence—and his lifetime mixture of text and image, William Cumming is also the bridge to the postmodern moment of our day.

NOTES

1. William Cumming, interview with the author, March 4, 2005.
2. William Cumming, *Sketchbook: A Memoir of the 1930s and the Northwest School.* Seattle: University of Washington Press, 1984.
3. William Cumming, interview with Bill Hoppe for the Archives of Northwest Art, Allen Library, University of Washington, August 2, 1972, is the most extensive. Others will be noted as quotations arise for attribution. See also Jeane Taggard, "A Man's View: Art and the Artist/An Interview with William Cumming," *Seattle Women*, December 1980, 8–9.
4. William Cumming, interview with the author, March 3, 2005.
5. Hoppe interview, 24.
6. Ibid.
7. Application to the Federal Bureau of Investigation, U.S. Department of Justice, was made by Cumming under the Freedom of Information Act on February 26, 2005. As of this writing, the files have not been released.
8. Clement Greenberg, *Art and Culture: Critical Essays*. Boston: Beacon Press, 1961, vii.

9. William Cumming, letter to Margaret Bundy Callahan, May 3, 1942.

10. Deloris Tarzan Ament's *Iridescent Light: The Emergence of Northwest Art* (University of Washington Press, 2002) attempts—and fails—to explain the rise of twenty-one artists in relation to climatic conditions on Puget Sound.

11. Hoppe interview, 26.

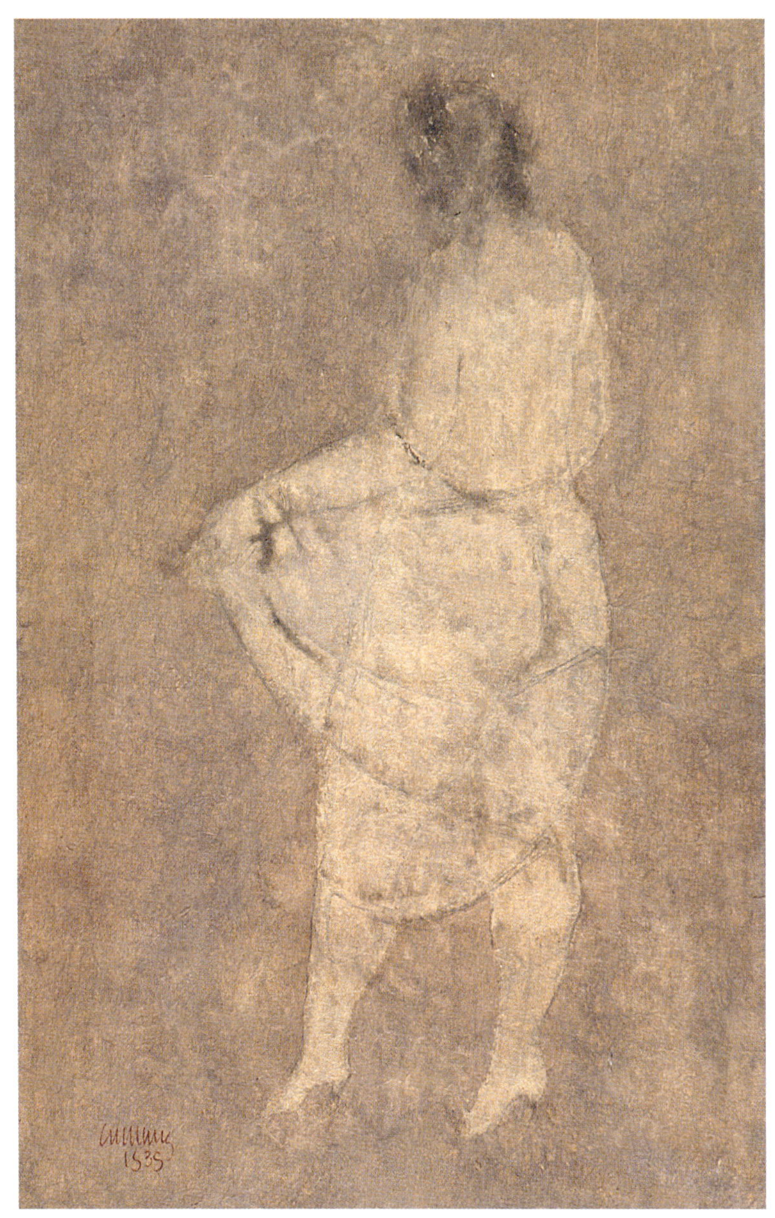

FIG. 7
Untitled (Female Figure), 1935
Gouache on paper
17 1/4 x 11
Collection of B. T. Callahan

CHAPTER ONE

Youth: Idyll, Crisis, and Discovery

I am extremely uneducated, an autodidact.
—William Cumming to author, January 10, 2005

Seen in retrospect, William Cumming's childhood and youth carry all the signs of a young man bound to become an artist. Encouraged by his parents, James and Helen Cumming, to pursue his interests in reading, art, and music, Cumming's several moves with his family—from Kalispell, Montana (where he was born on March 24, 1917), to Portland, Oregon, and thence to Foster (now Tukwila), Washington—did not preclude the continuation of his boyhood hobbies.

In this way, long before he met the artists who were to become known as the Big Four—Guy Irving Anderson (1906–98), Kenneth Callahan, Morris Graves (1910–2003) and Mark Tobey—the Cumming boy was already embarked on various cultural activities on his own, albeit as a small town boy not a city kid. His classical piano lessons, constant sketching, and an avid absorption of contemporary cartoonists like George Herriman ("Krazy Kat"), Phil May of *Punch* magazine, and Montana cowboy artist Charles M. Russell (1864–1926) were formative influences on his overall development.

In addition, as he told Hoppe in an interview for the Archives of Northwest Art in 1972, an "unofficial aunt" agreed in 1927 to pay for an art correspondence course for the ten-year-old from the International Correspondence School. Always interested in drawing the figure in motion, he was later surprised upon meeting veteran Alaska scene painter Eustace P. Ziegler (1881–1969), who challenged Cumming's football game sketches; he was convinced the youth had copied them because it seemed impossible to "Zieg" that someone so young could draw so dynamically.[1] "I was always drawing the figure in motion. It attracted me much more than a static model."[2]

Cumming has concentrated in his writings and interviews on the experiences of the 1930s, after he became part of the circle of Margaret Bundy Callahan, the poet, author, and editor married to Kenneth Callahan who became, according to Cumming's extended accounts, the center of the Big Four. Before that, however, it's important to give the teenager credit for his burgeoning talent and voracious reading.

The family's move to Foster-Tukwila in 1924 stabilized them for a while, as Cumming's father worked as an insurance agent and they lived in Spartan comfort in a small house. Cumming completed grade school and went on to Foster High

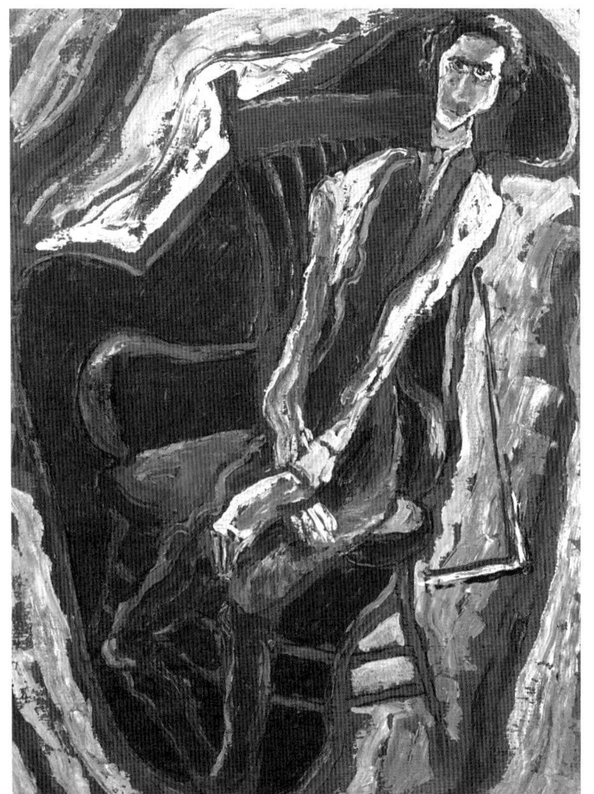

FIG. 8
MORRIS GRAVES
(American, 1910-2001)
Portrait of Bill Cumming, c. 1940
Oil on canvas
43 1/2 x 32 1/4
Portland Art Museum 49.7
Caroline Ladd Pratt Fund

School, where he became valedictorian for his graduating class of eighteen students in 1934. As he recalled later, "I was always at the head of my class. We knew we were expected to be at the top in our family."[3] All that had come crashing down, however, after Black Thursday, 1929, with the failure of the Wall Street stock market and Cumming's father's loss of his job.

Eighteen years before *Sketchbook* was published, Cumming wrote an earlier memoir of those years in *Puget Soundings*, a publication of the Seattle Junior League, in what he called an "imaginary interview," replete with staged questions and answers:

> Lack of money wasn't the only advantage of the Thirties. The young artist was under no pressure to attempt success. . . . None of us really dreamed of ever earning a living by the sale of our work. . . . The shadow of Hitler fell over us, but it would not be until the Forties that we would have to face up to it.[4]

Until then, the teenager frequently commuted via the interurban trolley line into Seattle after graduation. Instead of college, which was out of the question even for so bright a student as Cumming, he received a partial scholarship to a short-lived art school in downtown Seattle run by veteran realist painter Ernest Norling (1892–1974). Cumming's classes at the Northwest Academy of Art included perspective drawing, life class, and paint preparation. Despite the honor of the scholarship, Cumming felt cramped by the courses and moved on after a few months to where the action was: the National Youth Administration Photographic Project.

Part of a broader, New Deal series of Depression-era make-work projects, the N.Y.A. was Cumming's first exposure to government support of the arts, an integral part of the artistic, social, and political milieu of 1930s America. There was great excitement as well as anxiety in the country at the time. As one art critic put it in *The Nation*, "The depression of 1929—? may prove to have been the best thing that ever happened to American art."[5]

Although his father got a Works Project Administration job as a construction-site foreman for the building of a gazebo at a park in Tukwila, Cumming felt some pressure to share his part of the burden that resulted from the family's new economic exigencies. Therefore, despite his pride in the National Youth Administration work and the $25-per-month salary, the young Cumming felt fortunate to get hired

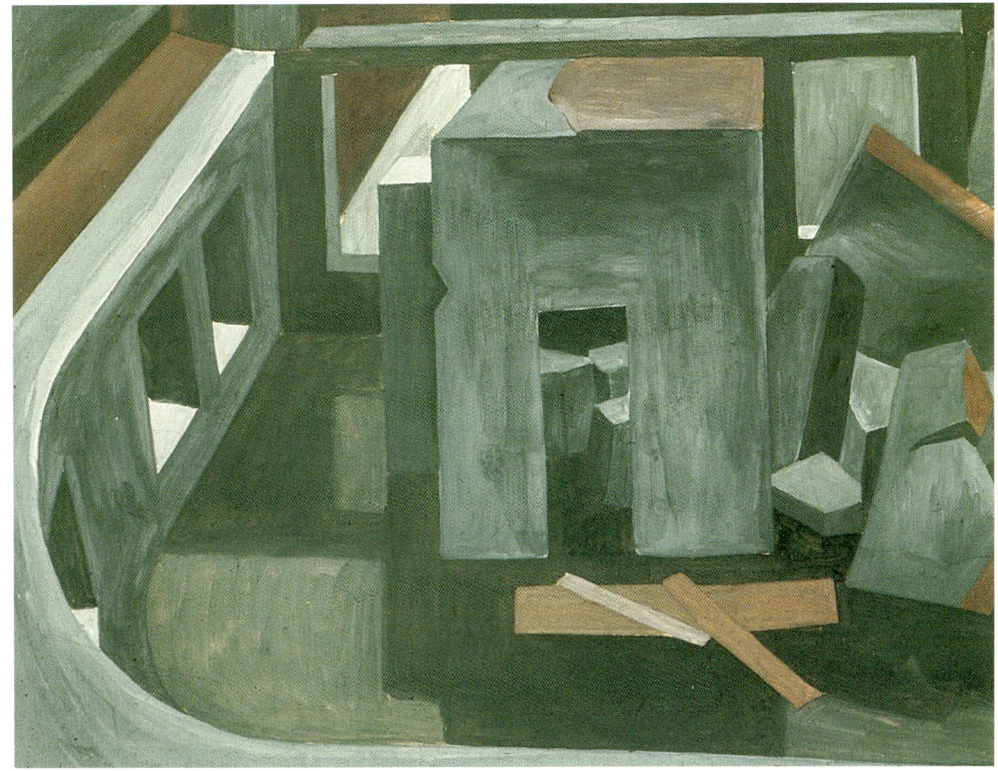

FIG. 9
Abandoned Factory, 1939
Tempera on board
$9^{7}/_{8}$ x 13
Seattle Art Museum 41.46, Eugene Fuller Memorial Collection

as a laborer and ditch digger by the W.P.A. on the building of the new Memorial Stadium at what is now called Seattle Center.

Before leaving the National Youth Administration, however, he had made a good friend, Betty MacDonald (1908–58), head of the N.Y.A.'s Division of Information, who would later become the celebrated best-selling author of a memoir of her unsuccessful attempt to run a rural poultry farm, *The Egg and I* (1945). Her subsequent physical collapse and tuberculosis were chronicled in another book, *The Plague and I* (1948), one that sadly echoed Cumming's case. When he was diagnosed a few years earlier and sent to Firland Sanatorium for his long recuperation in the mid-1940s, it was MacDonald who drove him to the hospital.

Still too young to be on the Federal Art Project, Cumming concentrated on his reading and writing while working his W.P.A. job. He met Lancaster Pollard, a writer and editor-in-chief of the *Town Crier*, a *New Yorker*–like weekly magazine that even emulated the *New Yorker*'s stylish typeface and layouts. Reading and writing at night and still living at home with his parents, Cumming led a full life, and his immersion in working-class conditions at the job site would remain vivid to him forever, including the intemperate boss who eventually picked a fight with the younger man.

Plunging headfirst into his cultural enthusiasms with the confidence and arrogance of youth, the nineteen-year-old took up Pollard's tentative suggestion that he try writing art and music reviews for the *Town Crier*. William Cumming, arts critic, debuted in the spring of 1937. He immediately took on Kenneth Callahan (whom he had not yet met) and went after him with some equivocation in his review of the Seattle Art Museum's "Northwest Annual" exhibition:

> Kenneth Callahan's *Man in the Grey Hat* is undoubtedly worthy of mention beside the best works of the larger group. Callahan, I think, suffers at times from his tendency toward intellectual content in his paintings. At the same time, he is technically one of the finest artists in the Northwest.[6]

With up to one-third of the country unemployed, social conditions in Seattle grew grim. Homeless people and the unemployed, what the police still call "vagrants," became everyday sights that often moved the young man deeply. Such sights and the experiences at Memorial Stadium became a catalyst for the incipient image of consequence in his art: a kind of blue-collar, pre-proletarian realism. These experiences were reinforced by the general down-at-the-heels milieu rapidly transforming the American middle class, including Cumming's family. Instead of their former upwardly mobile social standing, they became unwittingly downwardly mobile:

> Most of the men I knew were workers. . . . The fathers of my friends were working stiffs. I saw them on the street. There was no idea at the time that this could become timeless subject matter.[7]

What some other men of that generation would later call the "college of hard knocks" was handing out diplomas right and left; Cumming got right in line. Between his jobs as a photographic assistant at the National Youth Administration, digging

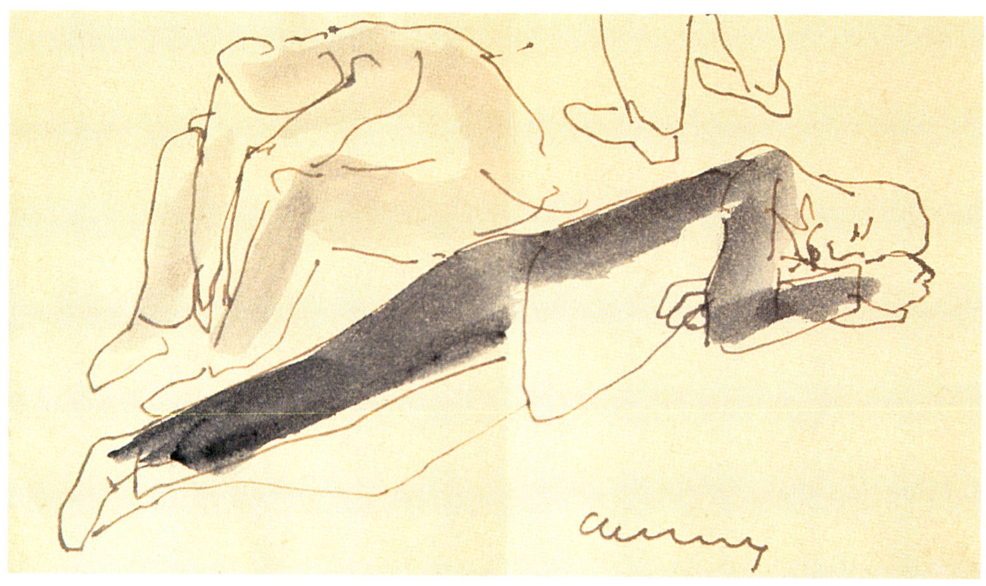

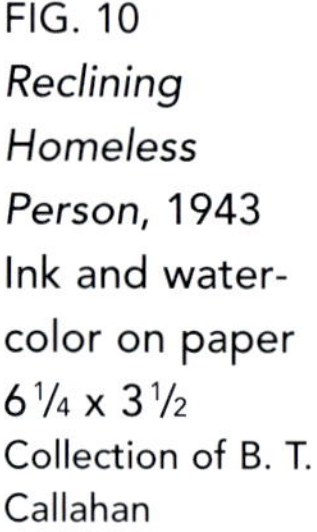

FIG. 10
Reclining Homeless Person, 1943
Ink and watercolor on paper
$6\frac{1}{4} \times 3\frac{1}{2}$
Collection of B. T. Callahan

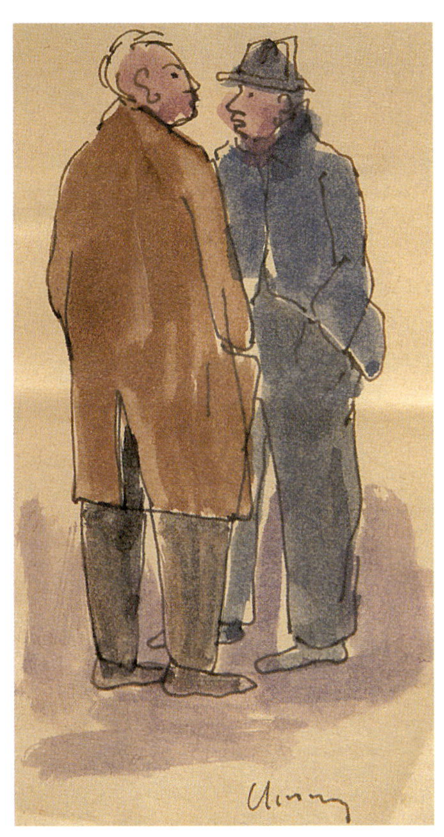

FIG. 11
Two Homeless Men, c. 1943
Ink and watercolor on paper
6¼ x 3½
Collection of B. T. Callahan

ditches for the W.P.A., and sporadic writing at the *Town Crier*, Cumming was getting an education in reality, culture, and economic determinism with unusual speed. Finally, in 1938, he was hired for $68 per month on the Federal Art Project. Working under the unpopular but effective director, painter, and printmaker Robert Bruce Inverarity (1909-99), with whom Cumming would repeatedly butt heads, the younger artist felt an exhilarating pride. At first, the Federal Art Project groups were housed in the Maritime Building on Western Avenue near the historic Pioneer Square area. Later, they shared studio space in the basement of Bailey Gatzert Elementary School near Beacon Hill.

Recent art historical scholarship has drawn analogies between New Deal art projects and simultaneous programs in Germany, Italy, and the Soviet Union. As Erika Doss has noted in *Drawing on America's Past*, there were 2,500 public murals painted in 100 different communities, along with 108,000 easel paintings created under the auspices of the Federal Art Project: "In contrast to contemporaneous government arts patronage in Nazi Germany, fascist Italy and Communist Russia, New Deal notions of cultural nationalism focused on affirming aesthetic pluralism and championed local, regional cultures."[8]

Cumming's reminiscences of his freedom and feuds on the Federal Art Project are dealt with extensively in *Sketchbook*. For our purposes, it is important to remember that, for an artist who subsequently concluded that art should be at the service of the working class, his youthful apprenticeship as an artist occurred under unusually freewheeling and relatively unrestricted circumstances. Instead of undergraduate and graduate instruction, Cumming's activities between 1936 and 1940 comprised a crash course in art as well as in literature, music, and film.

The artist's nascent left-wing politics made itself felt as the equivalent of fraternity pranks aimed at the nearest authority figure, Inverarity, such as when the younger man affixed a red star to a mural in order to offend the boss.[9] His help in founding the Washington Artists Union also proved to be a futile activity, initiated by a friend of Cumming's as a plan to get rid of Inverarity. As Cumming told Hoppe, it was Spokane union members Carl Morris (1911–93) and Hilda Morris (1911–91) (herself a member of the Communist Party USA) who backed Inverarity in the final vote, thereby thwarting the union's efforts. When Cumming had finally had enough and simply told the director he was leaving, Inverarity responded blandly, "I think that's probably a good idea."[10]

Still, the seeds of the image of consequence had been planted. Far from the obvious and inexorable shift toward proletarian subject matter that Cumming sometimes suggests was unstoppable, there were other choices in Seattle at the time, namely, the French-style modernism of University of Washington faculty members

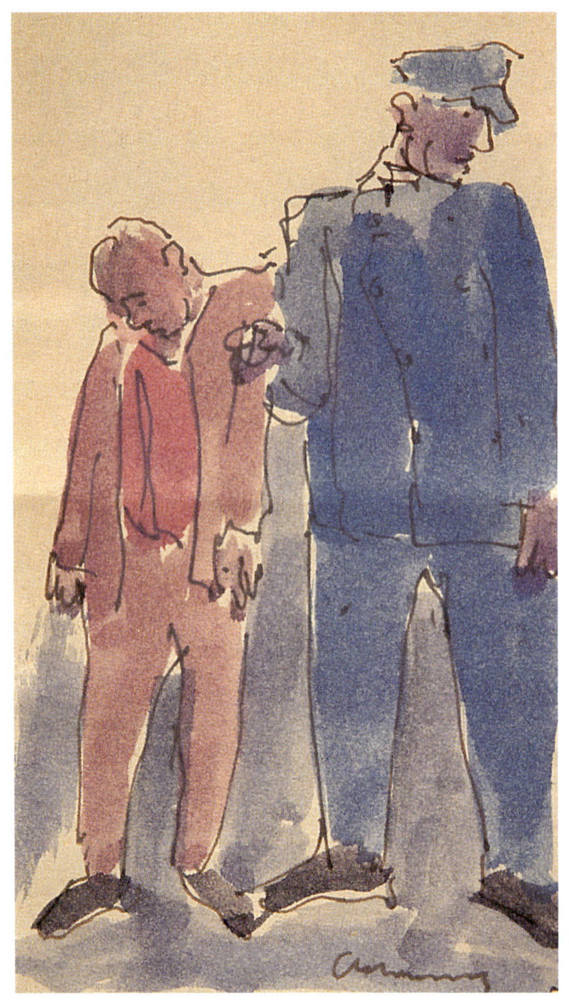

FIG. 12
Policeman and Citizen #1, 1943
Ink and watercolor on paper
6 1/4 x 3 1/2
Collection of B. T. Callahan

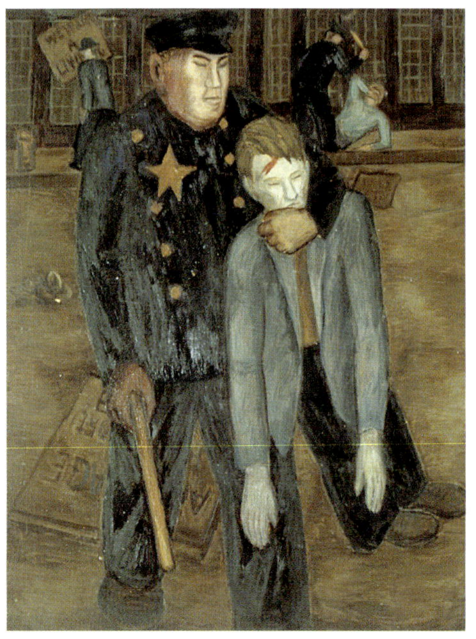

FIG. 13
ARTHUR RUNQUIST
(American, 1891-1971)
Law and Order, late 1930s
Oil on board
27 3/8 x 21 7/16
Seattle Art Museum
83.23
Gift of the Pacific Northwest Art Council

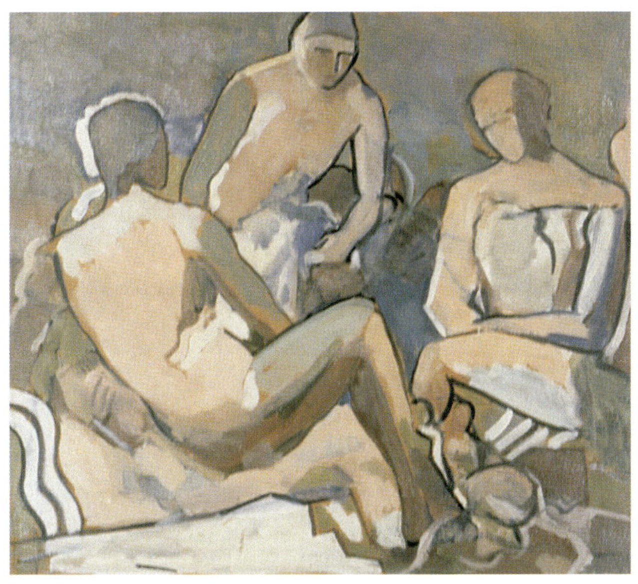

FIG. 14
WALTER F. ISAACS
(American, 1886-1964)
Bathers, 1935
Oil on canvas
27 x 30¼
The Estate of Walter F. Isaacs and Francine Seders Gallery

such as Ambrose Patterson and long-time dean Walter F. Isaacs (1886–1964), both of whom had exhibited in Paris with, respectively, Monet and Picasso. Fascinatingly, it would be another forty years before Cumming would meet them on their own ground of close-value color, flattened Cubistic space, and the generalized, de-individuated figure. His confrontation and reconciliation with European modernism would occur long after Patterson's and Isaacs's deaths and be delayed for decades because of the greater urgency of the social distress of the Great Depression and World War II, as well as the young man's stubborn determination that art must serve the working people.

By the time Cumming finally met Graves in 1937 and was subsequently inducted into the elite Margaret Bundy Callahan salon as its youngest member and intellectual plaything, Cumming was facing a bigger challenge than assimilating Parisian painting styles: how to become a leftist intellectual and artist while remaining true to his gradually forming vision. As we shall see, despite Mrs. Callahan's gracious literary tutelage, other forces took charge, and the World War II years proved to be a period of both triumph and tragedy.

As it turned out, the only significant W.P.A. art project Cumming completed was a mural for Burlington High School in Skagit County, which was destroyed in a fire in the late 1950s. The stamp of a social-realist style was indelible, however, and had set in motion the artist's first mature phase.

NOTES

1. William Cumming, interview with Bill Hoppe, Archives of Northwest Art, Allen Library, University of Washington, August 2, 1972.
2. William Cumming, interview with author, March 5, 2005.
3. Ibid., December 30, 2004.
4. William Cumming, "Fragments of a Journal," *Puget Soundings*, June 1966, 20–25.
5. Suzanne LaFollette, "Review," *The Nation*, October 10, 1936.
6. William Cumming, "Art," *Town Crier*, July 23–August 5, 1937, 10.
7. William Cumming, interview with author, December 30, 2004.
8. Erika Doss in *Drawing on America's Past: Folk Art, Modernism, and the Index of American Design* (Washington, D.C.: National Gallery of Art, 2002), 69.
9. Hoppe interview.
10. Ibid.

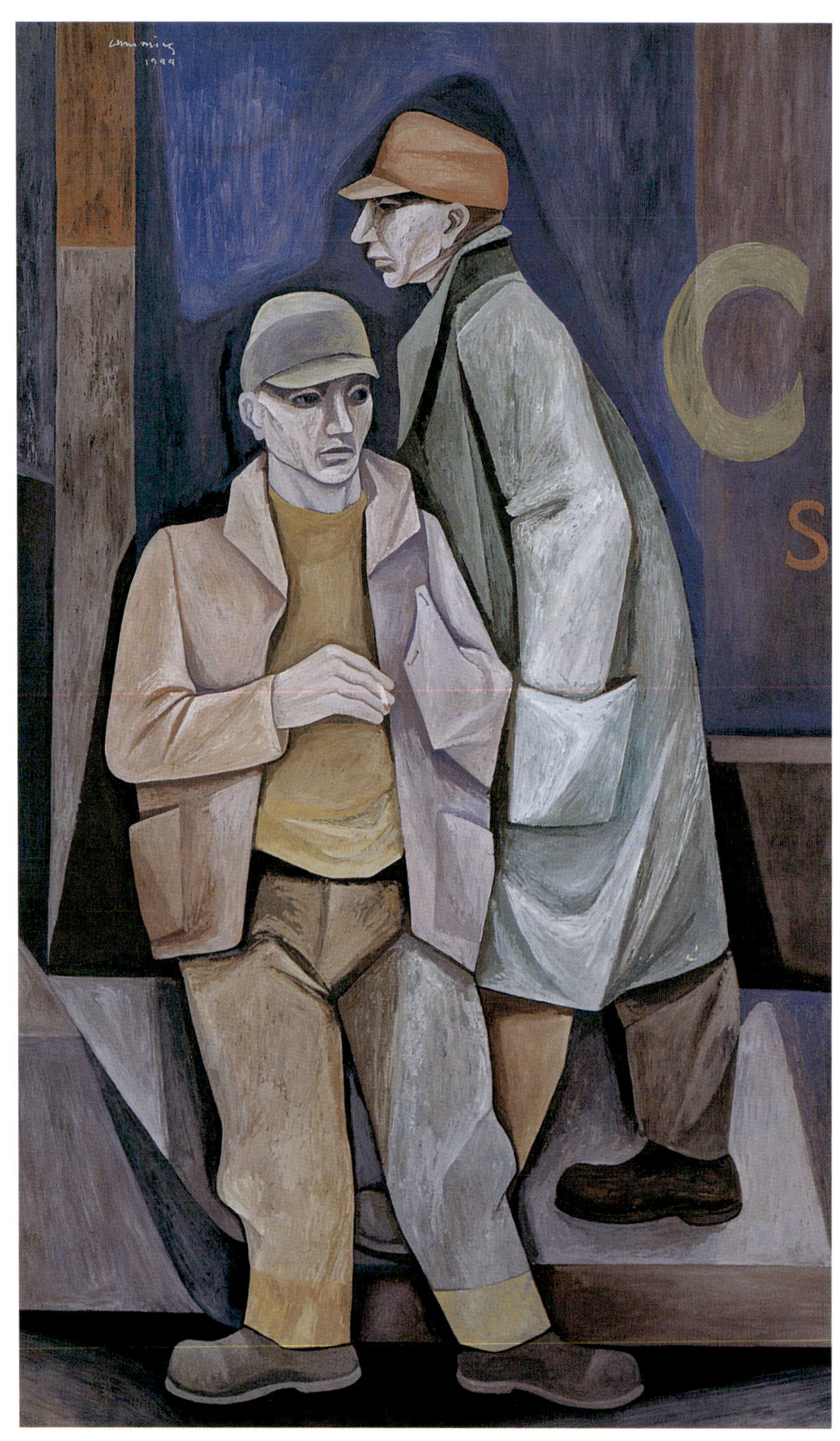

FIG. 15
Two Loggers, 1944
Tempera on board
23 3/8 x 15 1/2
Seattle Art Museum 46.207

CHAPTER TWO

Cumming's Cultural Nexus

Bill's been reading Lenin and Marx for the first time and is a dialectic materialist with a vengeance . . . whole hog. . . . Tomorrow evening the group meets at Mark's, attempting to work out ideas in painting dealing with war, symbolism, etc.

—Margaret Bundy Callahan's diary entry, November 30, 1943[1]

Bill Cumming was already at Firland Sanatorium when Maggy Callahan wrote her diary entry. Cumming remembers that it was probably his second wife, Virginia Hoyt, who brought the fateful volume of Marx at his request. It was Maggy Callahan, though, along with Elizabeth Bayley Willis (1902–2003), who sent him most of his reading matter, unless it was picked up off the sanatorium library cart.

After the modest splash he had made with Maggy and her friends, it seems a sorry pass that the young artist had come to. At twenty-five, he had only been married for a few months (to Dorothy Werst) when his bride fled to California in 1938. He subsequently married Virginia Hoyt in 1941, before he learned of the diagnosis of tuberculosis. His jobs had come to an end due to his poor health, possibly exacerbated by the collapse of his first marriage and poor nutrition. The year he went into the hospital, 1942, his mother died of TB. Cumming was convinced he would share her fate as well as that of his older brother, James, who had died of TB eight years earlier at the age of twenty-four.

FIG. 16
MARK TOBEY
(American, 1890–1976)
Two Men on a Bus, 1927
Oil and tempera on board
20 x 16
Location unknown
Courtesy of the Estate of Mark Tobey, Seattle Art Museum

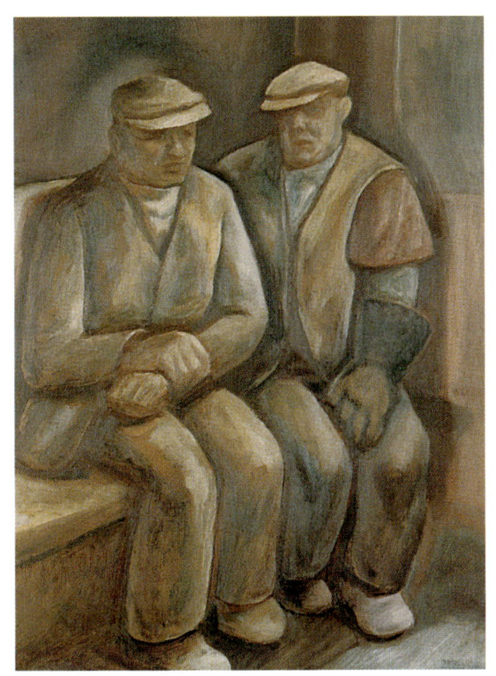

Promise and potential seemed more likely than defeat and death when he was first taken up by the Callahan circle. The older artists were fascinated by the young art critic writing about them, and each took a shine to the fellow. As Cumming points out in *Sketchbook*, Kenneth Callahan went out of his way to show the young man his W.P.A. murals at the Marine Hospital.[2] Years later, Cumming reflected on the Callahans' marriage:

> He was not a painter who was ever totally sure of himself. He would sit and paint and she

> would read to him. What with all my reading, I was full of all that literary stuff, *la vie de bohème*, but the Callahans were more domesticated, older and less adventurous.[3]

Cumming's art changed markedly after he formed friendships with the city's future regional masters. Up until then, before 1938, Cumming had commented on how he had "done all the usual things, and was more influenced then by [illustrator] Edward Abbey and the N. C. Wyeth illustrations for *Treasure Island*."[4] Within a very short time, Cumming came to share with the older artists "my dull color, my use of tempera and my reliance on draftsmanship."[5]

Besides the greyed color of Callahan and Tobey, Cumming feels that, in general, tonality, not primary color, became more important. Building on the mixture of oil and tempera that he learned from Callahan, Cumming's early paintings use color as a telling accent rather than the dominant orchestral element present after 1984.

Worker Lifting a Rock (1940; fig. 17), his first purchase prize in the Seattle Art Museum's "26th Annual Exhibition of Northwest Artists," balances a long red sleeve beneath a short-sleeved white work shirt near a blue-grey rock. Having noticed Callahan's comparatively static mural figures, Cumming made use of his proven control over dynamic figure movement to aid his new paintings. The powerful presence of Cumming's figures, their nobility and dignity despite the backbreaking nature of their roadwork, also came out of Callahan's example: "I preferred Kenneth's figures to Mark's. Kenneth didn't draw fluently; he drew awkwardly and I liked that."[6]

Two Loggers (1944; fig. 15) recalls Tobey's *Two Men on a Bus* (1927; fig. 16), the unhappy alienated figures not in communication with each other but caught in a public setting. *Two Loggers* won a watercolor purchase prize in the "32nd Annual Exhibition of Northwest Artists," news of which reached Cumming in the form of a letter from the Seattle Art Museum director, Richard E. Fuller (1897–1976), while the artist was in the sanatorium.

Despite the American entry into World War II in 1941, Cumming's extraordinary feat of gaining a one-man show at the Seattle Art Museum that year seemed to portend a great future. The exhibit, undoubtedly helped by Kenneth Callahan's position as curator, was also warmly endorsed by Dr. Fuller, a trained geologist who had built both the museum's collection and its Art Déco building in 1933. Cumming had an alternately friendly and stormy relationship with Fuller over the years. It was Fuller, though, who forgave and forgot years later when he gave Cumming his second Seattle Art Museum exhibit in 1961, after the artist's political debacles of the early Cold War period.

The social panorama Cumming encountered in the Skid Row area of Seattle's Pioneer Square inspired the first important works of his early maturity, the birth of the image of consequence. Although a few pictures of rundown houses on Yesler

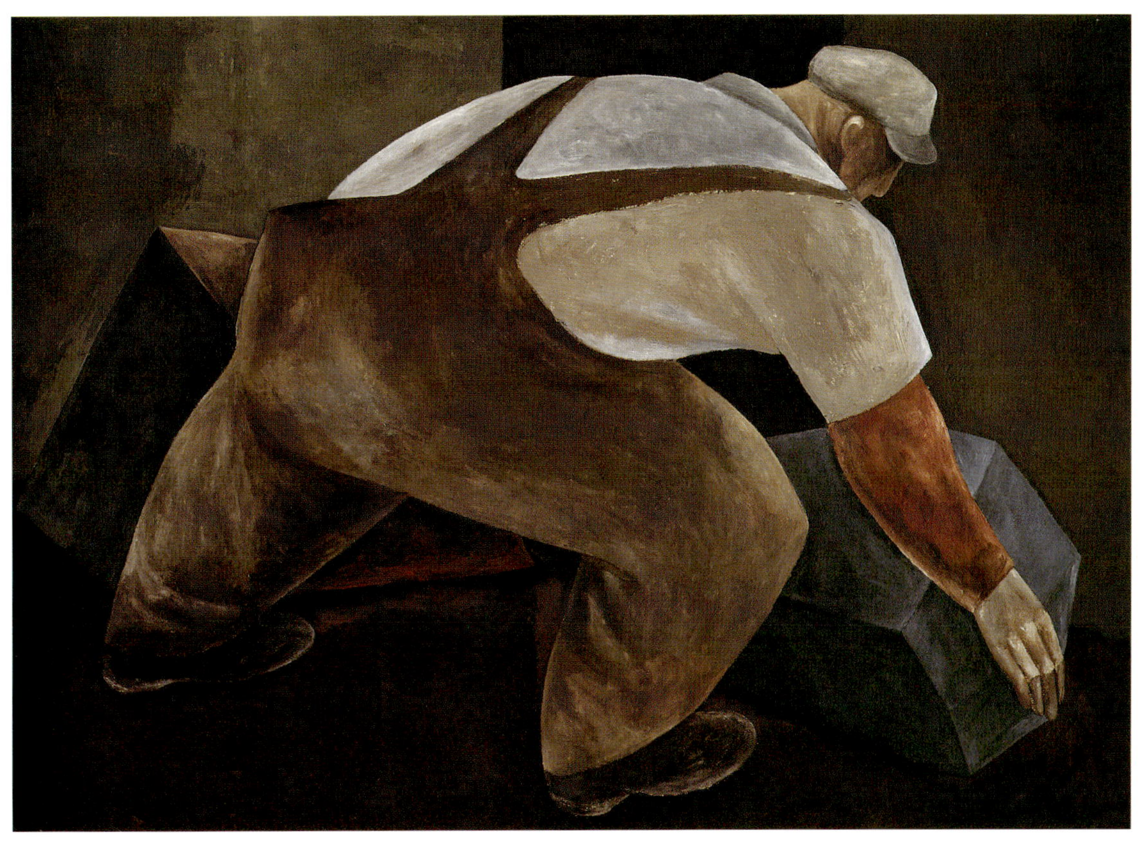

FIG. 17
Worker Lifting a Rock, 1940
Tempera on board
27 3/4 x 37 1/2
Seattle Art Museum 40.71

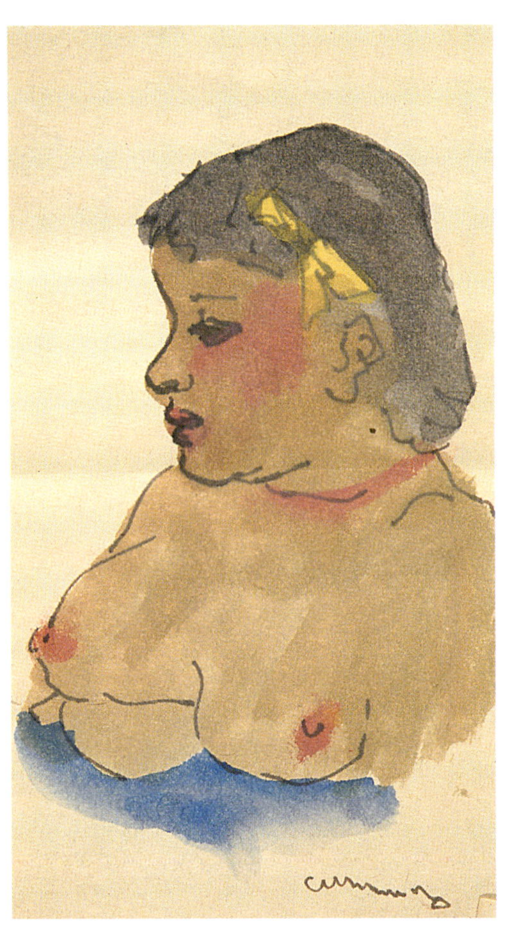

FIG. 18
Working Girl #1, 1943
Ink and watercolor on paper
6 1/4 x 3 1/2
Collection of B. T. Callahan

Way remain haunted by their dark, nighttime light, it is the figures that dominate this period.

Although male figures outnumber them, female figures are far from absent in Cumming's work. The elegant nudes Margaret Bundy Callahan derided are not so bad (see, for example, *Untitled* [Female Figure], 1935; fig. 7), but they suggest a searching desire for the female form. By 1943, they are replaced by the less elegant but more lively quick watercolor sketches of prostitutes and burlesque strippers (see *Working Girl #1*, 1943, fig. 18). At this stage, Cumming retains the male and female figures' individualized facial features, but they can hardly be called portraits.

There is a poignancy and sadness to all the works that were in the 1941 Seattle Art Museum exhibition and those that followed before, during, and after Cumming's first hospitalization. Because he was unable to paint or, indeed, leave his bedroom ward, reading became the trusty frigate of his imagination, the vehicle of a journey that would be both a solace and a tempest in years to come. A wealth of letters Cumming wrote to Margaret Bundy Callahan was released in 2004 to the author. They reveal the highs and lows of Cumming's feelings and thoughts, along with refreshing insights on writers of the past and present. Eventually, the letters reveal his incipient political thoughts and theories of rebellion and revolution. As to the latter, it is important to remember that despite the shakily improved economy, due to the New Deal and America's entry into World War II, many anti-fascist Americans such as Cumming sincerely believed that capitalism had caused the war, fascism being an extreme form of capitalism.

Cumming pours all this out in his letters to Mrs. Callahan, bitterly attacking what we can only surmise were her thoughtful, liberal objections to his increasingly strident positions. While Cumming's frustrated political activism was put to the test after his release from Firland, the extremities of his illness (and subsequent surgeries in 1949, 1954, and 1956) must have had a great deal to do with the despairing frame of mind that drove him to the consolations of Communism.

Cumming's substantial literary apprenticeship can be discerned from his reading and his letters from Firland. As a child, his favorite writers had been adventurer and explorer Ernest Thompson Seton (1860–1946), poet and novelist Robert Louis Stevenson (1850–94), and William Makepeace Thackeray (1811–63), author of *Vanity Fair*.

Once Mrs. Callahan (and the art patron and private dealer Elizabeth Bayley Willis, 1902–2003) began sending books, his "sentimental education" began to be supplemented by more meaty fare. Mrs. Willis had promoted Graves and Tobey to New York dealer Marian Willard and was also herself an important cultural figure during this period. He wrote to his mentor that Thomas Wolfe (1900–38), author of *Look Homeward, Angel* (1929), stood "far above any other American writer," and, regarding the writer's last works, *You Can't Go Home Again* (1940) and *The Hills Beyond* (1941), Cumming found that Wolfe "was on the way to a more mature, more objective idiom."

Some of Cumming's enthusiasm for Wolfe lay in the American writer's passionate and poetic evocation of a young man's coming of age intellectually and sexually. Wolfe's final illness, tuberculosis of the spine and brain, had been contracted in Seattle (according to Cumming, the rumor was that Wolfe had sat next to a TB victim on the ferry going up to Victoria, British Columbia)[7] and, after a long train trip back to Baltimore, he died. While in Seattle, Wolfe had been entertained by the Callahan set shortly before their first dinner party with Cumming. It may be that, in some ways, Cumming reminded the Callahans of the young Wolfe: impassioned, impetuous, greatly talented, and grievously stricken.

Cumming finds his voice as a literary critic and political polemicist in his Firland letters. In one, he tells Mrs. Callahan that *You Can't Go Home Again* is "far more mature than anything else he or any American has done."[8] In another letter, he announces his preference for Shakespeare over James Joyce. D. H. Lawrence's novels exert a strong tug as well.

At the same time, Betty Willis had him reading "*War and Peace*, Emerson, Thoreau, Voltaire, Roger Fry and is now threatening me with Spinoza and [Vernon] Parrington."[9] Cumming adds in his next letter, "Betty added Marco Polo's *Travels* and the *Philosophy of Spinoza*. . . . I got back at her by lending *State and Revolution* by Lenin."[10] Ominously, we read in the same letter what Cumming had hinted at earlier: "Marx and Lenin have done a lot to organize my thought processes."[11] After six months in the hospital on a steady diet of great books of Western Civilization and the tracts of Marx, Lenin, Stalin, and Trotsky, the die of ideological restrictions was finally cast:

> I really get little from the literature of the past. . . . Too many ideological differences from my outlook—Altho' I guess Marx was contemporary with Tolstoy—but Marx doesn't share Tolstoy's illusions which irritate me.[12]

Gradually the twenty-six-year-old invalid opens up to Callahan. By January 1943, after seven months in bed with limited time to walk around, he confesses, "It's hard to face certain things within myself in this life of no privacy and my only refuge is in screwballish humor of deprecation."[13]

Reading remained Cumming's other refuge. Revealing a self-education worthy of any graduate student in literature, he adds as an aside in the same letter:

> January reading: *Ulysses*, Malraux's *Man's Fate*, Muriel Rukeyser's *Willard Gibbs*, Hart Crane's *Collected Poems*, more Whitman and some Emerson.[14]

An avid magazine and political journal reader as well, Cumming proudly quotes to Callahan a letter he received from prominent liberal cultural critic Malcolm Cowley (1898–1989), author of *Exile's Return* (1934) (which may have served as an additional model for *Sketchbook*). Cowley's response to a TB patient's fan letter is thoughtful, mildly encouraging, and respectful:

> New York is full of people living in the past of other countries. [Parker] Tyler and Charles Henri Ford in Paris 1924; the Trotskyists in Petersburg 1905; the German exiles are still in the Weimar Republic—and all that world is gone, gone, and am I, are you, living in the present? Cordially, Malcolm Cowley[15]

In one of Cumming's loneliest passages, he comments to Callahan, "I hope he *will* have time to write at length. You can feel his intense integrity and his ability at communicating ideas."[16]

Much of the rest of the correspondence to Callahan deals more depressingly with the "closing of an American mind," to use Allan Bloom's phrase, the rigidifying of Cumming's political ideas, his defense of Marx and Stalin, and his elaborate, repeated defenses of his convictions. These become noteworthy as the preface to the artist's "lost years," 1944 to 1960. As we shall see in chapter 3, despite the artist's deflecting comments years later in *Sketchbook*, Cumming's politics were absolutely serious and sincere.

Cumming's hospital reading was a crucial part of the cultural nexus that formed him as an artist. The middle-class cultural pursuits provided by his parents, the reading encouraged by Callahan and Willis, and the young man's own voice as an art and music critic (for barely six months) all combined to create an urban sensibility, one open to experimentation and cultural experiences, but also, because of tough times and a debilitating illness, perilously open to the temptations of totalitarian idealism.

With Cumming's shift from liberal artistic pluralism to Communism, his life thus far was broken in half. Nevertheless, the power of his paintings of the 1930s and early 1940s brought Northwest art into a mainstream of politically committed art of the period. While the Callahan circle was seeking nebulous images of "war, symbolism, etc.," Cumming remained doggedly on track, honoring and chronicling the working man.

A constellation of factors—the Great Depression, the New Deal, World War II, and a huge gulp of intoxicating cough syrup in the form of Marxist Communism—shaped the appearance of Cumming's first mature period. During his stay at Firland, his subsequent release and abortive move to San Jose, California, and his return to live with his father and stepmother in Spokane, a political figure was born. Art was not yet called into question or abandoned, but it was sorely tested and challenged. Old friends, however, were tested, quizzed, and, in some cases, abandoned.

NOTES

1. I am indebted greatly to Margaret Bundy Callahan's son, Brian Tobey Callahan, for not only providing copies of Cumming's letters to his mother between 1942 and 1946, but for also providing the page from his mother's diary for the chapter epigraph.
2. William Cumming, *Sketchbook: A Memoir of the 1930s and the Northwest School* (Seattle: University of Washington Press, 1984), 42.
3. William Cumming, interview with the author, December 30, 2004.
4. Ibid.
5. Cumming, *Sketchbook*, 228.
6. William Cumming, interview with the author, February 14, 2005.
7. Ibid., March 5, 2005.
8. William Cumming to Margaret Bundy Callahan, July 4, 1942.
9. Ibid., November 1, 1942.
10. Ibid., November 11, 1942.
11. Ibid.
12. Ibid.
13. Ibid., January 30, 1943.
14. Ibid.
15. Malcolm Cowley, quoted in ibid., March 16, 1943.
16. Ibid.

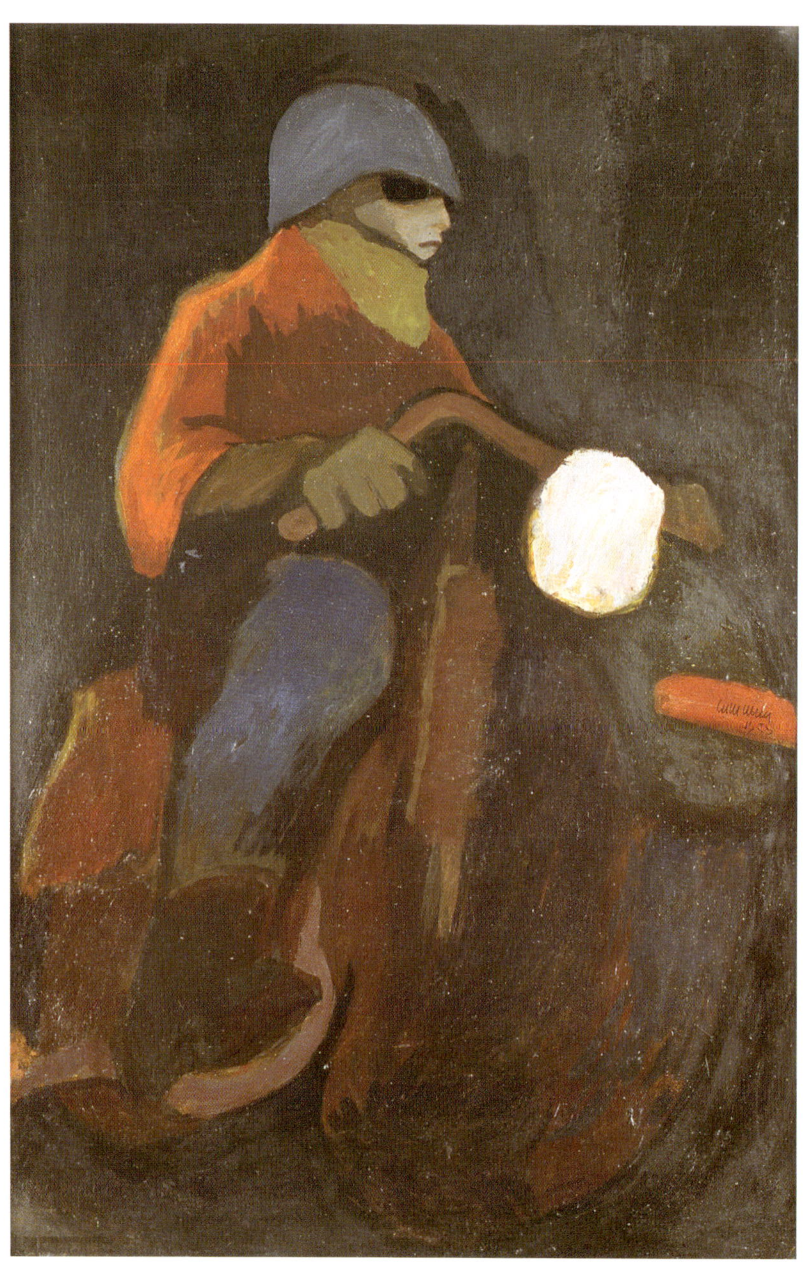

FIG. 19
Cyclist, 1955
Oil on panel
40 x 27 1/2
Tom Robbins, La Conner

CHAPTER THREE

The Dark Wood

Mi ritrovai per una selva oscura,
Chè la diretta via era smarrita.
(I found myself in a dark wood
where the straight way was lost.)
—Dante Alighieri, *Inferno*, Book I (1321)

William Cumming's hospitalization had multiple results: plenty of time for reading, an opportunity to create the equivalent of an artistic and literary manifesto through letters, and the transition from a curious young working man into a dedicated Communist. Cumming has commented at length in later years to interviewers Bill Hoppe, Deloris Tarzan Ament,[1] and others about his path into the political wilderness of the American Communist Party, but it is useful to reexamine as far as possible the precise extent of that commitment, how it developed, festered, and finally dissipated with a raging disenchantment and repudiation.

Bearing in mind that all foreign press stories leaving the Soviet Union were subject to censorship, it is not surprising that Cumming, like many others, did not have the full story on the Moscow purge trials or even the existence of the Gulag prison camp system. Thus, his startling comments to Margaret Bundy Callahan must be put into perspective, taking into account also the frustration and depression the TB patient may have been experiencing. He begins by commenting on how pro-American-involvement radio broadcasts are the product of "upper bourgeoisie . . . parasites" that are not "pulling their weight" compared to the labor movement. "And the sooner we have a New Deal dictatorship (if it's to be called that), the better. Stalin showed us how to purge the traitors and it's time we followed suit."[2] Cumming's paramount concern at this point is how to win the war.

In another letter, two years before Cumming's membership in the CPUSA begins, he defends the Party officials Earl Browder (1891–1973) and Harry Bridges (1901–90) as figures assisting and promoting the war effort,[3] which the patient follows closely in newspapers, magazines, and on the radio.

At this point, despite being "fed up with middle-class ideology," he clarifies his political position to Callahan. "I'm no more a Marxist than ever—I don't believe in the feeble 'proletarianism' of *New Masses* and the *Daily Worker*—culturally they are exactly the same middle-class slop as the *Saturday Evening Post*."[4]

Within a few months, however, Cumming's tune changes considerably. "I have been reading Lenin . . . I do believe . . . that [Stalin] has carried out Lenin's plan fully—much better than Trotsky would have done."[5] At the same time, Cumming's patriotism and anti-fascist sentiments are not in question. He laments that, due to his illness, he is "helpless to do anything at all in the fight against fascism"[6] and looks back on the Depression and the 1920s with rare insight: "I see a nation grown atrophied through its years of senseless, cruel commercialism."[7] The apocalyptic confidence in Lenin's theories has a near-religious conversion impact on the young patient who predicts:

> in the long run—the eventual struggle—the battle will resolve itself into civil-war between the forces of oppression and the mass of "workers." On no basic issue have the premises of Lenin-Marx-Engels been proved wrong. On the contrary, they have worked out with the precision of a mathematical formula.[8]

He soon responds to Callahan's counterarguments by asking, "You ask what I am? Have I not the right to call myself a proletarian? . . . What is an artist, if not productive?"[9] A month later, further chided by Callahan, he replies in a long letter, "Yes, I do feel a bit smug over my Marxism. But I know that I will eventually drop the dogmas and retain the principles—which is one of Lenin's main pillars."[10] Emulating the style of Communist propaganda, he also delineates an eight-part response to Callahan's criticisms of his increasing dogmatism.

Despite the doldrums, Cumming is heartened yet dismayed to receive notice that one of his paintings has received an honorable mention in the Northwest Annual at the Seattle Art Museum: "Feel quite cheered. Will I ever paint again? Will I ever bring order and meaning into my life?"[11]

Cumming's letters to Callahan gradually take on the tone of harangues rather than the earlier student-to-mentor or even artist-to-colleague voice. By March 28, 1943, he corrects her terminology of "Stalin regime" and denies that the death of Leon Trotsky (who had been killed in Mexico City in 1940) was a "political assassination." "Trotzky and his followers were engaged in a worldwide struggle to sabotage and overthrow the Soviet regime."[12] A long defense of what Callahan called "repression" in the U.S.S.R. follows, along with a justification of the "mistakes" of the Party. In his sternest tone, Comrade Cumming reduces Callahan's no doubt cogent, pleading arguments: "My whole argument is that your hatred of Communism is entirely expressed in terms of personal rancour [*sic*]."[13]

After Cumming's initial release from Firland that month, he travels to stay with a cousin, James Edmiston, and his family in San Jose, California. The stay ends with Mrs. Edmiston's insistence that the relative is still a health hazard to her children. Cumming returns to the Northwest, this time to be with his father and stepmother in Spokane. He was proud of at least having stopped smoking entirely at this time.

Once in Spokane, not only does he feel well enough to work part time, but he also begins painting again. Writing to both Kenneth and Margaret Callahan, he engages in self-praise and self-criticism (what would become a frequent Cumming recipe), conducting his own Party cell group meeting of one. "Am studying Marx's *Capital* and find it amazingly lucid. . . . Marx-Engels-Lenin have done more to free my thinking from the fault of carelessness, loose terminology, meaningless rhetoric . . . than anyone with whom I've ever come in contact."[14]

With the isolation of illness and the geographical distance, Cumming's assessments of his artist friends change, too. He writes to Guy Irving Anderson to request help in getting $25 per month from either Dr. Fuller or prominent arts patron Emma Baillargeon Stimson (1887–1963) so that he can continue painting in Spokane and pay ongoing monthly medical bills. "I miss you all a great deal, and I miss the Northwest earth even more."[15]

A few weeks earlier, he commented on Graves's and Anderson's weaknesses as artists to Mrs. Callahan:

> Morris seldom achieves anything beyond shallow kineticism . . . nervous movement, with no sense of structure whatever. Guy, I believe, has both qualities, but has trouble getting them together: i.e., one painting will have movement without structure, another will be just the opposite, or they will both be present yet seem to never quite establish "contact."[16]

On a more sobering note, the internment of Morris Graves for conscientious objection to fighting in World War II is mentioned by Cumming in a letter. Graves was confined for several months and released on March 1, 1943, with an honorable discharge, which he refused. Cumming's heretofore unpublished response puts Graves's wartime activities and artistic output in a different light than that of Ray Kass, Graves's sympathetic biographer:[17]

> You are more lucky than anything else to be avoided by snob-Graves and I say that he is definitely NOT an artist. If he were a true artist, he wouldn't have been a draft dodger. . . . To think of the decent, fine kids who are fighting and dying, wanting a decent world, and then to think of that coward and traitor. . . . What is he but the filthiest of treasonable collaborators of fascism, no matter how "passive" his activities?[18]

Cumming doesn't stop in his diatribe against Graves the pacifist and conscientious objector, but extends his comparison between cowards and heroes to other figures of greater cultural status than Graves, such as "Jean Cocteau, [André] Derain, [Arthur] Honegger, collaborators," comparing them unfavorably to French intellectual (and

Communist) Louis Aragon. He finally adds, "I despise Morris, and, if he condescends to exhibit at the Annual next year, I will personally protest (and there will be others behind me) to Dr. Fuller against allowing his work on the Museum walls."[19]

Working as a Party recruiter and youth worker in Spokane, Cumming returned to painting. He opens up the sunlight in his work, demonstrating for the first time that the darker ground oil-and-tempera-based admixture can allow for brighter, less "greyed out" colors. *Spokane Backyard* (1943; fig. 20) is one of a number of works completed at the time. Within a few months, its light and airiness are superseded, however, by the stricter proletarian imagery of *Two Loggers* (1944; see fig. 15) and one of the first of many representations of African Americans, *Planting the Flare* (1945; plate 8), both of which were acquired by Dr. Fuller for the Seattle Art Museum's permanent collection.

While in Spokane, Cumming's work with the Russian War Relief (a nonprofit, nongovernmental group) combined with his participation as an adviser in American Youth for Democracy (a college-age group that was possibly a Party front or target for Party takeover). Coupled with his increased painting came a rise in Cumming's morale as well as in recuperation from TB. He clarifies his role in the Party in a letter to Maggy Callahan:

> My activity time is pretty much given to the party. . . . I am only interested in one thing, strengthening the party. The party is my second homeland and my first is the Northwest earth. . . . I love my country and I love mankind, but the party represents the only thoroughly conscious and thoroughly organized form of struggling for the good of humanity.[20]

As Cumming's political position hardens, so does his animosity toward Morris Graves, about whom Mrs. Callahan comments in a letter to Cumming that must have been written shortly after Graves's second successful show in New York at Willard Gallery. Cumming lashes out in an undated letter:

> As to such people as Graves and his "success," what is there to say? It is the same success as that which his friends, Hitler and Goebbels, once enjoyed and it will fade, along with the "work" of Dalí, Ernst, Calder . . . as genuine people's art grows out of the democratic front of political-economic coalition. . . . Morris paints with direct intention of bolstering the intellectual position of the snobs and dilettantes of the M[useum] of M[odern] Art group, all of whom are either latent or actual fascist sympathizers.[21]

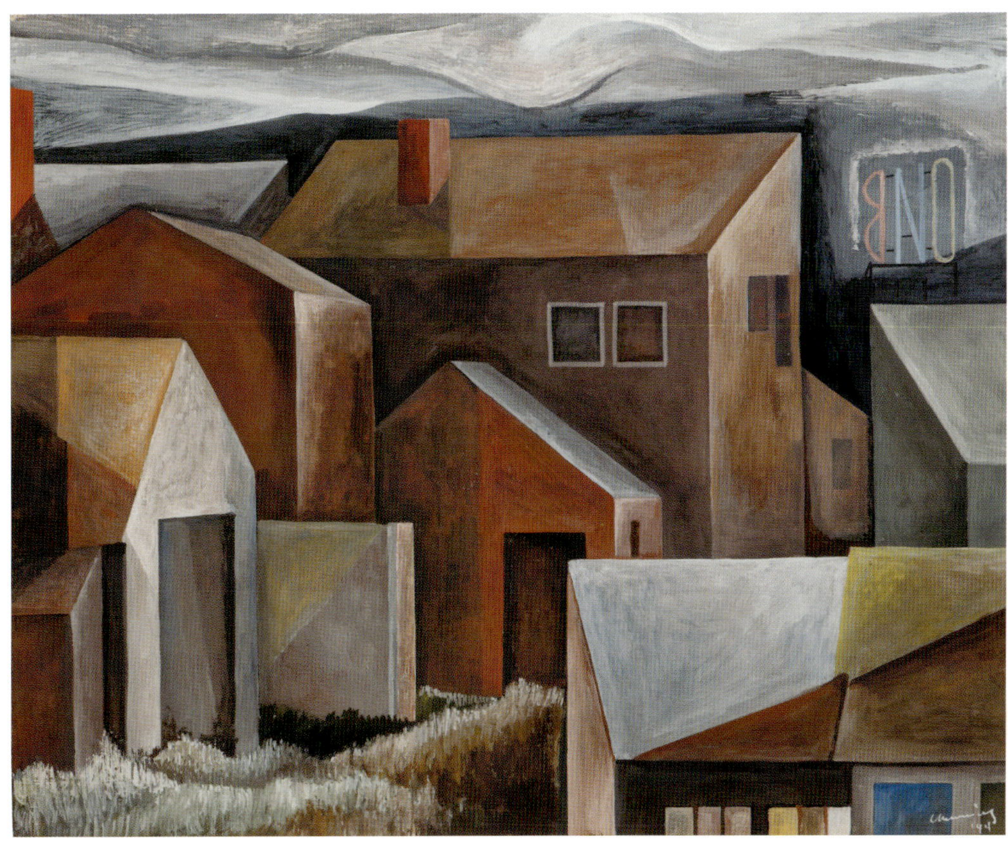

FIG. 20

Spokane Backyard, 1943

Gouache on composition board

$14\frac{1}{2}$ x $17\frac{1}{2}$

Collection of the Northwest Museum of Arts & Culture, 3921.1

Eastern Washington State Historical Society, Spokane

Gift of Glenn and Judith Mason and Museum Purchase

He concludes the letter with a fiery soapbox valedictory:

> Let the fascists tremble. We will destroy them on the cultural front, and we will then cut them to pieces politically and economically.[22]

Comrade Cumming

With the war winding down and Cumming settled down with his father and stepmother, Midge, his life was full. While he had been ill, his second wife, Ginny Hoyt, filed for divorce and, with Cumming's grudging consent, put up their son, Kevin James, for adoption (father and son would be reunited in 1967). Shortly thereafter, Cumming met Dorothy Loft (1925–72), a labor organizer and member of the miners' union. She was also working for Russian War Relief. If anything, her politics were more radical than those of her new husband. They married in 1947 and moved back to Seattle. A son, Phillip, was born the same year, followed by two daughters, Claudia Ann (b. 1949) and Karen Irene (b. 1950).

Cumming's wrangling with Maggy Callahan continued in his letters from Spokane, which took issue with what she called her "stout disappointment" in Communist policy toward the arts. Besides roughly quoting the polemicist Anna Seghers, whose article "The Task of the Arts" had recently appeared in *New Masses*, he states his personal position:

> I don't try to tell the individual artist what he or she should do but I do say that, to be the anti-fascist . . . they must stick to the masses, to the people and derive their strength from the people.[23]

Unable to find full-time work once back in Seattle, Cumming continued his Party organizing and went on welfare disability. Fortunately, he began teaching at a small commercial art school, the Burnley School of Professional Art (where he continues to teach today in its present incarnation, Art Institute of Seattle).

Gradually, the postwar euphoria in Seattle changed to a grim awareness of the Soviet Union as a threat, especially after the Russians exploded their first hydrogen bomb in 1952. In a growing national hysteria, individuals once praised as sympathetic to wartime allies were now deemed "premature anti-fascists." Cumming's wartime and postwar activities in Spokane and Seattle came under increasing scrutiny. The Communist Party's rapidly diminishing numbers were exacerbated by Soviet Premier Nikita Khrushchev's surprising denunciation of Stalin in a 1954 speech. Cumming was torn. As he recalled in 2005:

> Khrushchev's speech set me on fire and made me question everything I believed in. I was disappointed that it led to no changes [in the Soviet Union]. He was called a traitor but by

> that time the American Communists were a bunch of bleacher coaches.[24]

Asked why, if he was so disillusioned and, as would soon become apparent, in peril, he did not leave the Party after the revelations about Stalin. Cumming replied, "I couldn't desert the Party under fire because of the McCarthy period. To leave at that time would have been cowardly."[25]

Despite such courage, the other foot of the McCarthy era, the Canwell Committee, soon fell on Cumming. An old friend and mountain-climbing pal, Barbara Hartle, decided to "name names" to the Joint Legislative Fact-Finding Committee on Un-American Activities of Washington State.[26] Both Cumming and his wife, "Lofty," were named by Hartle, along with dozens of other individuals. Especially painful for Cumming was the embarrassment his Republican father (now a Spokane auto dealer) experienced once the names appeared in the national press. The Hartle Affair was similar to the case of Elizabeth Bentley (1908–63), the so-called "Red Spy Queen," who had also simultaneously been a government employee and twenty-year Party member.[27]

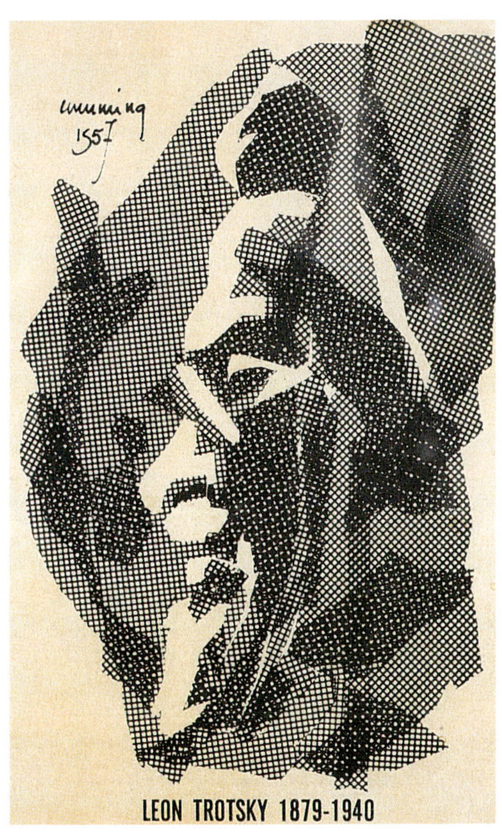

FIG. 21
Leon Trotsky, 1957
Mixed media on paper
10 x 8
Collection of Frank Krasnowsky

Hartle's unexpected courtesy visit to the Cumming family home on a sunny Saturday morning preceded what would shortly become one of the most sensational chapters in the Red Scare. The following Monday morning Hartle named both Bill and Dorothy as well as claiming to the Canwell Committee that "'well over 1,000 Negroes belonged to the Communist party in this area at one time."[28] After the Khrushchev speech and now the explosive Hartle Affair, the Cummings were approaching the low point of the decade. To be fair, more trouble was to come, including the FitzGerald Affair (a court case involving plagiarism) and his ghostwritten role in the Gates-Foster Debate (a public brouhaha involving leaders of the CPUSA). The fallout, according to Ament, resulted in "six years, during the era of Senator Joseph McCarthy's Communist witch hunts, [in which] Cumming was blacklisted."[29]

But was Cumming blacklisted? It has been difficult to prove. The artist, in his thirties, continued to teach at Burnley and even began an additional part-time job at Cornish Institute. Remaining on full disability, Cumming's health was not 100 percent improved, regardless of his re-entry into the world of radical politics in Seattle. Some of Cumming's Communist friends, such as Stan Iverson at City Light, lost their jobs; others were more fortunate, such as radical Frank Krasnowsky, who lost his steelworkers' union position in a purge, but did not lose his job.

More pertinently, within a few years of the Khrushchev speech, Cumming transferred his loyalties to the Trotsky faction in Seattle, the group already long estranged from the CPUSA, a Stalinist stalwart group. With the Party still dominated by individuals who refused to believe Khrushchev's charges, Cumming turned to the city's most prominent radical figures, Frank Krasnowsky,[30] Richard Fraser (1923–88), and Clara Kaye Fraser (1925–99). As Cumming remembers it fifty years later:

> I was in the CP but I was more a literary communist. I read the texts of the [Moscow Purge] trials. Most of the Stalinists were awful except for misguided fools like me. Reading the transcripts, that's how I learned of the power of words, how you can turn a word into a weapon, like the Trotskyists did.[31]

Clara Fraser and her second husband (she had previously been married to Krasnowsky) counseled Cumming on his transition from Stalinism to Trotskyism, one shared by many American intellectuals in the period after Stalin's death. Cumming later designed the portrait-cover for Fraser's collected writings, *Revolution, She Wrote*.[32] He might have been returning a favor to Fraser, although her memoirs contain no mention of Cumming or his conversion to Trotskyism. By now, Cumming's affinity to Communism was shaped substantially by the Frasers:

> The Frasers appealed to people who were sick of the CP. A kid like me would see the CP adapting itself into one of the strong parties. In 1939, it seemed to the left; then after 1940, it went to the right. In 1950, it was repressed by the Smith Act. Looking back, I was a Marxist by misapprehension.[33]

By 1957, Cumming had had enough. Under Clara Fraser's direction, he composed a sixteen-page, double-spaced typewritten letter resigning from CPUSA and ridiculing internal party squabbles between *Daily Worker* editor John Gates and Party chair William Z. Foster.[34] The Soviet invasion of Hungary was the final straw for Cumming, although, thanks to the Frasers (who had already joined the Trotskyist splinter group, Socialist Workers Party), Cumming's separation had been building steadily. Perhaps to counter the negative publicity he had received at the time of Hartle's "naming names," he wrote:

> I have decided to make my resignation public in the pro-Soviet press. . . . I take this step of publicly resigning from the Communist Party. I call upon all the radicals and socialists, all cultural workers, to demand the immediate liberation of the imprisoned Hungarian revolutionaries. Fraternally, William L. Cumming[35]

It was the artist's last public political statement—on anything. After the debacle of the dreary Party work, the exposé of the Canwell Committee, and even an abortive, last-ditch effort to work with the Frasers in the Socialist Workers Party, Cumming never again was active politically, nor did he make any further political statements during the Vietnam War, the Gulf War, or the Iraq war. To this day, he does not vote.

With hindsight in 2005, Cumming commented on his CP membership and why he was attracted to a group that may have begun as anti-fascist but that became, soon enough, anti-democratic:

> It was one of the stupidest things I ever did. I'm not an organizational person. There's a rather romantic idea that I did so because I owed something to the Great Proletariat who had sweated through the War. . . . Nobody persuaded me; I forced my way in. It's a wonder they didn't suspect me as an F.B.I. stooge. Within a short time, I was a functionary for them. . . . I've often wondered if I was a puppet.[36]

What with all the political shenanigans going on in his life, it may be surprising to learn how prolific Cumming was with his art. It is as if after the split from the Party and then from the Frasers that the artist felt released into a new period of productivity; the image of consequence was maturing.

In what was perhaps an act of even greater courage, considering the potential side effects, Cumming resigned from his TB disability payments and resolved to paint full time. He had a small studio sale in 1959, with drawings selling from $5 to $10; they attracted the attention of a new patron, Manfred Selig, who bought dozens of drawings that Cumming had done of street people in the mid to late 1950s. They remain among the few examples left of Cumming's art during the McCarthy era. Including figures in movement, fashion sketches, children, and old people, they capture in capsule form the evolution of the image of consequence. One of his subjects, new clothing, was not exactly a hard-core proletarian image, but it served as an image of changing times.

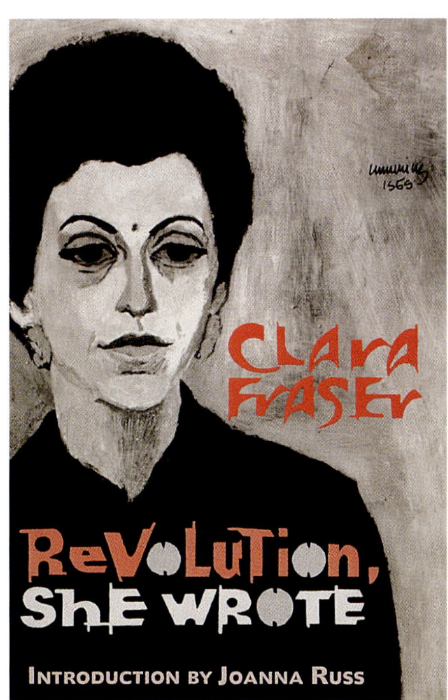

FIG. 22
Book cover for Clara Fraser's *Revolution, She Wrote*, 1998

Another suite of drawings was acquired by a sympathetic collector-couple, Spencer Blair Kirk (1912–2004) and his wife, Lucille (1913–2001). These comprise drawings in ink and wash on paper of an African American female nude and mark a high point of Cumming's control over dynamic figure movement (see, for example, *Untitled* [Running Female Figure], 1959, and *Untitled* [Crouching Female Figure], 1959; figs. 25 and 28). Seen together, they resemble a cinematic montage—sitting, rising, crouching, kneeling, running—and further underscore

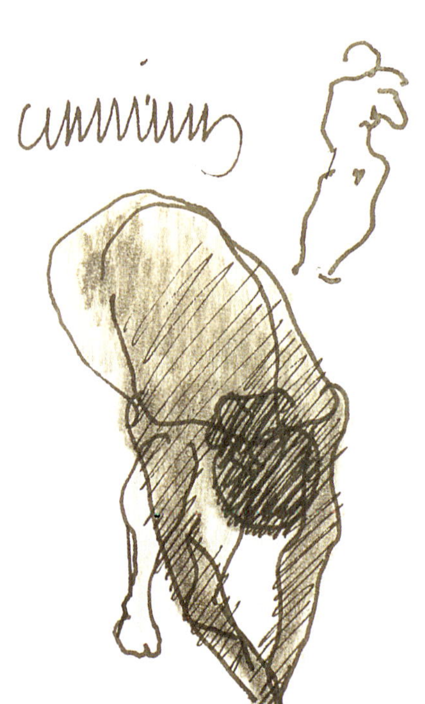

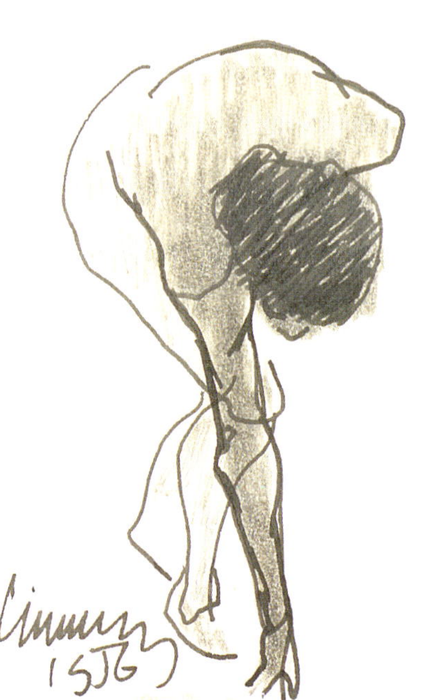

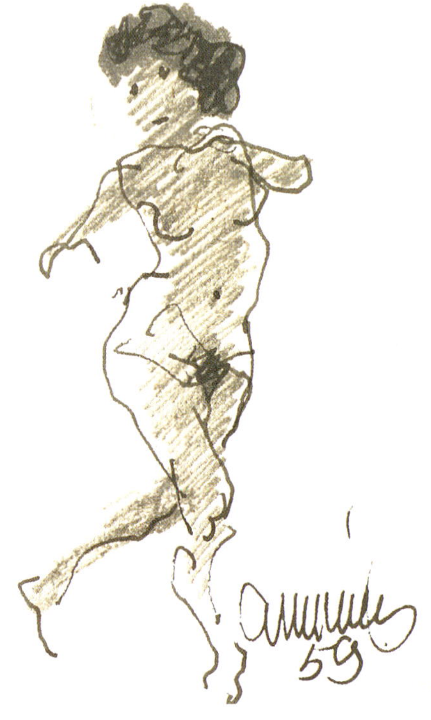

FIG. 23–28 (from left to right)
Untitled (Female Figure—Bending Over), 1956

Untitled (Female Figure—Hand Touching Floor), 1956

Untitled (Running Female Figure), 1959

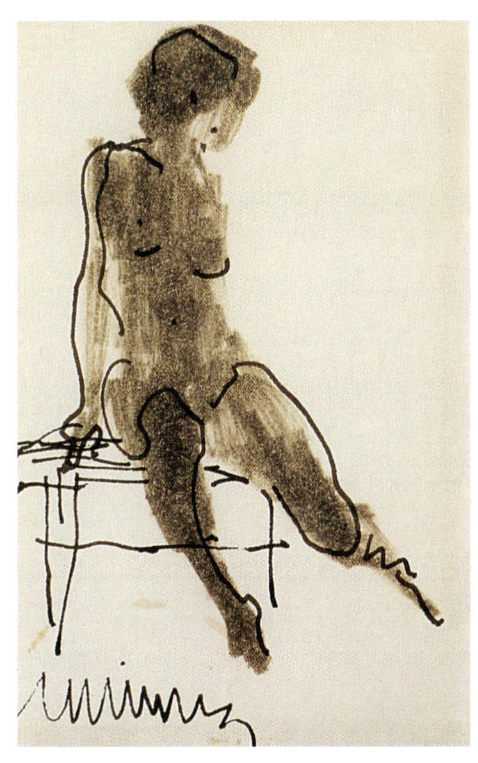

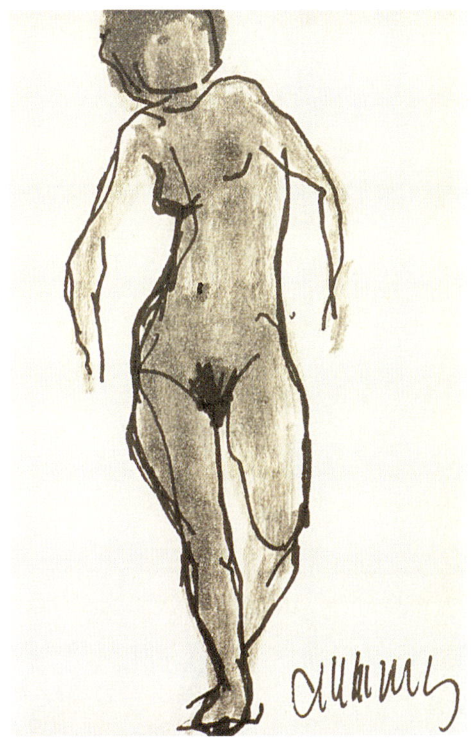

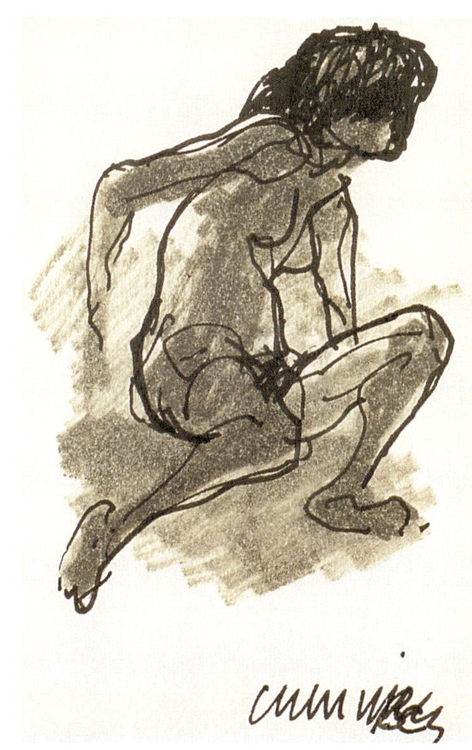

Untitled (Seated Female Figure), 1959

Untitled (Female Figure—Arms at Sides), c. 1956

Untitled (Crouching Female Figure), 1959

Ink and wash on paper
Museum of Northwest Art 2004.138.103
Blair and Lucille Kirk Collection

Cumming's interest in and support of minority groups.

Besides the figure studies that Selig and the Kirks purchased, a few smaller paintings, such as *Cyclist* (1955; fig. 19) (a kind of Hell's Angels figure) and *The Child* (1958; pl. 11), remain of the period. Other portrayed children include *Boy on Stilts* (1959; fig. 29), another African American subject, and the group *Swimmers* (1959; pl. 12). *The Roots of Heaven* (1959; pl. 13), an image of two nuns, had its title borrowed from a popular novel of the day by Romain Gary. It won first prize in the 1960 "Puget Sound Area Exhibition" at the Charles and Emma Frye Art Museum. That same year *Two Girls* (1960; page 6) was purchased by the Frye out of its first invitational exhibition for local artists.[37]

Things were looking up for Cumming, although his third and fourth marriages, the latter to an African American woman named Clyde Carter (1919–86), had ended. There appeared to be light at the end of the "dark wood" of Cumming's long political odyssey. Adding to the recognition of the Frye prize and purchase, Cumming returned to the gallery scene with an exhibition at the top avant-garde forum of the era, Scott Galleries, in 1964.

Later that year, Cumming was contacted by Seattle Art Museum curator Millard B. Rogers, who, at Dr. Fuller's discreet urging, offered him his second one-man show at the Seattle Art Museum. In retrospect, this was an extraordinarily conciliatory gesture on Fuller's part. In addition to having given Cumming his first solo exhibition anywhere, in 1941, and buying six important paintings in a five-year period, the Asian art connoisseur had also assisted the artist with small cash gifts while he was hospitalized. Cumming, in an incredible gaffe that can only be attributed to his blind political convictions of the time, took the city's leading art establishment figure to task for displaying a show of Mexican printmakers in the museum's basement activity room instead of in the main floor galleries in Volunteer Park. The review appeared in a 1948 issue of the West Coast edition of *People's World*, a Party organ. Fuller wrote a letter expressing hurt, and Cumming responded with the typical anti-bourgeois bosh he had perfected.

Barely more than a decade later, the old man was offering the battered and beleaguered Cumming another solo show. With all due respect to Thomas Wolfe, perhaps Cumming had proved that you *can* go home again.

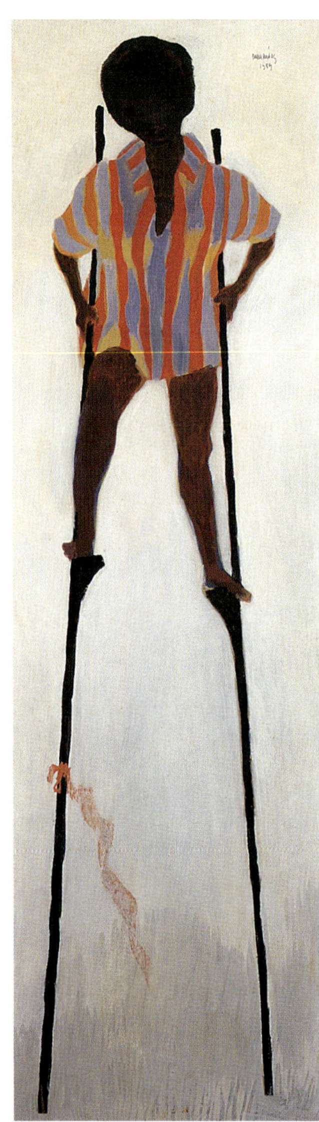

FIG. 29
Boy on Stilts,
1959
Oil and tempera on board
65 x 23½
Collection of Fredda and Steven Goldfarb

NOTES

1. Deloris Tarzan Ament, "William Cumming: 'The Willie Nelson of Northwest Art,'" in *Iridescent Light: The Emergence of Northwest Art* (Seattle: University of Washington Press, 2002), 171–72.
2. William Cumming to Margaret Bundy Callahan, May 3, 1942.

3. Ibid., May 28, 1942.
4. Ibid., July 4, 1942.
5. Ibid., August 13, 1942.
6. Ibid., August 28, 1942.
7. Ibid.
8. Ibid.
9. Ibid., September 6, 1942.
10. Ibid., October 1, 1942.
11. Ibid., October 5, 1942.
12. Ibid., March 28, 1943.
13. Ibid.
14. William Cumming to Kenneth and Margaret Callahan, June 16, 1943.
15. William Cumming to Guy Irving Anderson, October 2, 1943.
16. William Cumming to Margaret Bundy Callahan, October 29, 1943.
17. Ray Kass, *Morris Graves: Vision of the Inner Eye* (New York: Braziller, 1983), 38.
18. William Cumming to Margaret Bundy Callahan, February 5, 1944.
19. Ibid.
20. Ibid., 1944.
21. Ibid., n.d.
22. Ibid.
23. Ibid., January 19, 1945.
24. William Cumming, interview with author, January 25, 2005.
25. Ibid.
26. "Mrs. Hartle, Ex-Red, Freed From Prison," *New York Times*, February 2, 1956, 26.
27. Kathryn S. Olmsted, *Red Spy Queen: A Biography of Elizabeth Bentley* (Chapel Hill, N.C.: University of North Carolina Press, 2002).
28. Lawrence E. Davies, "Witness Admits Inquiry Contempt," *New York Times*, June 17, 1954, 25.
29. Ament, "William Cumming," 171.
30. Frank Krasnowsky, interview with author, March 7, 2005. Krasnowsky is the only living Trotskyist who takes full credit for easing Cumming away from the clutches of Stalinism into the Trotskyist faction. As he told me, "Yes, we recruited him. He was ready."
31. William Cumming, interview with author, January 25, 2005.
32. Clara Fraser, *Revolution, She Wrote* (Seattle: Red Letter Press, 1998).
33. William Cumming, interview with author, January 31, 2005.
34. Archives of the Communist Party USA and Archives of Northwest Art, William Cumming files, Collection #2553-002, Boxes VF896 and VF1388, Allen Library, University of Washington.
35. Ibid., Box VF1388.
36. William Cumming, interview with author, February 7, 2005.
37. Walser S. Greathouse to William Cumming, January 21, 1960.

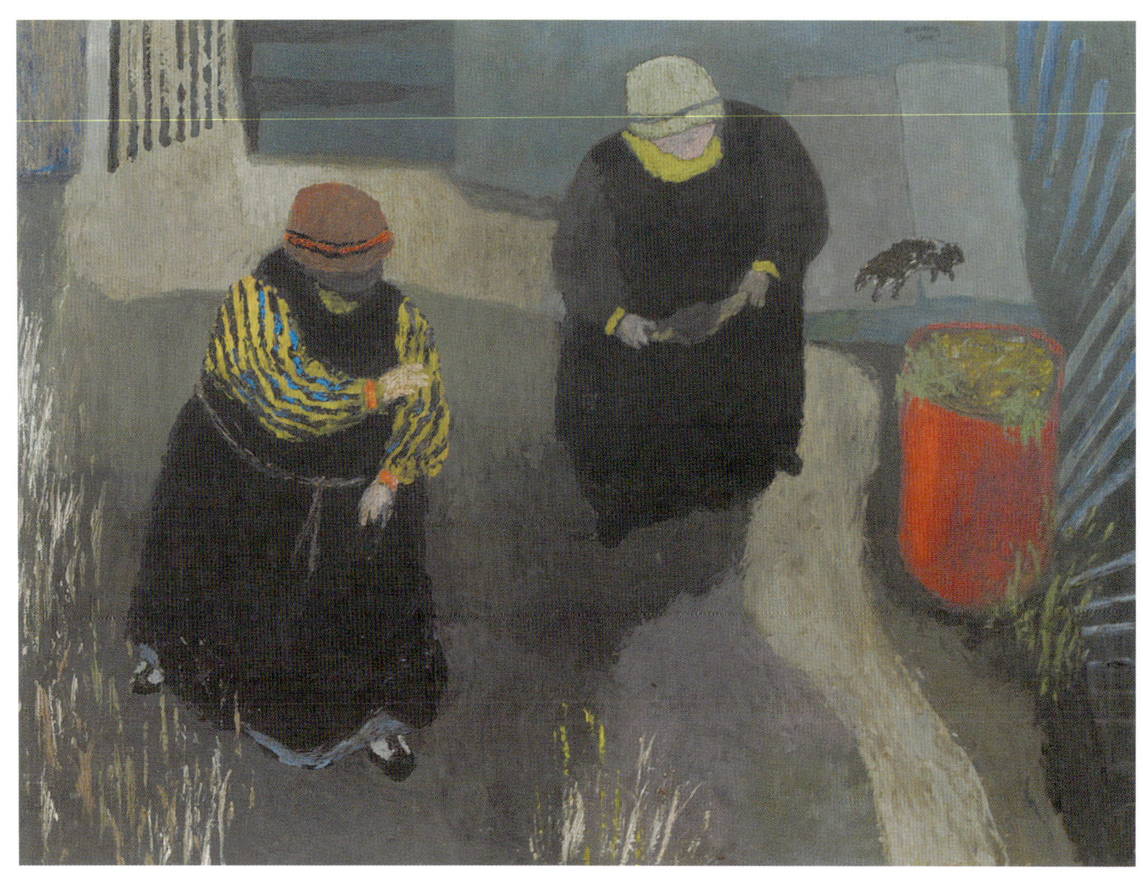

FIG. 30
The Sisters, 1960
Oil and tempera on masonite
36 x 48
Collection of Philip and Mary Serka

CHAPTER FOUR

The Search for the Populist Subject

I agree with Bonnard when he said, "Moi, j'observe."
—William Cumming, 2005[1]

William Cumming's 1961 Seattle Art Museum exhibition contained fourteen paintings (including two that are a part of this exhibition: *The Sisters*, 1960, fig. 30, and *The Little Nun*, 1961, pl. 27) and eight ink drawings. They build on the street sketches Cumming had sold to Manfred Selig. One painting in particular, *Song of the Cranes* (1961; fig. 31), is a tribute to playwright Bertolt Brecht (1898–1956) and his composer-collaborator Kurt Weill (1900–50); it is a scene from *Rise and Fall of the City of Mahagonny* (1929), the musical that first expressed Brecht's conversion to Marxism. *Song of the Cranes* displays a Lotte Lenya–like figure in cabaret attire, and words from the songs are inscribed on the painting in German with Cumming's characteristic lettering.

Curator Millard B. Rogers's brief statement in the accompanying brochure was extremely circumspect and flattering. He notes that Cumming studied privately with Burnley instructor Nikolas Damascus but was otherwise self-taught. As to the "lost years," Rogers simply mentions that "ill health forced him to give up painting for almost a decade in the late forties and early fifties."[2] We now know this is not entirely true but, despite considerable efforts, little of the art of the "lost years" has been found, apart from the sketches Manfred Selig bought and a few other works.

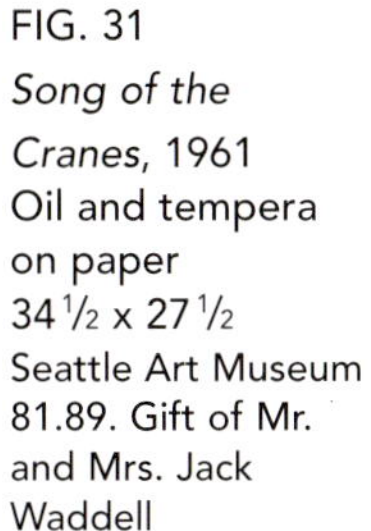

FIG. 31
Song of the Cranes, 1961
Oil and tempera on paper
34 ½ x 27 ½
Seattle Art Museum 81.89. Gift of Mr. and Mrs. Jack Waddell

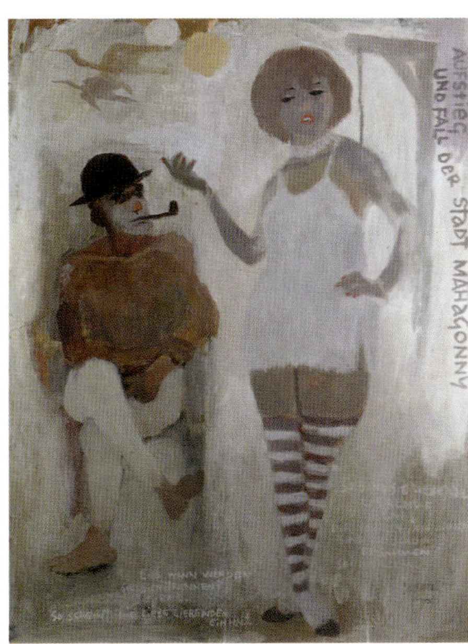

One work, however, *Steelworkers' Strike* (ca. 1959; fig. 32), was saved by Frank Krasnowsky and suggests the more socialist-realist tangent taken under pressure from the Party to make proper proletarian pictures. Far more realistic and propagandistic, it may honor a 1939 Seattle steelworkers' union strike march that led to police clashes.[3]

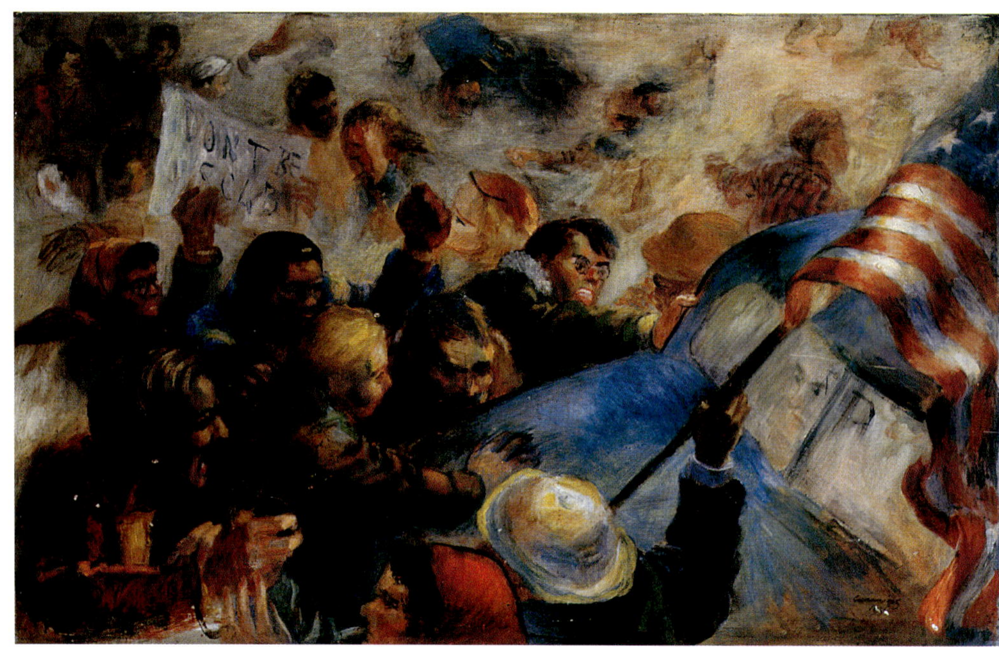

FIG. 32
Steelworkers' Strike, ca. 1959
Mixed media on board
24 x 36
Collection of Frank Krasnowsky

Leaving all that behind, Cumming's SAM show looked like a new leaf had been turned in the artist's life. But had he been rehabilitated? The subjects are still accessible, and perhaps there is a ratcheting down to populist rather than socialist realism. Cumming has mentioned in passing the direct and indirect effects of pressure on his art from Party members once he joined their ranks.[4] Furthermore, it is possible that many of the works of the Party years were dispersed or even destroyed after the revelations of the Hartle Affair for fear of future embarrassment or even arrest.[5]

More importantly, Seattle was coming of age culturally. This happened to coincide perfectly with Cumming's comeback. New galleries besides Scott included Zoe Dusanne, Otto Seligman, Gordon Woodside, and Henriette Woessner, as well as the Cellar Gallery in Kirkland, east of Lake Washington.

Within a year, Rogers would borrow *Song of the Cranes* for "Northwest Art Today," the huge catchall survey for Century 21, the 1962 Seattle World's Fair. Eighty-eight paintings and sculptures were displayed in the sleek new Exhibition Hall on the fairgrounds designed by leading International Style architect Paul Thiry. In an important setting, the Big Four were set alongside the University moderns like Ambrose Patterson and Walter F. Isaacs, and Wendell Brazeau (1910–74) and Spencer Moseley (1925–89) (the latter two had been postgraduate students at Atelier Fernand Léger). As Millard Rogers astutely pointed out:

> The present exhibit may reinforce such beliefs about the "Northwest School of art," but the evidence presented here will certainly modify some of the clichés concerning a particular muted color sense, a strong influence of the forest and the sea, and even the Oriental flavor. These factors are modified by rapid communication in the field of art today.[6]

Scholars will continue to argue for decades about the beginning and ending dates of the "Northwest School," a term for the Big Four that Cumming both uses in the subtitle to *Sketchbook* and thoroughly repudiates therein. For example, art historians and co-curators Sheryl Conkelton and Laura Landau use the year 1954 as a cut-off date for their investigations.[7] Rogers's bold modernization of Northwest art in his World's Fair essay strongly suggests 1962 as a terminal point. In Cumming's case, an earlier date, 1945, coinciding with his joining the Communist Party, proves even more persuasive, at least in terms of his own interactions with the Callahan circle. It could also be argued that both Tobey and Callahan produced their greatest works between 1941 and 1945.

For our purposes, the important thing is that Seattle had grown up, Cumming had recovered, and the entire art scene became livelier, less parochial, and even, for a few, profitable. The advent of art critics like Jean Batie, Anne G. Todd, and Tom Robbins at the *Seattle Times* and Ann Faber, Sally Hayman, and Thelma Lehmann at the *Seattle Post-Intelligencer* in the 1960s changed everything. Exhibitions were covered regularly, reputations were measured and revised, and the cultural status of the visual arts in general rose steadily. Cumming, who had eighteen solo exhibits between 1962 and 1978, benefited substantially from the improved level of critical writing. In fact, the success of the SAM exhibition, six cash prizes in various competitive juried shows, and a raft of favorable reviews and interviews drew Cumming close to the top of the Seattle art world.

In a 1966 radio interview on KING-FM with Jim Wilkie and Rolon Bert Garner touching on the history of the Northwest Annual, Cumming reminisced about past Annuals and spoke at length about the "52nd Annual" at the new Seattle Art Museum Modern Art Pavilion on the former World's Fair site (now called Seattle Center), renovated with funds from contemporary art collector Virginia Wright's mother, Virginia Merrill Bloedel (1902–89). Cumming observed, "The trouble with this kind of show is that while it purports to be a definitive prestige show for the area for a given year, it becomes a sort of grab bag, and you . . . still have a very unsatisfactory sampling of work."[8]

It would be another decade before Cumming's suggestion that the Annual be junked and replaced with an invitational was implemented by SAM modern art curators Charles Cowles and Sarah Clark. Until then, in each of the subsequent other invitational exhibitions of the decade, Cumming was always included.

Some of Cumming's press coverage in the 1960s and 1970s took the form of thinly veiled interviews and profiles rather than reviews or critical analyses. Ann Faber's 1960 article hangs on his every word as he pontificates on the human

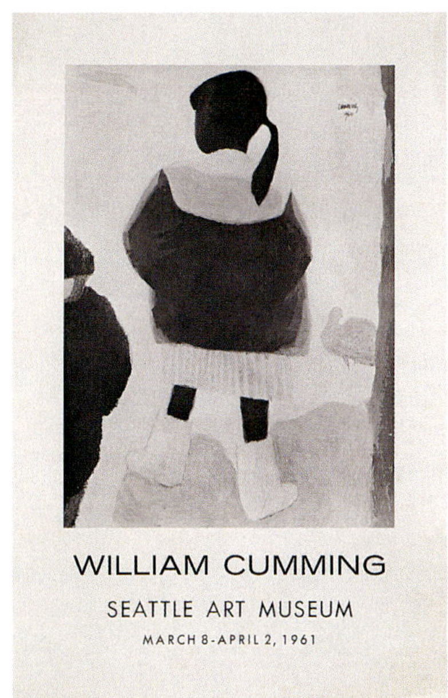

FIG. 33
Seattle Art Museum exhibition catalogue cover illustrating *The Spectator* (1959)
Collection of the artist

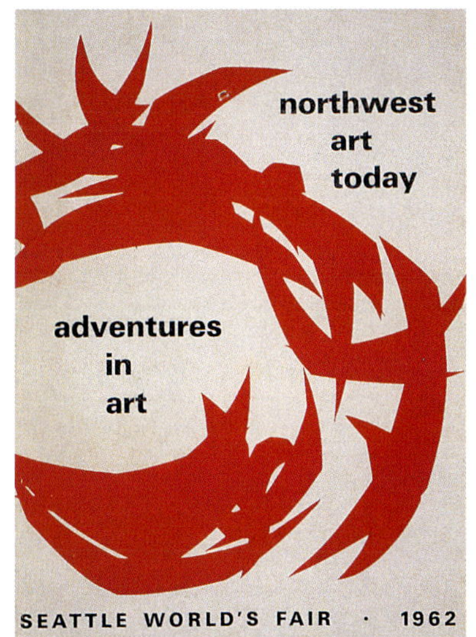

FIG. 34
Catalogue cover for exhibitions at Century 21, Seattle World's Fair, 1962

FIG. 35
Little Boy on Parade, 1969
Ink and pencil on paper
17 ½ x 15
Courtesy of Gordon Woodside / John Braseth Gallery

figure.[9] A Sunday supplement article in the *Seattle Times* calls him piquantly, "Seattle's Artist 'Of the People,'" accompanied by several pages of black-and-white photographs of the artist sitting in the street sketching a road crew.[10] *Boy on Stilts* (1959; see fig. 29) appears behind the artist in a staged studio shot. Even a woman in pedal pushers at a laundromat is worthy of intent observation.

Despite a fifty-fifty split between interview and analysis, Robbins's 1963 preview of Cumming's shows at PANACA Gallery in Bellevue and at the University Unitarian Church Fine Arts Gallery is really the first piece of serious writing the artist received. Calling Cumming a "geriatrical Tom Sawyer," Robbins captures the artist's mordant wit and laconic manner. While Robbins notes that Cumming is "probably the most popular painter in the Northwest today," he also praises him for resisting the sentimentality and kitsch of Norman Rockwell and Walter Keane. Robbins brings a darker tone into the discussion when he notes how "the inescapable fact of death, which is the greatest absurdity, hangs heavy in Cumming's work."[11]

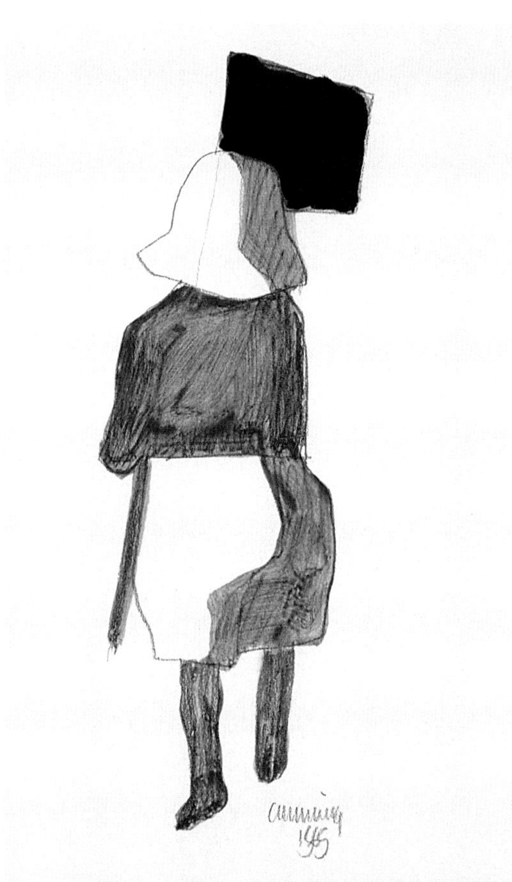

Anne G. Todd delves more deeply into the morbidity and danger visible in Cumming's work in her review of the artist's first solo show at Gordon Woodside Gallery in 1965. Sidestepping Robbins and other critics' fascination with the forty-eight-year-old artist's line of blarney, she quietly states, "What I gather from the paintings in the show . . . (and I have not asked him whether I am right or wrong) is that Cumming feels like the past was lived by people identical with ourselves."[12] The many references in the works' titles to Greek tragedy, the *Iliad*, and other works of Classical literature suggest the example of Michael Spafford, a University of Washington professor of art who moved to Seattle in 1963 and who also favored Greco-Roman mythology in his similarly de-individualized figure paintings.

Cumming soon published a pedagogical manifesto in the *Seattle Times*. "Art Students Need Fundamentals" is a ringing indictment of art instruction in the Seattle Public Schools. Lamenting that his Burnley students arrived unequipped technically, he ridicules the then-prevalent notion that creativity rather than technical skills is the proper goal for secondary art education curricula. It is a thoughtful, well-argued polemic that elevates Cumming's community stature and provides a counterpoint to the bland city school arts programs in existence at the time.[13]

Children and African Americans dominate much of Cumming's art from 1960 to 1978 and may have been a further outgrowth of Cumming's brief marriage to fellow radical Clyde Carter, the Trotskyist he had met through Krasnowsky and the Frasers. Besides *Boy on Stilts* and *The Spectator*, which appeared on the cover of the SAM catalog for the 1961 exhibition, numerous other paintings and sketches revealed the artist's search for a populist subject, one that addresses all facets of American society, including racial minorities.

The determined use of the figure became less and less fashionable as the 1960s and 1970s continued, causing Robbins to remark in another interview in 1967 that "you're one of the few artists anywhere still working with the figure in any kind of vital, formally significant way."[14] Cumming agreed and confessed that he paid very little attention to the art world. Fascinatingly, much of the rest of the interview involves a defense of the use of the figure—but in modernist/formalist terms. For example, Robbins tells Cumming "the only significant thing in your work . . . is the dialogue you set up between movement and volume." Thus, as early as 1967, critics were paving the way for the artist's transition from a social-realist practice to a figurative-formalist position with strong modernist tendencies. Cumming would dispute this for many years to come and, to a certain extent, still does, but when confronted at this time by Robbins, he replied, "What you're saying is valid but you're the one who'll have to explain it. You're the critic."[15]

The FitzGerald Affair

Cumming had avoided going to court or testifying as a result of the Hartle Affair, but he was not so lucky in 1965, when he was commandeered by his sculptor friend, James FitzGerald (1910–73) to appear on FitzGerald's behalf in a plagiarism suit that was the talk of the town and the subject of an unprecedented four-thousand-word article in *Seattle Magazine*.[16]

FitzGerald became convinced that a sculpture of his, *Rock Totem* (1958), had been plagiarized by a University of Washington graduate student, Robert Hopkins, for a work in a parking lot adjacent to the Ballard branch of Washington Federal Savings and Loan. His suit for $50,000 was countered by Hopkins' $25,000 suit for libel and slander.

Hopkins's *Transcending* (1965) was so similar to FitzGerald's work that the case went to trial on January 4, 1965, in Room 745 of the King County Courthouse in downtown Seattle. Judge Edward E. Henry presided. Before Cumming's testimony, FitzGerald's other witnesses included painter William Ivey (1919–92), who helpfully explained, "Creativity lies in the concept—that is the one thing that an artist has to offer—not in the product." FitzGerald's dealer, Don Scott, also testified.

According to the author of the *Seattle Magazine* article, Suzanne Braun, it was Cumming's testimony that attracted the most attention. Alternately soft-spoken and angry, Cumming was obviously uncomfortable. Looking back, he said, "It was absurd to sue in the first place that bum boy for [University of Washington sculpture head Everett] DuPen, that incompetent boob."[17]

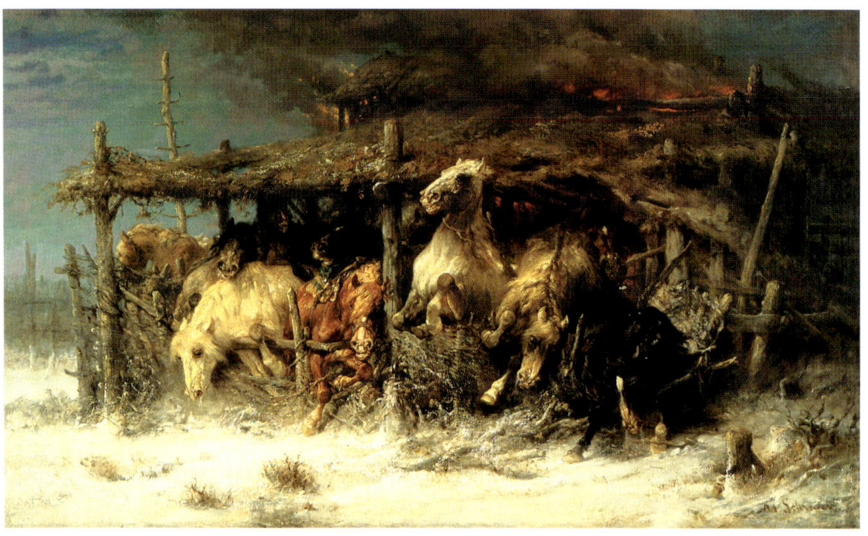

answer is a qualified yes. The dignity of work is preserved at the same time the artist's lifestyle approaches a down-home squirehood. What saves Cumming from romanticizing his already romantic Western subjects is the absence of facial features and the careful, dusty yet luminous color (see, for example, *Driving Cattle*, 1975; fig. 36). Given a potentially limited topic, the artist achieves a very wide range of approaches with, as usual, drawings that were equally as important as the paintings, such as *Figure on Horseback* (1981; pl. 56).

FIG. 38
ADOLF SCHREYER
(German, 1828-1899)
The Burning Stable, c. 1880
Oil on canvas, 47 3/4 x 79 1/4
Charles and Emma Frye Art Museum
1952.154.

One crucial development in the late 1950s through the late 1970s is the perfection of the de-individuated figure. A focus for form, event, movement, and volume, the faceless figures took on an even greater universality that sidestepped the social realism to which Cumming had become allergic (see, for example, *Cast a Cold Eye*, 1973; pl. 44). Far better at paying homage to Everyman and Everywoman, the faceless figure paintings had political and artistic advantage. Without precise identity, portraiture was never a possibility. Unlike Barbara Hartle, to "name names" in his paintings was unthinkable for Cumming, as if it would allow identification through portraiture and facilitate investigation and invasion of privacy. With his great powers of observation, Cumming would never turn his humble street-sketcher identity into a tool of oppression.

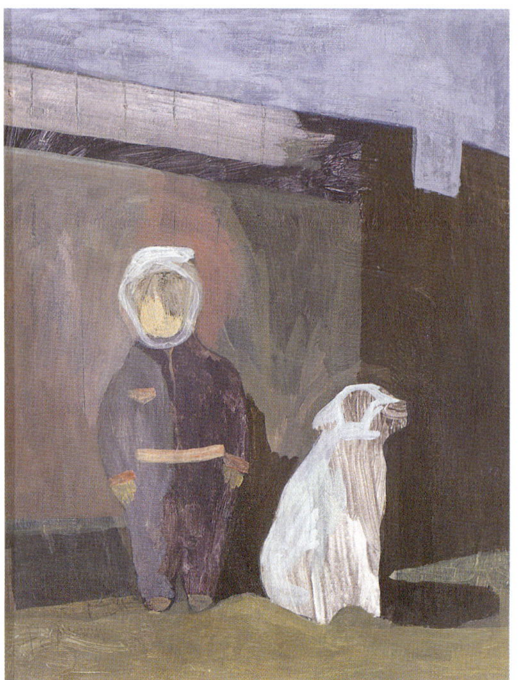

FIG. 39
Snapshot—Boy with Dog 1922, 1976
Oil and tempera on board
20 1/2 x 16 3/4
Private collection, Bellevue

As the pain of the "lost years" receded, Cumming's art took on new energy. Before he turned his back completely on the dissolving pressures of the Party to create the proletarian subject—the image of ideological consequence—Cumming had one more painting he had to complete, his ultimate "good-bye to all that," *Structural Steel Shop*.

NOTES

1. William Cumming, interview with author, February 14, 2005.
2. Millard B. Rogers, *William Cumming* (Seattle: Seattle Art Museum, 1961), unpaginated.
3. Frank Krasnowsky, interview with author, March 8, 2005.
4. William Cumming, interview with author, March 7, 2005.
5. Ibid.
6. Norman Davis and Millard B. Rogers, *Northwest Art Today* (Seattle: Century 21 Exposition, Inc., 1962), 7.
7. Sheryl Conkelton and Laura Landau,. *Northwest Mythologies: The Interactions of Mark Tobey, Morris Graves, Kenneth Callahan and Guy Anderson* (Tacoma, Wash.: Tacoma Art Museum and the University of Washington Press, 2003), 15.
8. William Cumming, interview with Jim Wilkie, "Talking About Art," KING-FM, transcript, Archives of Northwest Art, University of Washington, October 1966. Accession 2553, Box VF896.
9. Ann Faber, "People Equal Motion in Cumming Paintings," *Seattle Post-Intelligencer*, September 18, 1960, 15.
10. C. L. Anderson, "Seattle's Artist 'Of the People,'" *Seattle Times Pictorial*, April 9, 1961, 50–55.
11. Tom Robbins, "Testy Prophet Hits Stride as Major Painter," *Seattle Times*, October 20, 1963, 33.
12. Anne G. Todd, "Cumming Views a Few Heroes," *Seattle Times*, November 28, 1965, 14S.
13. William Cumming, "Art Students Need Fundamentals," *Seattle Times*, October 10, 1965, S11.
14. "Whither Goest Cumming?" Interview with Tom Robbins, *Seattle Magazine*, September 1967, 11–16.
15. Ibid.
16. Suzanne Braun, "The Great Courtroom Hassle that Made History Here: Did He Slander? Did He Plagiarize?" *Seattle Magazine*, March 1965, 16.
17. William Cumming, interview with author, February 14, 2005.
18. Ibid.
19. Ibid.

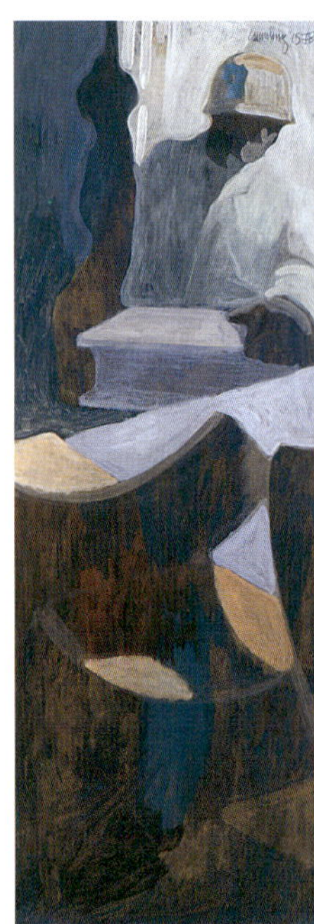
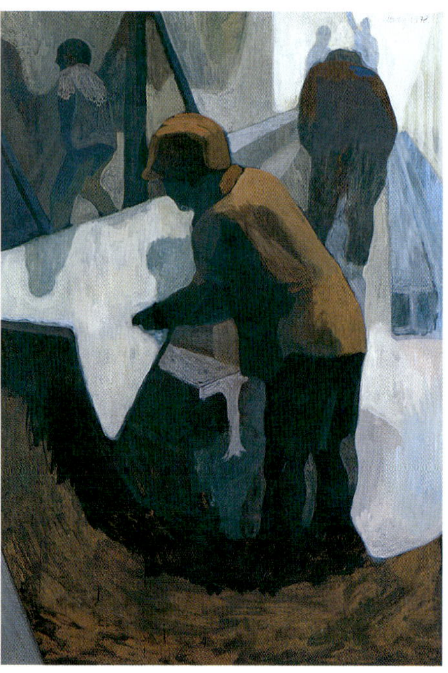
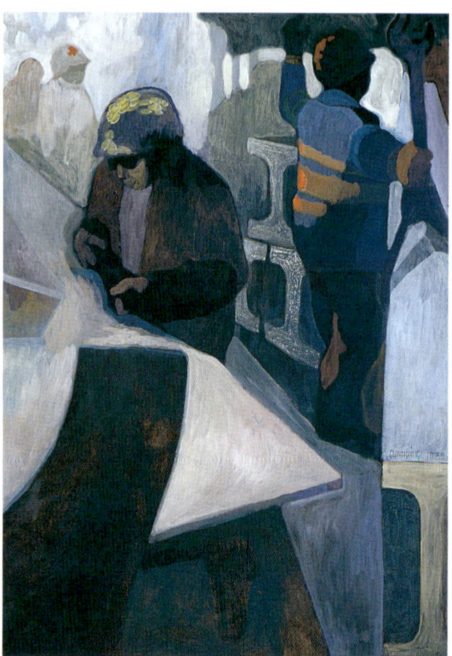
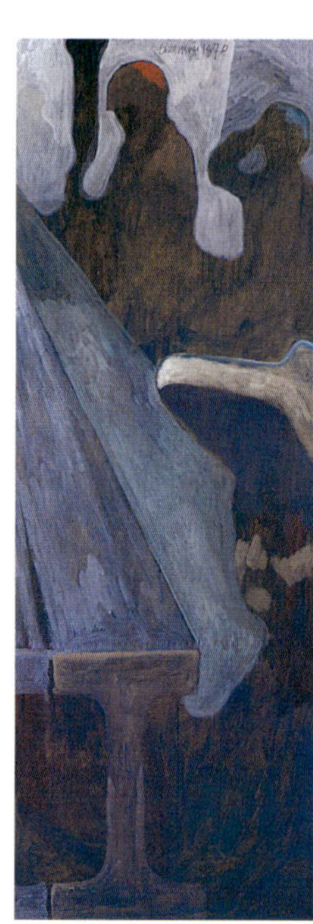

FIG. 40
Structural Steel Shop,
1978
Oil and tempera on
masonite quadriptych
48 x 120
Preston, Gates and Ellis, L.L.P.

CHAPTER FIVE

Sketchbook: Subtext of an Imagination

When I was young, I could remember anything whether it happened or not. . . . Truth is stranger than Fiction, but it is because Fiction is obliged to stick to possibilities. Truth isn't.

—Mark Twain, *Pudd'nhead Wilson's New Calendar*, 1894

Cumming's memoir took nearly two decades to write and covered the same span of time that produced some of his finest paintings. Midway through the writing, *Structural Steel Shop* (1978; fig. 40) formed a grand, creative farewell to both politics and the proletarian art of the people that fellow Party members kept pressuring Cumming to produce. Like *Sketchbook, Structural Steel Shop* represents a finishing up—with a twist.

Highly composed, divided into four sections like a Renaissance altarpiece, the work takes place in the blazing cauldron of industrial labor, the site where Cumming's leftist friends, such as Frank Krasnowsky, had first infiltrated and then been purged from the union hierarchy. None of the workers is identified personally, yet each plays a crucial role in the creation of steel. *Structural Steel Shop* also makes up for the Federal Art Project mural at Burlington High School that was lost in a fire. We'll never know what that one looked like, but *Structural Steel Shop* no doubt more than measures up to the earlier painting's promise. It also talks back to Kenneth Callahan's logging murals, including *Weyerhaeuser Company Mill B* (1944), one of the paintings the older artist did for the timber conglomerate after the Federal Art Project ended.

Like *Sketchbook, Structural Steel Shop* is multi-paneled with one crucial point of view, a single, fire-red dot at its center, symbolizing the viewer. After its completion, Cumming never looked back in his art to the propaganda style of the 1940s and 1950s but, as we have demonstrated, he retained a loyalty to the concept of the image of consequence, the subject of everyday people's lives so dear to the Leninists and Stalinists of his youth.

After *Sketchbook* and *Structural Steel Shop*, Cumming broadened the image of consequence into middle-class subjects—childhood, family, leisure, recreation, fashion—and made it relevant to changing times. Cumming never forgot the poor and downtrodden; he just fit them into a less dreary, more colorful setting.

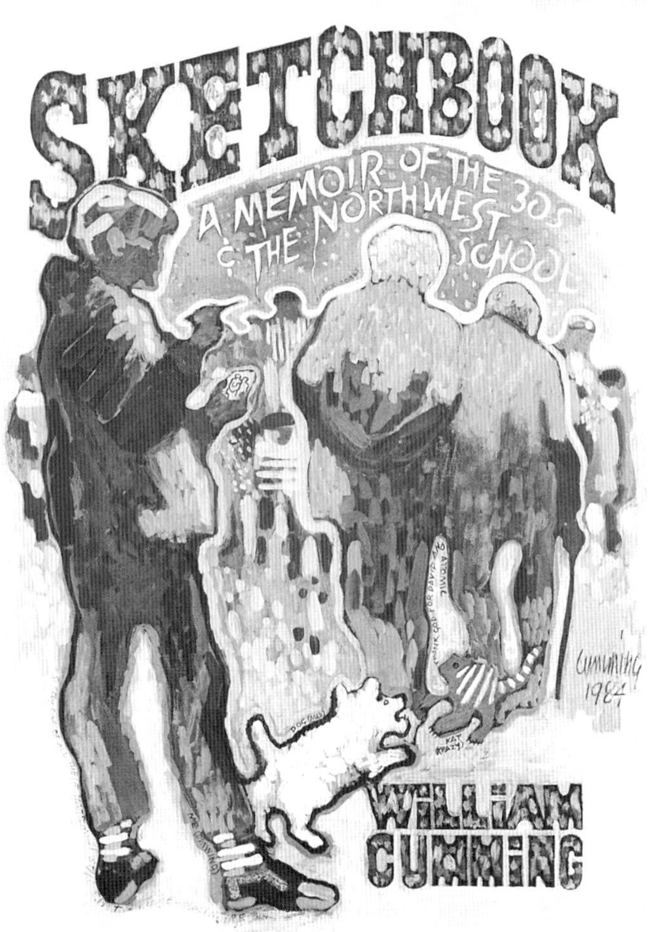

FIG. 41
Cover of
Sketchbook, 1984

Sketchbook: A Memoir of the 1930s and the Northwest School was finally published in the fall of 1984. It never would have seen the light of day were it not for one man, Donald Ellegood (1924–2003), longtime director of the University of Washington Press. Close to being a Maxwell Perkins of the Northwest (the legendary Scribners editor of Hemingway, Fitzgerald, and Thomas Wolfe), Ellegood prompted and prodded his friend and neighbor for over twenty years to get down on paper the rich lode of anecdotes and surprisingly poignant moments of his mentor-friends in the Margaret Bundy Callahan circle. Cumming has readily admitted that the structure and sequencing of chapters of *Sketchbook* were completely left up to Ellegood. None of the reviewers picked up on this, and if they were aware of it, they kept quiet about it.[1]

An additional twenty years after Cumming's book was published, *Sketchbook* now deserves to be called a classic of American autobiography. Although Cumming is careful to distinguish between autobiography and memoir, much recent literary history and critical scholarship tend to play down the differences between the two genres. As Roy Pascal writes in *Design and Truth in Autobiography:*

> There is no autobiography that is not in some respects a memoir, and no memoir that is without autobiographical information. . . . In the autobiography, proper attention is focused on the self, in the memoir or reminiscence on others.[2]

Thus, Cumming's shifting stories that dart back and forth in time are an authorial solution to the problem of straightforward autobiographical chronology. It is important to remember how the very origins of the English novel are intimately tied up with the conceits of memoir and autobiography. *Robinson Crusoe* (1720) and *Jane Eyre* (1847), both presented as putative true-life accounts, are two such examples told by a credulous narrator who, like Cumming, gains wisdom through crisis. We know now from his sanatorium reading lists that Cumming was thoroughly familiar

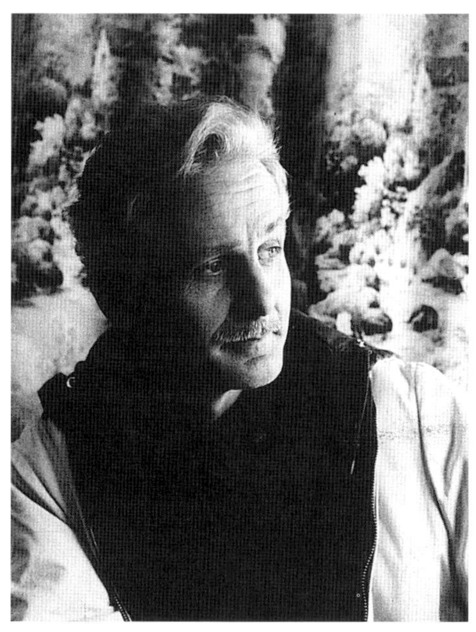

FIG. 42
DAVID HOWE
(American)
William Cumming,
c. 1980.
Black and white silver print photograph,
12 x 10
Collection of William Cumming

with James Joyce and aware of Marcel Proust, though he never read the latter's long masterpiece, *Remembrance of Things Past* (1913–27), a book that took the form of a novel masquerading as an autobiography.

What constitutes the greatness of Cumming's only published book? Its literary style, deeply subjective impressions of people, and richly allusive references. Even its opening lines, "Sometime in an autumn in the late fifties I called on an Old Friend," suggest the opening lines of Dante's *Inferno* ("Midway through life, I found myself in a dark wood"). The narrative's establishment shares that of any novel: the main character as storyteller and the other significant character, Margaret Bundy Callahan, the "Old Friend." Like Dante's guide to the underworld, the Roman poet Vergil, Maggy Callahan becomes Cumming's guide and moral mentor, replete with occasional scoldings and Cumming's falling out with her husband, Kenneth, which the opening chapter tries to repair years afterwards.

Cumming also published two article-length memoirs in 1965 and 1967, "Look Back in Laughter"[3] and "Fragments of a Journal,"[4] wherein he tries out various versions of the truth, assessing both his feelings and the strength of his memories. There never was a real journal to speak of, so even at the earliest stage of construction, literary artifice was helpful.

As autobiography scholar Timothy Dow Adams writes, "All autobiographers are unreliable narrators, all humans are liars, and yet . . . to be a successful liar in one's life story is especially difficult."[5] In Cumming's case, it will be left to future literary historians and biographers to pin down the precise refractions of the truth. As this book has tried to demonstrate, despite repeated references in *Sketchbook* to the artist's misbegotten politics ("my period of political unconsciousness," p. 57; "rote phrases of jargon dictated by Stalinist party line," p. 93; "desert of political activism," "iron cage of thirties Marxism," p. 106; and "facile and shallow materialism of authoritarian Marxism," p. 51), it is likely that much remains to be studied and analyzed about Cumming's immersion in radical politics. As the revelations of the letters to Maggy Callahan make clear, however, Cumming's positions *at the time* often differed sharply from his version filtered through *Sketchbook* many years later.

Perhaps playwright Lillian Hellman (1905–84) is a good contrast. Her three books, *An Unfinished Woman* (1969), *Pentimento* (1973), and *Scoundrel Time* (1976), all deal with radical politics during the same period as *Sketchbook*. As Adams points out about Hellman, large parts of her life are not included in *An Unfinished Woman* and, unlike Cumming, there is a constant "underplaying of her commitment to Stalin."[6] However, Hellman shares with Cumming a published recanting of her "errors." "Simply then and now I feel betrayed by the nonsense I had believed."[7]

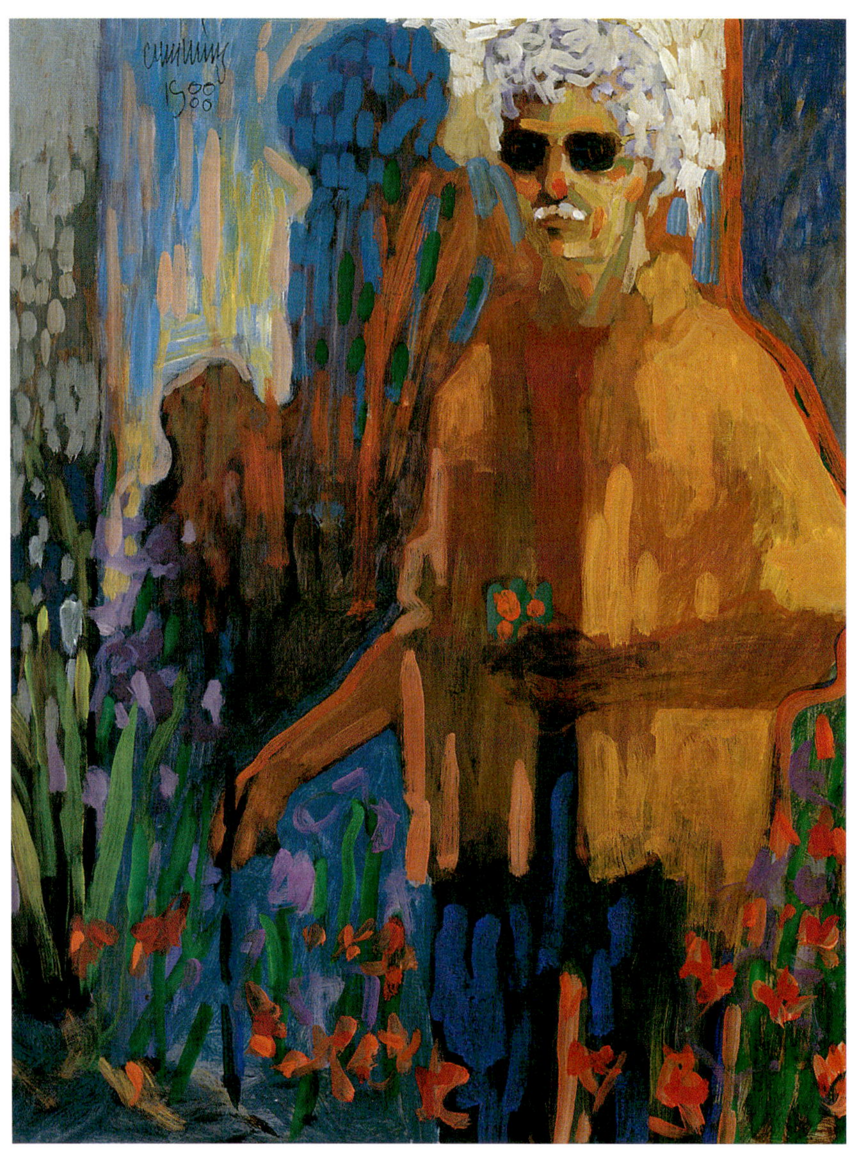

FIG. 43
Self-Portrait, 1988
Oil and tempera on
masonite
36¾ x 24
Collection of Dr. and Mrs.
Chester Woodside

Adams's explanation of Hellman's silence on Stalin's Great Terror and the Gulag Archipelago might also apply to Cumming's blind spots evidenced in his letters to Mrs. Callahan. Adams notes that "[Hellman] argues that what we now know about the 1937–1938 purges in Russia seemed then far less certain, part of a propagandistic smokescreen made out of equal parts of anti-Communist press releases and a Soviet determination to cover up what happened by never admitting it."[8]

Other literary influences to *Sketchbook* can be discerned in addition to Mark Twain and Thomas Wolfe, Cumming's admitted literary avatars. Although Cumming claims Ellegood made up all the chapter titles, such as "I Remember an Earlier Day," and "A Portrait and What Happened to It," silent film intertitles seem one source for them, as do the wide-eyed naïveté and up-by-the-bootstraps optimism of the novels of Horatio Alger Jr., written for boys (*Luck and Pluck, Tattered Tom*). The one novel Cumming re-reads every year is also an obvious source for the convention of the older man looking back at his boyhood, *Treasure Island* (1883) by Robert Louis Stevenson.

Cumming's vivid re-creation of events gives them an enduring quality that make one want to re-read *Sketchbook* again and again. Whereas Wolfe's novels have faded for Cumming into the excesses of overly enthusiastic and undisciplined youth, *Sketchbook* retains a similarly youthful credulity, a somewhat hurt sense of growing up, and a passionate attachment to ornate, if sometimes florid, prose style. Unlike Wolfe's tragic fate, which became legend in Seattle, Cumming lived longer than Wolfe's thirty-eight years, and his reminiscences thus take on the refractive patina of time.

Critical response to *Sketchbook* is worth touching upon briefly to underscore how great books are often underappreciated at first, with some comments positive and observant, some obtuse, and some gratuitously sniping.

Regina Hackett of the *Seattle Post-Intelligencer* drew attention to the "relation the writings bear to the painting style. . . . Just as the writing concentrates on significant moments, each painting concentrates on a highly colored, frozen instant of time."[9] Her main disappointment is that the book is a memoir and not a definitive history of Northwest art, which was never Cumming's or Ellegood's intention. Hence her carping that the University moderns (whom Cumming referred to as "diluted School of Paris") are left out or dismissed.

Prophetically, Hackett gives the last word of her review to the one writer who would be most influenced by the book: painter, collector, and all-around dilettante Wesley Wehr (1929–2004). Wehr was a younger acolyte of the Big Four and one with even broader interests than Cumming. As Wehr told Hackett for the final line of her review, "The book is a rich addition to the folklore of the area."

Wehr's two book-length memoirs, *The Eighth Lively Art* (2000) and *The Accidental Collector* (2004), both take the structure of *Sketchbook* for their model and share other aspects of the book, such as the unreliable narrator, the innocent youth looking up to elders, and vanity masquerading as self-deprecating humility.

One factor may explain everything: Donald Ellegood was once again the avuncular and fully involved editor. Wehr mentions Cumming in both books: first, in *The Eighth Lively Art*, where he quotes Cumming on Anderson,[10] and next, in *The Accidental Collector*, where he endorses Cumming's repudiation of the concept of the Northwest School.[11] Regrettably, Wehr goes on to recount a mildly embarrassing episode in Cumming's life, the affair between his fifth wife, Roxanne Johnston, and American poet and visiting professor at the University of Washington, Elizabeth Bishop (1911–79). Without detailing Wehr's distortions compared to Cumming's recollections,[12] it is fair to state that both of Wehr's books are indebted to Cumming's for their subject and format, as well as to their shared editor, Ellegood. Wehr's lifting of Cumming's unreliable narrator, the episodic structure that shifts back and forth in time, and the shared subjects—Anderson, Callahan, Graves, and Tobey, as well as Richard Gilkey, Walter F. Isaacs, and Wendell Brazeau—are also heavily affected by Ellegood's editorial eye. All this makes Wehr's reminiscences a future source for scholars and critics chiefly because of their debts to a greater book.

How else is *Sketchbook* like Cumming's art? In addition to Hackett's "frozen instant of time" metaphor, other analogies are feasible. Both the book and the paintings are somewhat blurred accounts of observed events. Like the book, the paintings posit an uninvolved yet attentive bystander. However, unlike the paintings, *Sketchbook* cannot exist without specific character and identity, whereas the art succeeds in de-individualizing people so as to better achieve a generalized sense of everyday humanity, or, Cumming's image of consequence. More "people's art" than intimate memoir, the paintings have their own modernist facets, such as the book's flip-flopping time sequence. The eradication of perspective space, the crowded compositions, and the increasing emphasis on color, shape, and form all intensify after the publication of *Sketchbook*. While Tobey confronted modernism by jettisoning the figure, narrative, and allegory, Cumming retained event, anecdote, and the figure in action. His progress toward a fuller assimilation of modern art would continue to occupy his late period, the years after the stocktaking, memory purging, and literary accomplishment of *Sketchbook*. The sustained act of writing had an unprecedented impact on an American painter of growing stature.

NOTES

1. William Cumming, interview with author, February 14, 2005.
2. Roy Pascal, *Design and Truth in Autobiography* (Cambridge, Mass.: Harvard University Press), 1960, 36.
3. Cumming, "Look Back in Laughter," *Puget Soundings*, January 1965, 16–17.
4. Cumming, "Fragments of a Journal," *Puget Soundings*, June 1966, 20–25.
5. Timothy Dow Adams, *Telling Lies in Modern American Autobiography* (Chapel Hill, N.C.: University of North Carolina Press, 1990), IX.

6. Ibid., 154.

7. Lillian Hellman, *Three: An Unfinished Woman, Pentimento, Scoundrel Time* (Boston: Little, Brown, 1979), 606.

8. Adams, *Telling Lies*, 155–56.

9. Regina Hackett, "Folklore It Is; Definitive Art Tome It's Not," *Seattle Post-Intelligencer*, November 10, 1984, C1.

10. Wesley Wehr, *The Eighth Lively Art: Conversations with Painters, Poets, Musicians and the Wicked Witch of the West* (Seattle: University of Washington Press, 2000), 84.

11. Wehr, *The Accidental Collector: Art, Fossils & Friendships* (Seattle: University of Washington Press, 2004), 147.

12. William Cumming, interview with author, March 10, 2005.

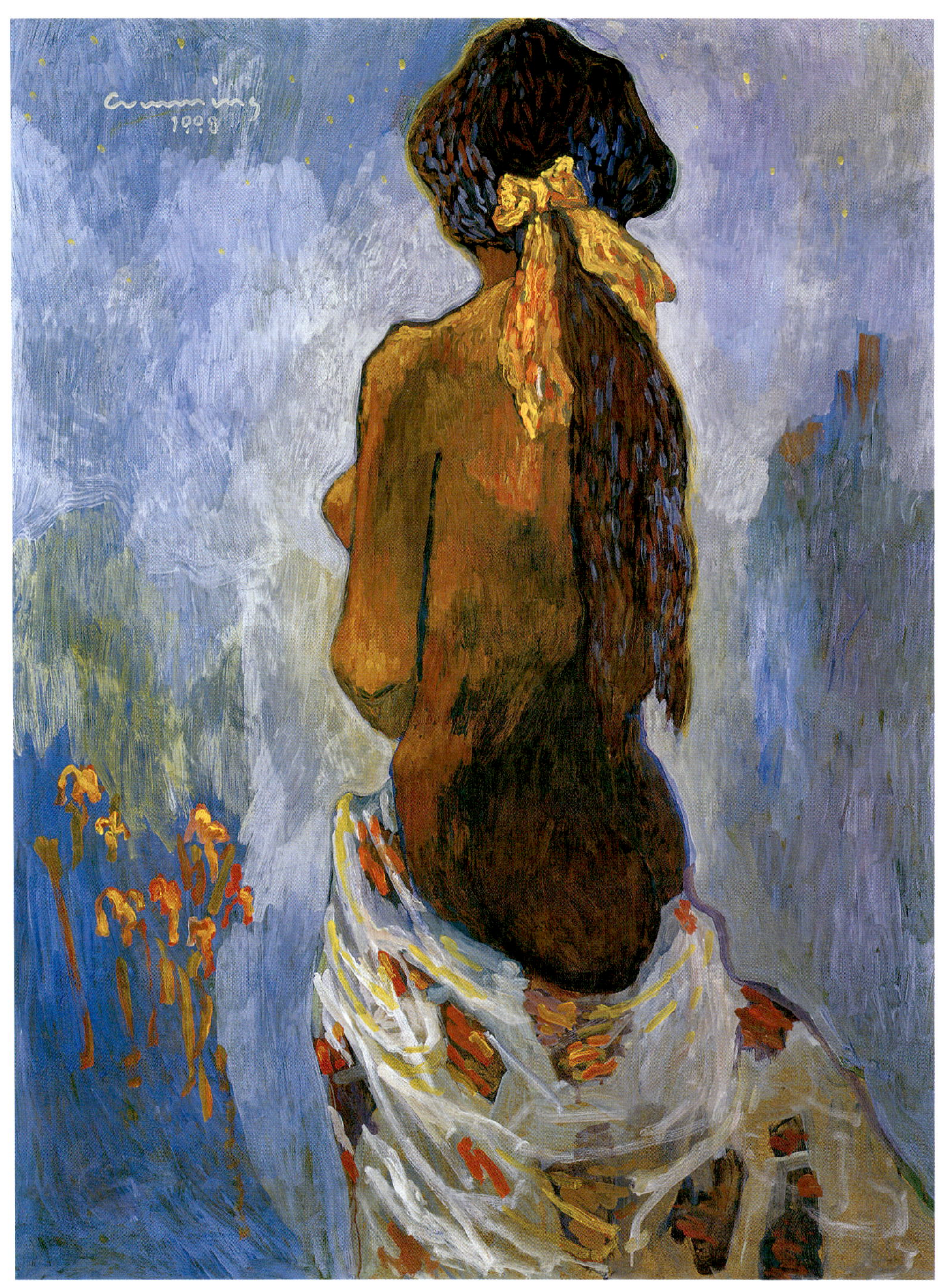

FIG. 44
Dream, 1998
Oil and tempera on masonite
55 x 43
Private collection, Bellevue

CHAPTER SIX

Transformation and Reconciliation: From Marxism to Modernism

It's too easy to put down critics. Most artists don't have the skill to be good nor the courage to be bad.
—William Cumming, interview with author, January 10, 2005

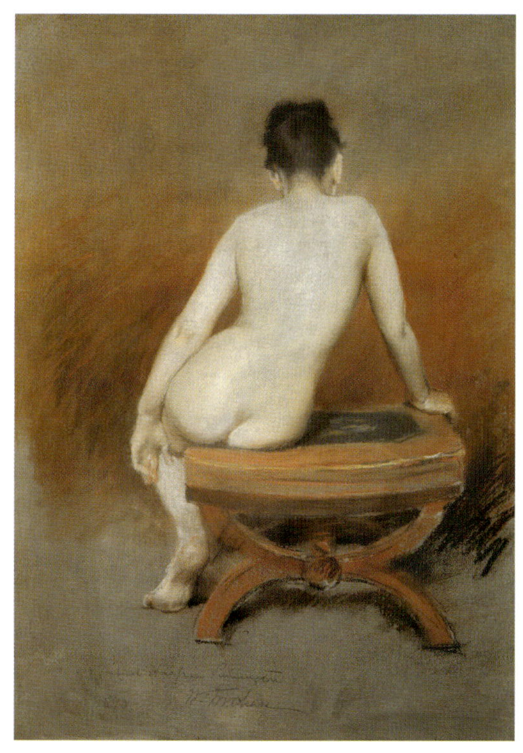

FIG. 45
WILLIAM MERRITT CHASE
(American, 1849–1916)
Back of a Nude, c. 1888
Pastel on canvas, 21 1/2 x 15
Courtesy of Berry-Hill Galleries, Inc.

Cumming's late period has lasted longer than most artists' working lives. His long life has meant outliving friends, lovers, and ex-wives, but also colleagues, other artists, and those whose brilliance or stupidity once impinged on his life in meaningful ways. With the welter of experiences he has had, Cumming has been "a child of the century" (as Ben Hecht referred to himself), eyewitness to and subject of many cultural and political trends and movements, actor in some, bystander in others.

As we have seen, the dedication to the image of consequence had taken care of the question, "What to paint?" What is fascinating is how late Cumming has come to terms with the dominant trend of the twentieth century, modernist abstraction. Cumming was always derisive of the University moderns and never fully succumbed to the non-objectivity or non-representationalism that Tobey, Graves, Callahan, and Anderson each eventually embraced. Cumming's case, as usual, is a more complicated one.

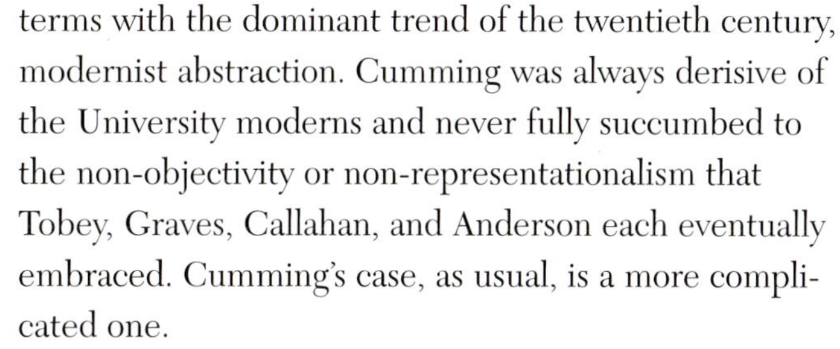

There is no way he ever could have shifted to the tangled "white writing" of Tobey or the gestural "wind patterns" of Callahan or the veiled, erotic Tantric geometrics of Graves. Nor could he have settled for the giant structures of form and design that so dominated the late period of Anderson.

Instead, Cumming formulated his own approaches to make more important the vital underpinnings of modernist abstraction: color, shape, contour, shadow, line, edge, pattern, and form. Because of his long teaching career at Burnley, Cornish, and the Art Institute of Seattle, Cumming has been able to share his opinions and skills with hundreds of students and yet, remarkably, never slow down in the studio. In the process, it could be that, for pedagogical purposes, he isolated various building blocks of painting and concentrated more on perfecting or mastering how each component could reinforce his search for the image of consequence.

Thus, drawing from lecture notes, one can see how Cumming's long transition from Marxism to modernism came about by reason, intuition, and skill, so different a philosophical path from the artist's earnest beliefs in radical political systems.

Avoiding the term "image" as too close to be confused with subject, Cumming tells his students that:

> The edge between a shape and its field is the primary factor in creating "near-far" space in a painting. When we want the shape to "advance" toward NEAR, we can increase the contrast. . . . "Losing" contour, impact or edge, or "gaining" such impact in . . . areas of the same shape approximates the dizzy pace of direct visual experience in the world of three-dimensional actuality.[1]

These comments bear direct relation to the paintings Cumming was working on in the period from 1985 to 2005. The figures hover and quiver in the tight space allotted them, both advancing and receding from the viewer and, indeed, often approximating the movement of a crowded street scene.

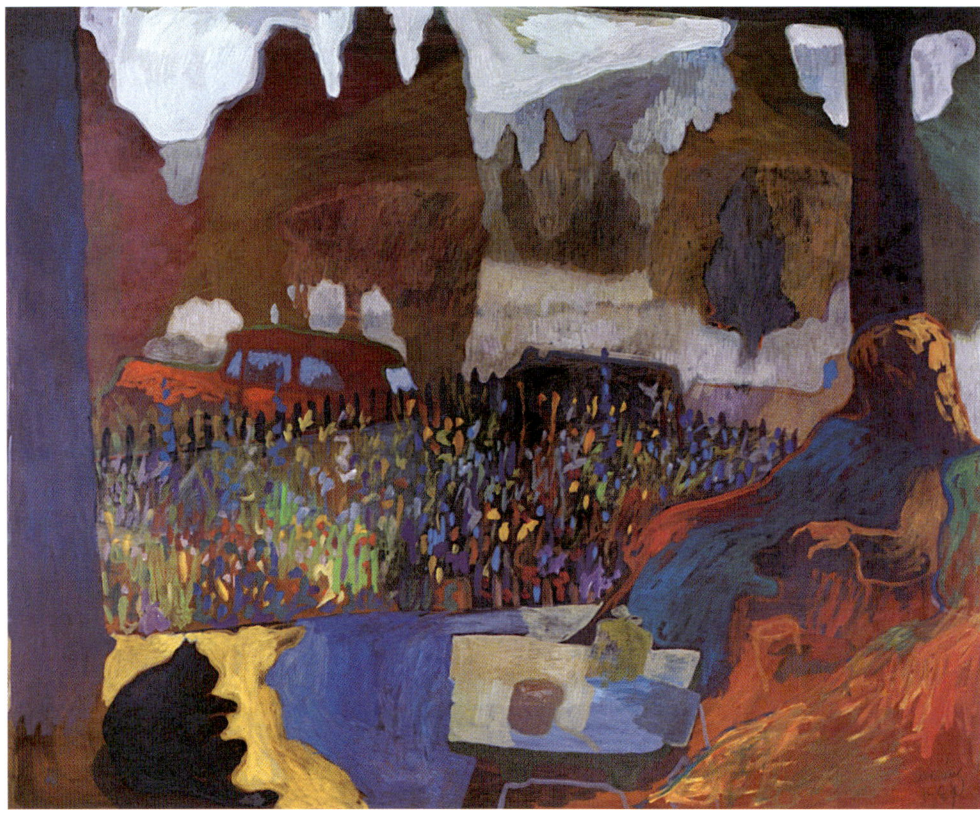

FIG. 46
My Garden, 1984
Oil and tempera on board
36 x 48
Collection of Swedish Medical Center

With contrasts of light and dark, a crucial factor given Cumming's chosen medium of mixed oil and tempera, shadow becomes an important player. As Cumming explains:

> The relationship of any material thing to its world is visually established by "shadow," i.e., by the fact that it intervenes between a surface and the light source, thus depriving a part of that surface from receiving its full share of light. The deprived area we call "shadow."[2]

It should not be surprising that the articulate former art critic and student of literature became a successful classroom art teacher for students of professional and commercial art. Cumming is touchy about the hierarchy between high and low, commercial and fine, claiming, in true postmodern fashion *avant la lettre*, that no such differences exist.

The single most startling development in Cumming's late period is the gradual introduction and refinement of bright color. As he said recently:

> This [bright color] is what I always fancied was my goal. However, lacking any education in these matters, I had a long struggle to get there. The heart of my color is the use of graying tricks, which act as a bed to set off the simpler touches of primary and secondary colors. . . . I began to think about color because I began to think of my art as ultimately more painting than drawing, which is how I had long thought of it. It took me forty years to master value. Before, color was tonality to me but, by the 1980s, I could identify color with value and see value and color as parallel tracks.[3]

FIG. 47
PIERRE BONNARD
(French,1867–1947): Bust in Profile, Red Background (study), c. 1920
Oil on canvas
46 x 52cm
Art Gallery of New South Wales, Sydney, Australia. Purchased with funds provided by the Art Gallery of New South Wales Foundation and the Margaret Hannah Olley Art Trust 2000. ©2005 Artists Rights Society (ARS), New York, ADAGP, Paris
Photograph: Brenton McGeachie for AGNSW

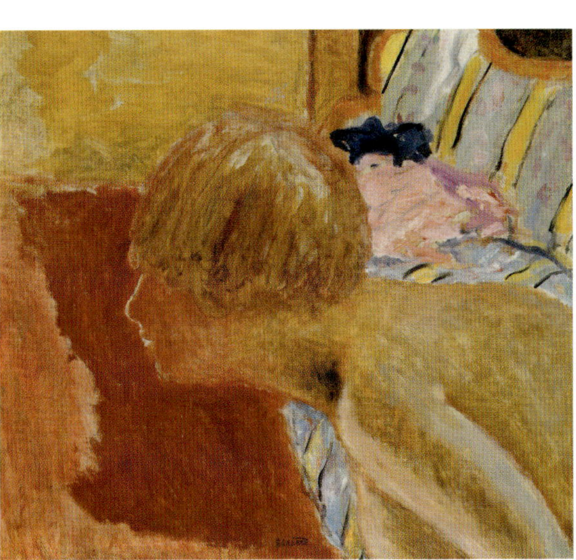

With color under control, Cumming's art bloomed. The street became the public arena of the outdoor recreational space: the park, the beach, or the backyard. Here he comes closer to the two artists most pertinent to his later work, Pierre Bonnard (1867–1947) and Édouard Vuillard (1868–1940). Both artists followed the generation of Post-Impressionists and concentrated on the subjects of middle-class French life. Like

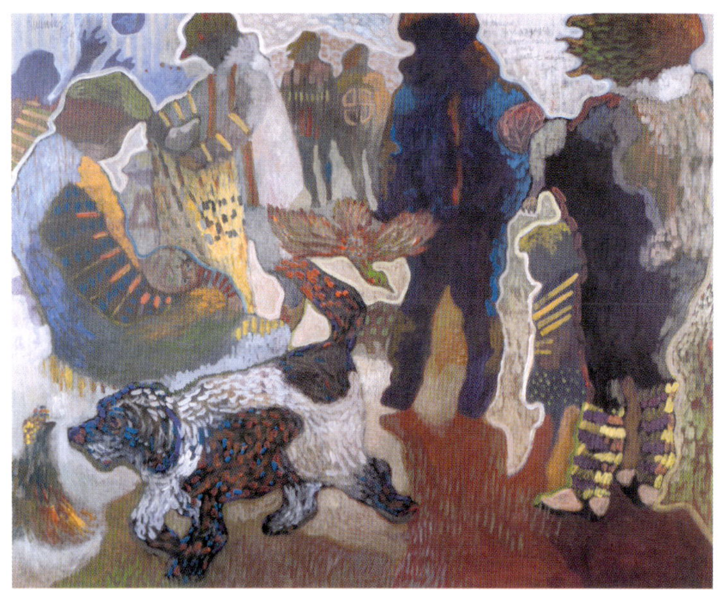

FIG. 48
Return of Odysseus (Tribute to Nikos Kazantzakis), 1984
Oil and tempera on board
47 1/2 x 59 1/2
Museum of Northwest Art
1992.027.001
Gift of Marshall and Helen Hatch

Cumming, they shared crowded compositions, tightly placed brushwork, and a clever dismantling of the expected, realistic image into a mixture of separated marks, solid color areas, and a heightened use of shadow.

Alluding to Bonnard and Vuillard in relation to his own art, Cumming commented: "Vuillard has a greyed color I identify with; to Bonnard, pure color mattered more. For them—and me—line is disappeared edge. A line represents a terminal edge of the plane."[4]

Two works of the mid-1980s suggest the heights to which Cumming's art was approaching. *Return of Odysseus (Tribute to Nikos Kazantzakis)* (1984; fig. 48) is far from an illustration of the Greek myth of the hero returning after ten years at sea to his patient wife, Penelope. It is a crowded scene in a park, a harbor, perhaps, where Odysseus's ship is awaited. Eight figures, a dog, and a bird present themselves to the viewer as dynamic, yet interlocked, shapes. Combining all the technical elements Cumming had been lecturing about to his students, *Return of Odysseus* is a joyous celebration. A basketball is tossed in the upper left corner, and a seated figure (Odysseus?) rests on the left side. A little girl profiled with a single meandering line of white watches a dog amble "offstage." Could it be that Cumming identified with the Greek hero, simply grateful to live a normal life after the long years of challenge and betrayal?

In *Sketchbook*, Cumming announced, "For forty years I have been working off and on around sketches for an ambitious painting to be called Belshazzar's Feast, which makes no sense at all."[5] The discussion of the painting is a prelude to one of the book's most touching passages, a glimpse of his old friend Lubin Petric, pal from the 1930s, now distraught and dying from cancer. Four years after the publication of *Sketchbook*, *Belshazzar's Feast* (1985–88; fig. 49) was completed. It is Cumming's late-period masterpiece, an extraordinarily vivid and complex work that is bright and dark, grim and celebratory, amusing and foreboding all at once.

The Old Testament figure from the Book of Daniel, King Belshazzar, is seated in the lower right corner with long hair and a crown, witnessing the extravagant and decadent behavior of the feast he organized after his father, Nebuchadnezzar, fled the city of Babylonia, only to be succeeded to the throne by his son in 539 B.C. In Cumming's version, we do not see the legendary handwriting on the wall that foretold Belshazzar's doom: "Mene Mene Tekel and Parsin" (Daniel 5:25). The last ruler of the Chaldean dynasty is surrounded by a carnival of dancers, diners, elephants, giraffes, a hyena, and a bird. Amusingly, Cumming has reinserted the red star at the

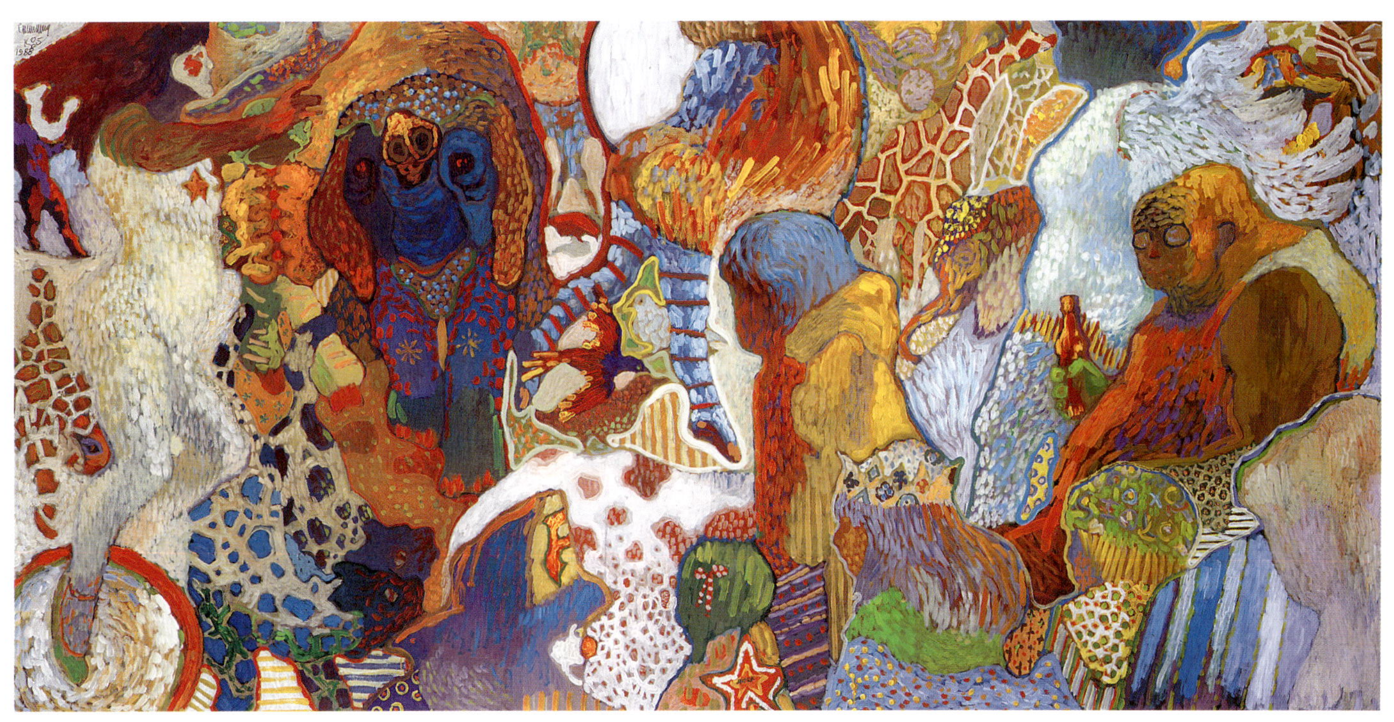

FIG. 49
Belshazzar's Feast,
1985–88
Oil and tempera on
masonite
52 x 100
Collection of the artist;
courtesy of Gordon
Woodside / John Braseth
Gallery

picture's base, which he had had to remove from his Federal Art Project mural fifty years earlier.

Just as Cumming may identify with Odysseus, so the unlucky king, Belshazzar (who is slain during the night following the big party), could be Cumming's symbol of the observer-artist. Or conversely, he could be identifying with the translator of the handwriting on the wall, Daniel, the sole author of the ancient account in the Bible. *Belshazzar's Feast*, despite its festive, celebratory tone, is an extended image of consequence—and doom. Formally, it is a series of interlocking areas of patterns in the dancers' dresses, the giraffe's skin, the revelers' robes, and the hyena. The banquet hall is crowded with event, colored in complementary tones of red and green, bringing together all the artist's abilities and the lessons of a long career. As Cumming commented on the work, "It's about my life. I'm a loner but I've always been drawn to humanity."[6] Other large, equally ambitious panels, such as *Triptych* (1992; pl. 61), painted for a senior citizen activity center when Cumming won the King County Arts Commission Honors Award, also display humanity in all its vanity and diversity, but none has the searing, fiery quality of *Belshazzar's Feast*.

FIG. 50
MILTON AVERY
(American, 1893–1980)
Bathers, Coney Island, 1939
Oil on canvas
32 x 48
Portland Art Museum 61.8. Gift of Mr. and Mrs. J. M. Kaplan

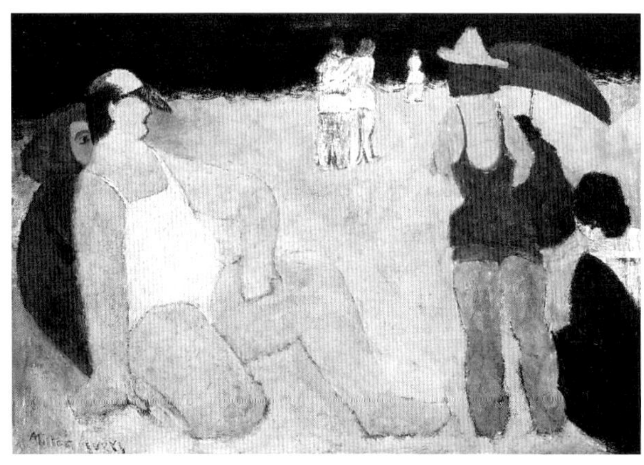

Works like *A Day at the Beach*, *At the Beach* (2004; fig. 51), and *At the Park* (2004; pl. 74) show Cumming in a mellower, less hortatory vein. The artist has accelerated his control over pattern, color, shadow, form, and shape, all qualities that pave the way for the artist's coming to terms with modernism in his own way.

Besides the images of humanity enjoying itself, more ponderous, quieter works have also been prevalent. *Evening Snow* (2003; pl. 72) and *Windy* (2004; pl. 73) hark back to greyer tonalities and typical Northwest weather. *Generations* (2004; pl. 76) depicts older men and women with younger children, perhaps grandchildren. Like Shakespeare's "seven ages of man," Cumming has chronicled infancy, childhood, youth, adolescence, maturity, middle age, and old age in his paintings. The "loner drawn to humanity" has indeed served humanity as a teacher and artist, becoming the "productive" member of society he so wanted to be when he was in the sanatorium.

A pair of female nudes, both called *Dream* (1998; fig. 44 and pl. 66), end our discussion on a peaceful note. They are distant echoes of a pastel by American Impressionist William Merritt Chase (1849–1916) (who was also an influential and widely loved teacher), *Back of a Nude* (ca. 1888). Cumming's *Dreams* are visions of his seventh wife and former model, Dena Lee. With alternately blue and yellow backgrounds, the female figures pose with their back to the viewer (and artist), facing a glowing light. Cumming at his most painterly, the *Dream* paintings are moody and mysterious, paeans to the eternal feminine. The ribbon at the neck is a symbol

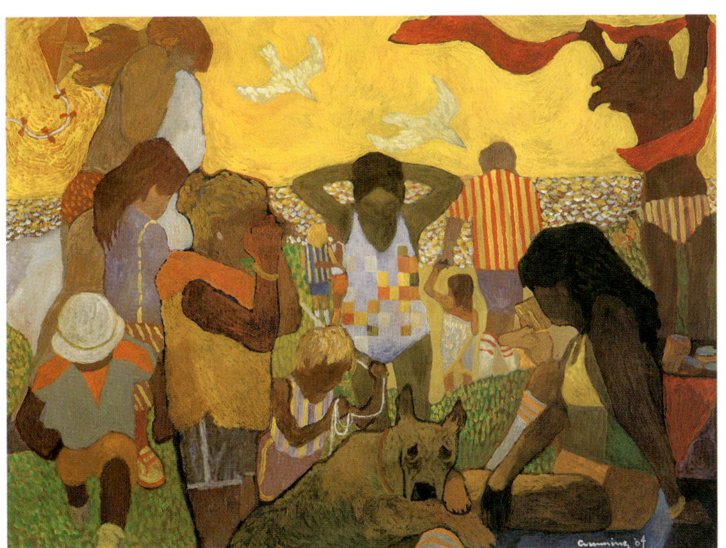

FIG. 51
At the Beach,
2004
Oil and tempera
on masonite
36 x 48
Private collection

of possession, as in Manet's *Olympia* (1863). But more than staking claim to the beloved, Cumming is letting loose, bringing to bear his tremendous energy and hard-earned, reconciled love of life and art. The "loner drawn to humanity" has often been caught halfway toward such a union, starting with his friendships and marriages. For our purposes, the relationship is one on one, artist to viewer, rather than uxorious.

Why is an artist of such great powers and achievement almost completely unknown outside the Pacific Northwest? There is no simple answer, but we could turn to Cumming's comments to Hoppe in 1972:

> I think that I felt the few times that I ran into Tobey and Graves that their success had been so disillusioning to them that I was willing to let them experience the disillusionment and avoid it myself.[7]

Such a decision led to an eventual outpouring of works that surely speak beyond Cumming's beloved "Northwest earth." As this book has attempted to situate Cumming within the narrower and wider contexts of American regional and national art and literature, so it is hoped that the early- and middle-period paintings, as well as the twilight masterpieces, will gain a more geographically dispersed audience, one that sees in Cumming a paradigm of courage and conviction as well as dedication, talent, and commitment to the image and art of consequence.

NOTES

1. William Cumming, handwritten lecture notes, undated and unpaginated.
2. Ibid.
3. William Cumming, interview with author, January 25, 2005.
4. Ibid., February 14, 2005.
5. William Cumming, *Sketchbook: A Memoir of the 1930s and the Northwest School* (Seattle: University of Washington Press, 1984), 124.
6. William Cumming, interview with author, January 10, 2005.
7. William Cumming, interview with Bill Hoppe for the Archives of Northwest Art, Allen Library, University of Washington Libraries, August 2, 1972.

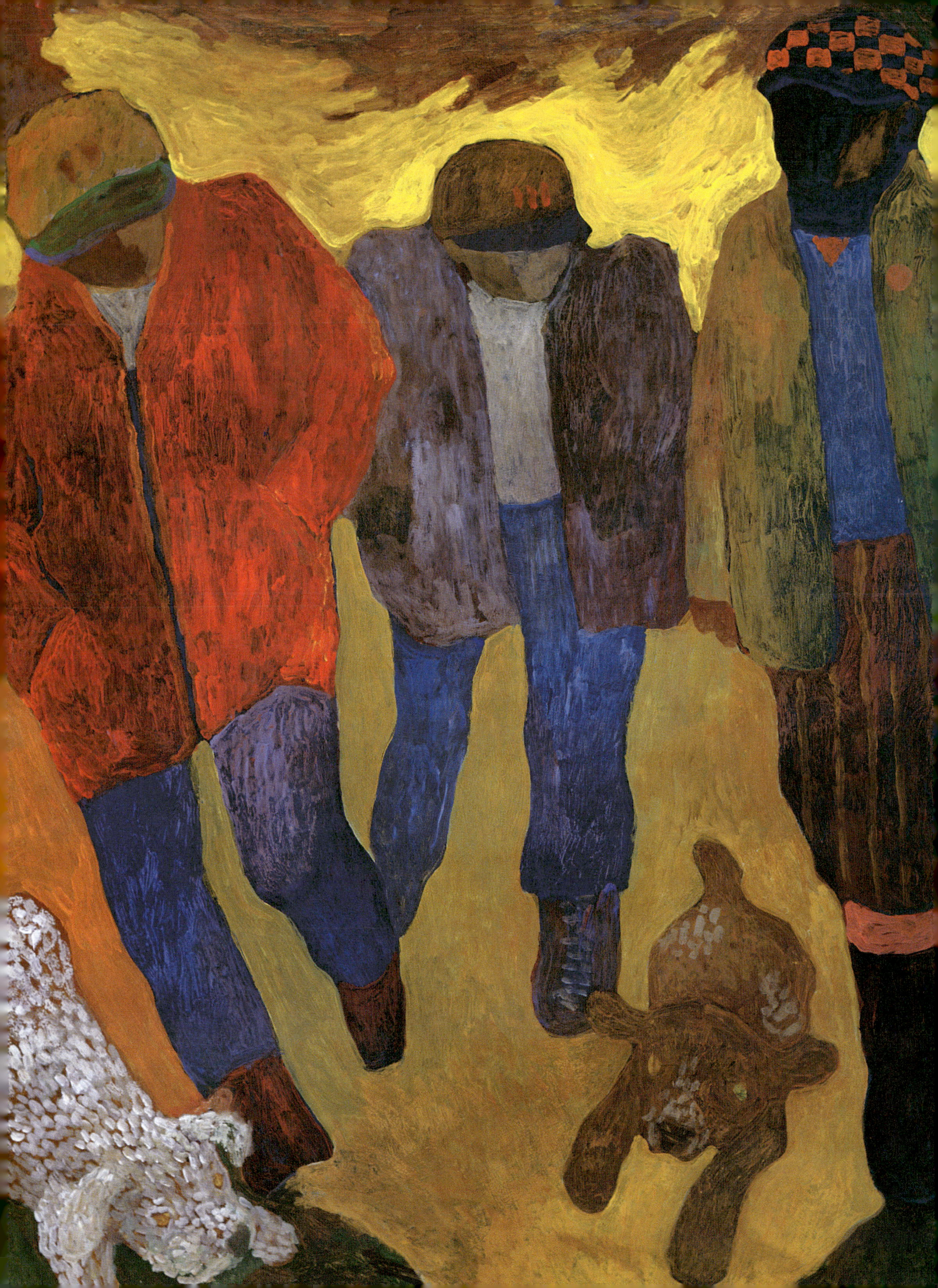

Plates

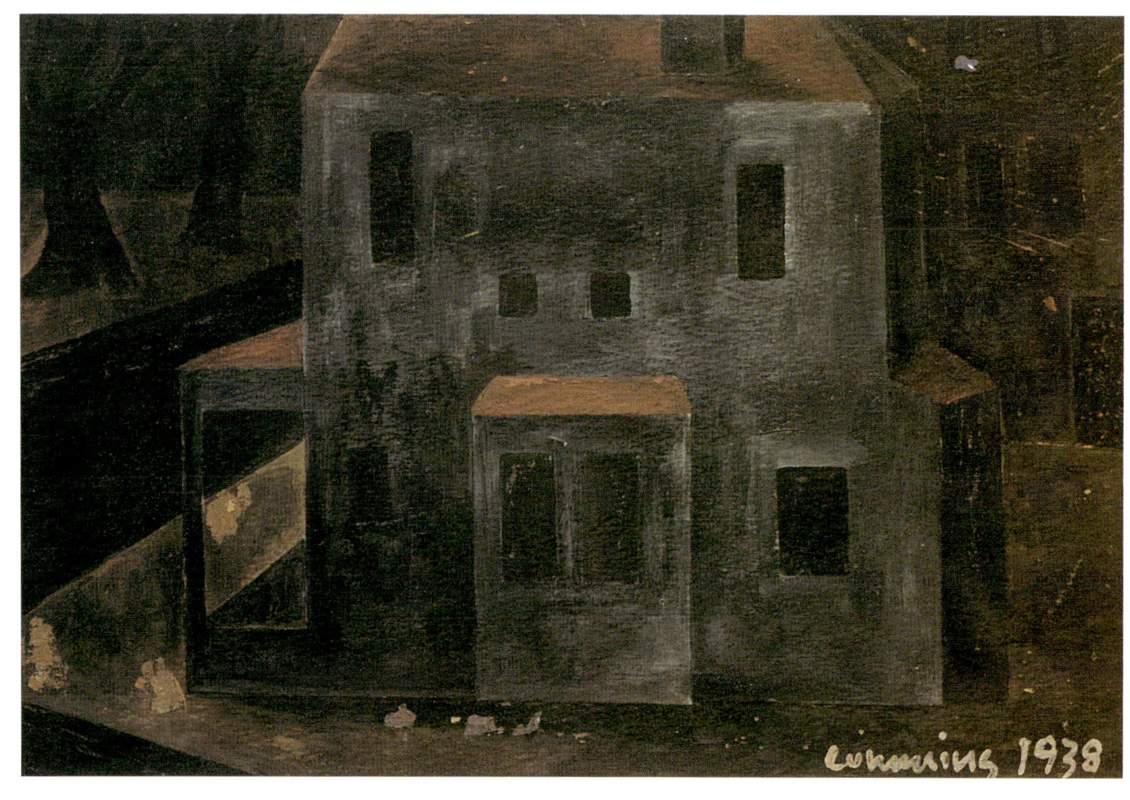

PLATE 1
Two-Story House, 1938
Tempera on board
17¾ x 22
Private collection, Seattle

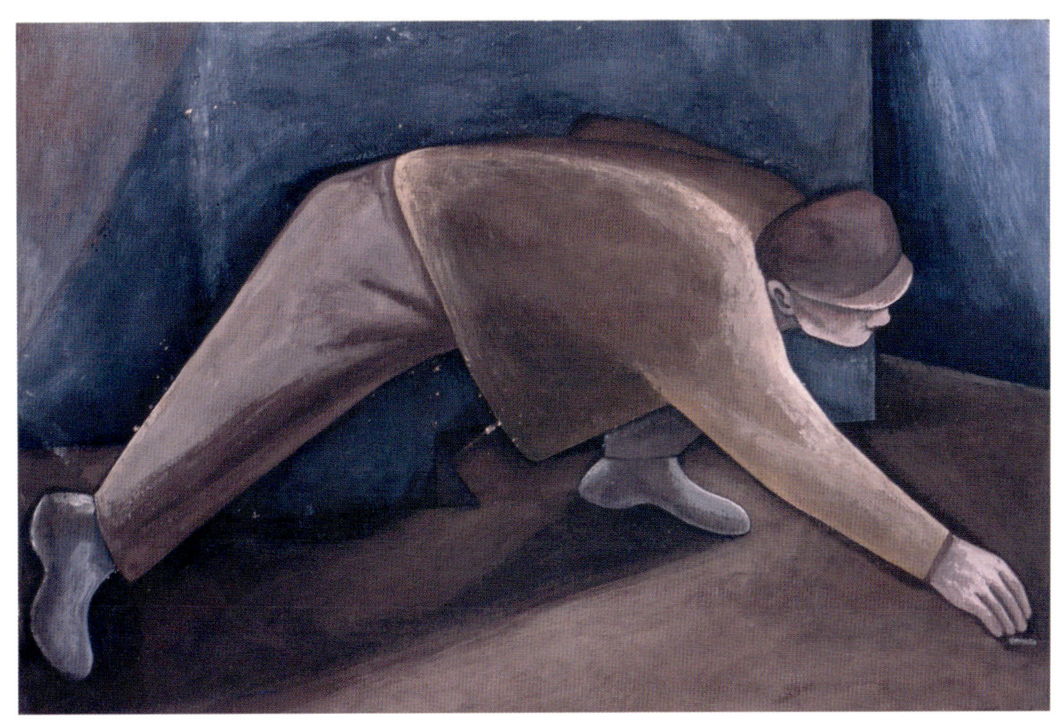

PLATE 2
Untitled (Man Reaching for Cigarette), c. 1940
Tempera on board
Unframed: 10¼ x 15
Museum of Northwest Art 1999.59.011
Bequest of James Odlin

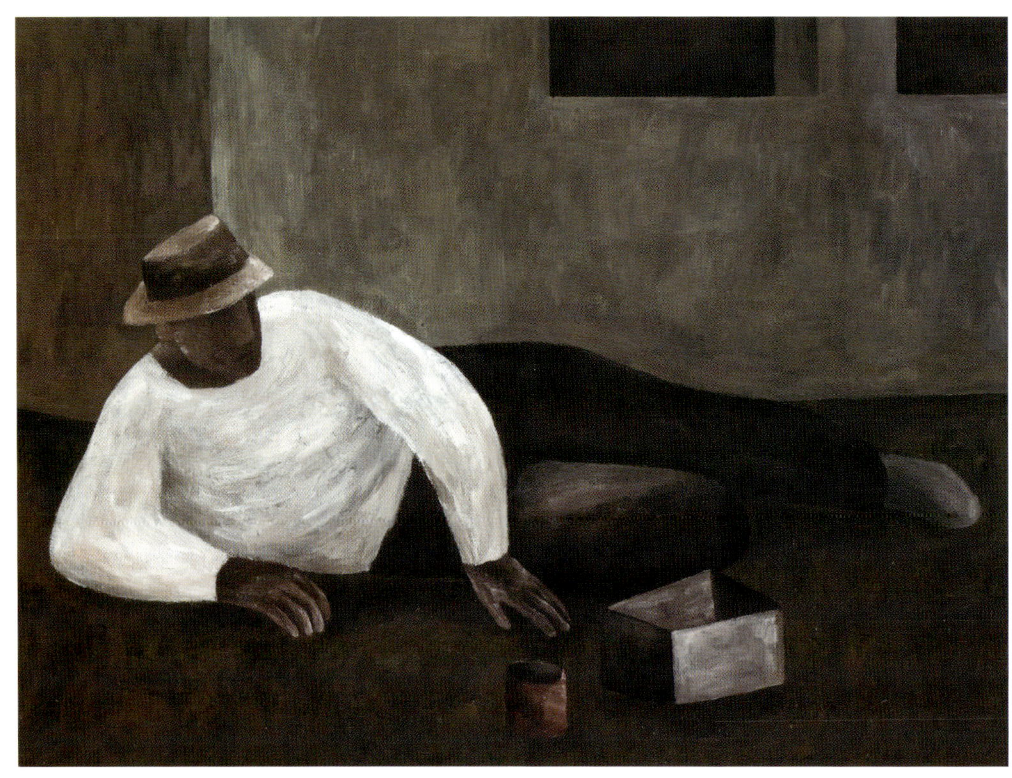

PLATE 3
Worker Resting, 1941
Tempera on board
Unframed: 15 x 19 3/4
Seattle Art Museum 41.44
Eugene Fuller Memorial Collection

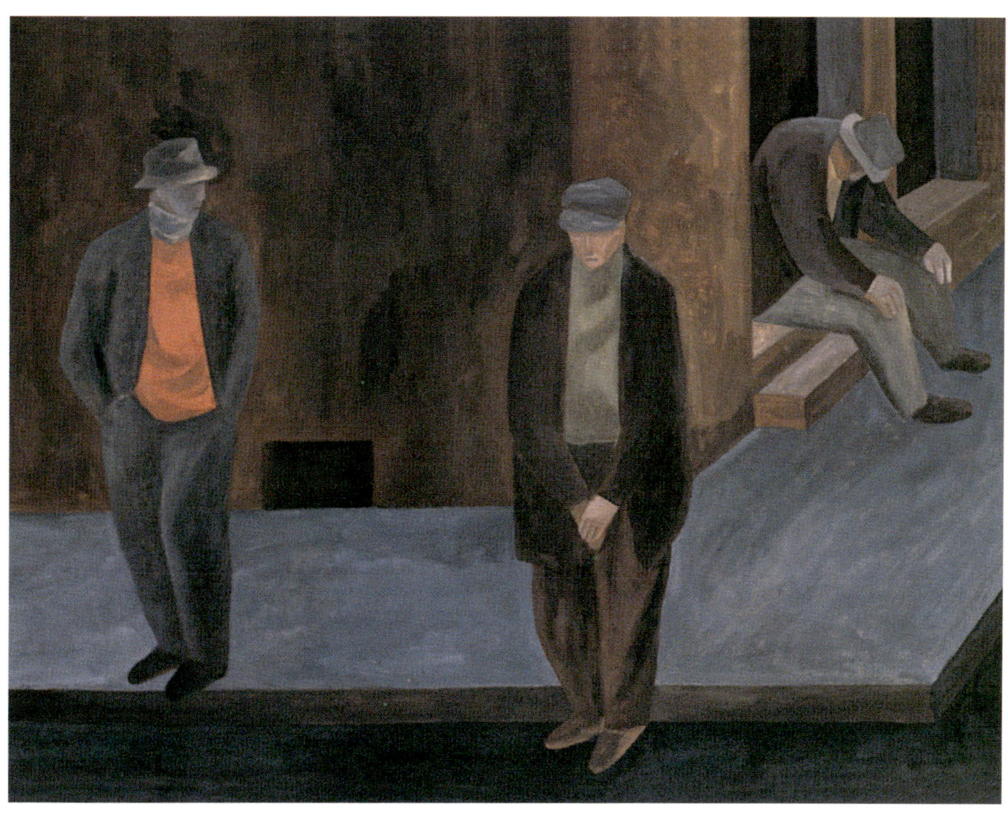

PLATE 4
Skidroad Group, c. 1940
Tempera on board
Unframed: 14 7/8 x 19 5/8
Seattle Art Museum 41.45
Eugene Fuller Memorial Collection

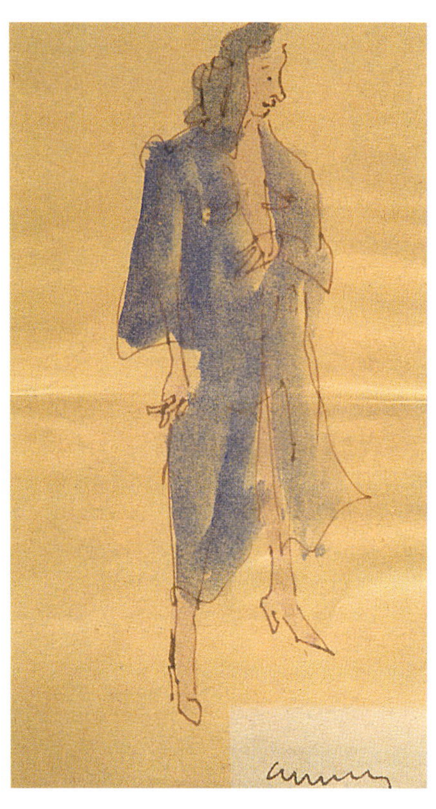

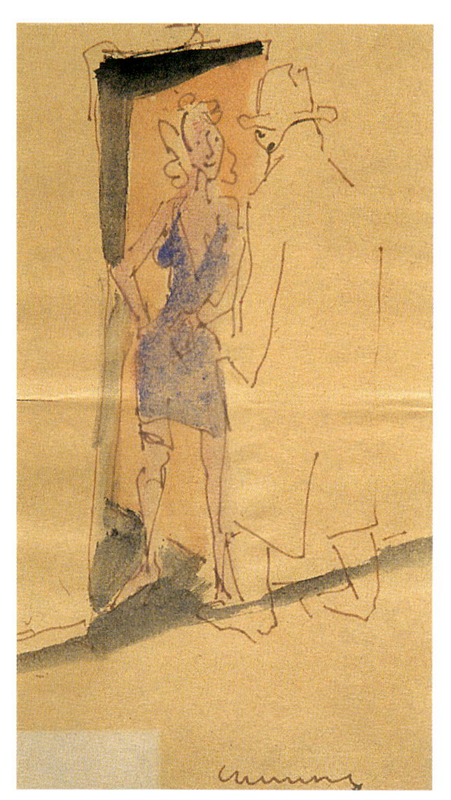

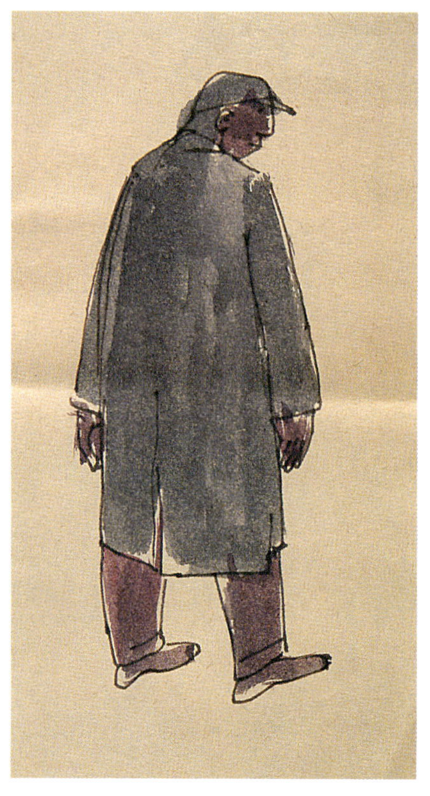

PLATE 5 (top left)
Working Girl #3, 1943
Ink and watercolor on paper
6 1/4 x 3 1/2

PLATE 6 (top right)
Working Girl with John, 1943
Ink and watercolor on paper
6 1/4 x 3 1/2

PLATE 7 (right)
Black Man in Overcoat, 1943
Ink and watercolor on paper
6 1/4 x 3 1/2

Collection of B. T. Callahan

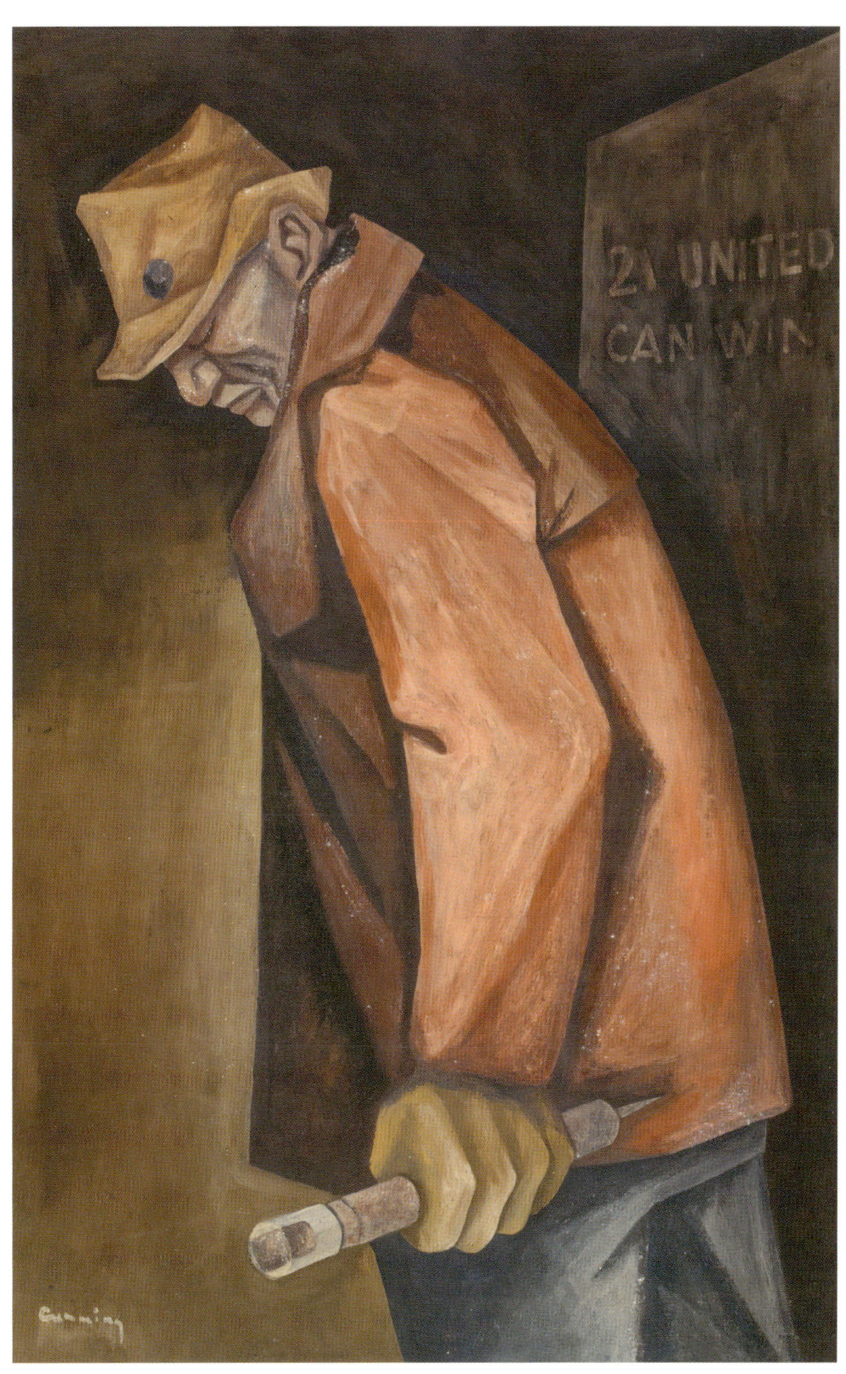

PLATE 8

Planting the Flare, 1945

Gouache on board

30 1/2 x 25 1/8

Seattle Art Museum 47.156

Eugene Fuller Memorial Collection

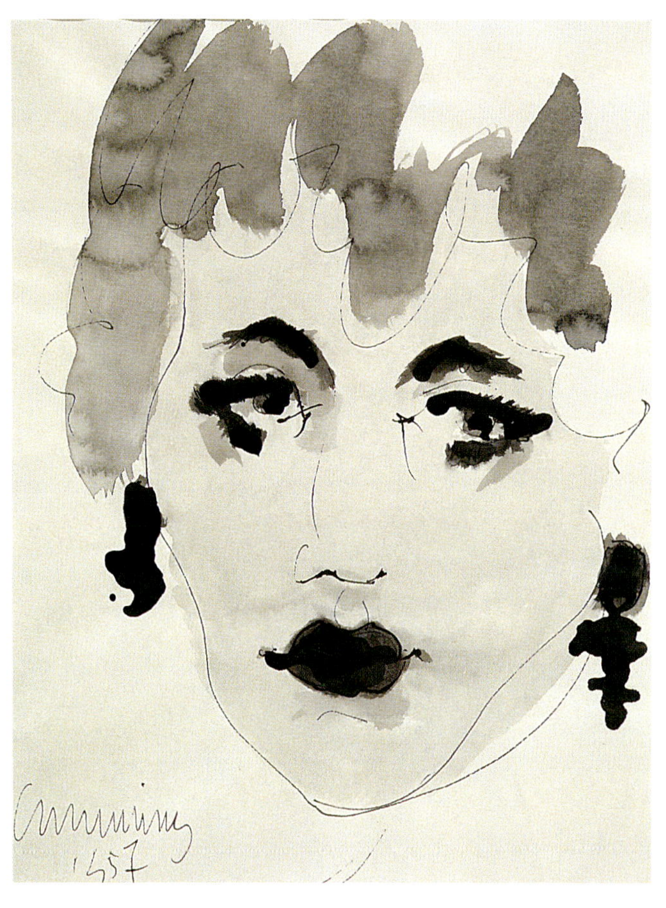

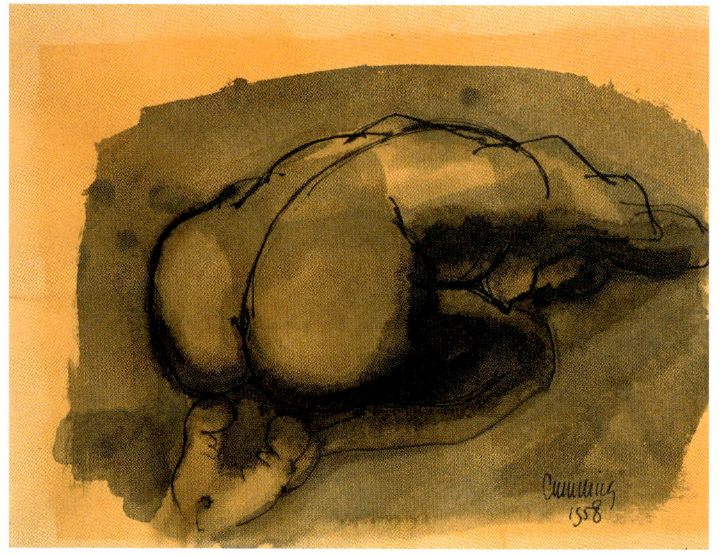

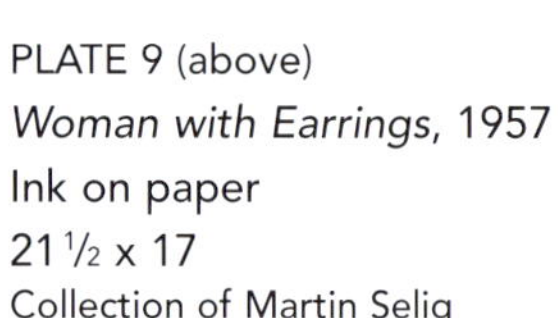

PLATE 9 (above)
Woman with Earrings, 1957
Ink on paper
21 1/2 x 17
Collection of Martin Selig

PLATE 10 (right)
Nude, 1958
Ink and wash on paper
14 1/4 x 16 1/4
Whatcom Museum of History & Art 1976.48.6
Gift of Virginia Wright Fund

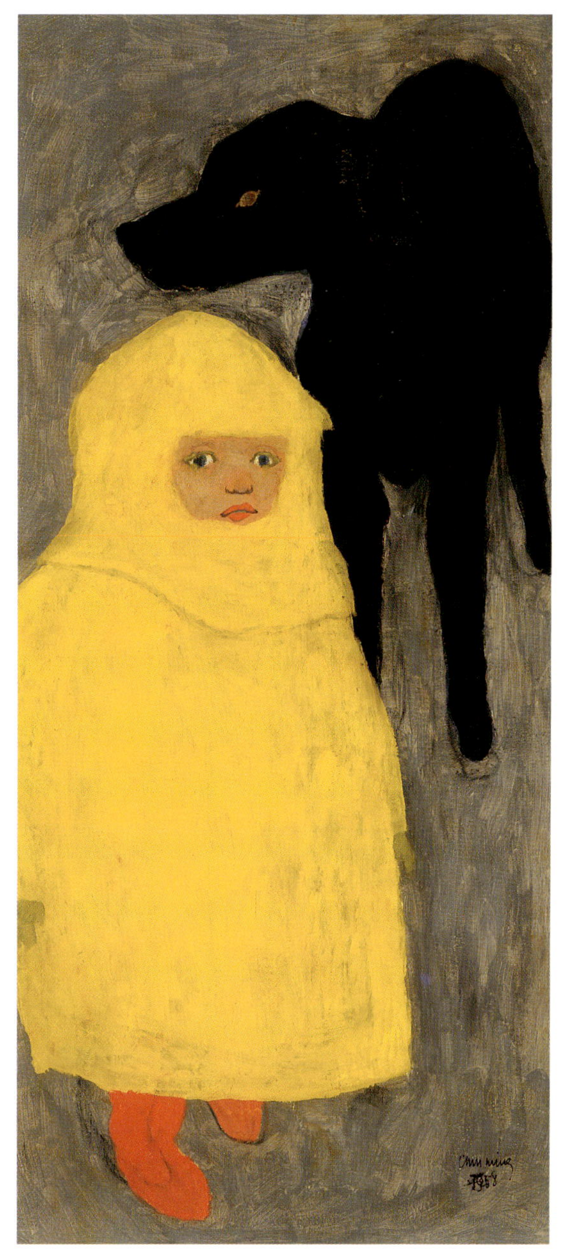

PLATE 11
The Child, l958
Oil on masonite
37 5/8 x 17 3/8
Tacoma Art Museum 1998.26.21
Gift of Bellevue Art Museum

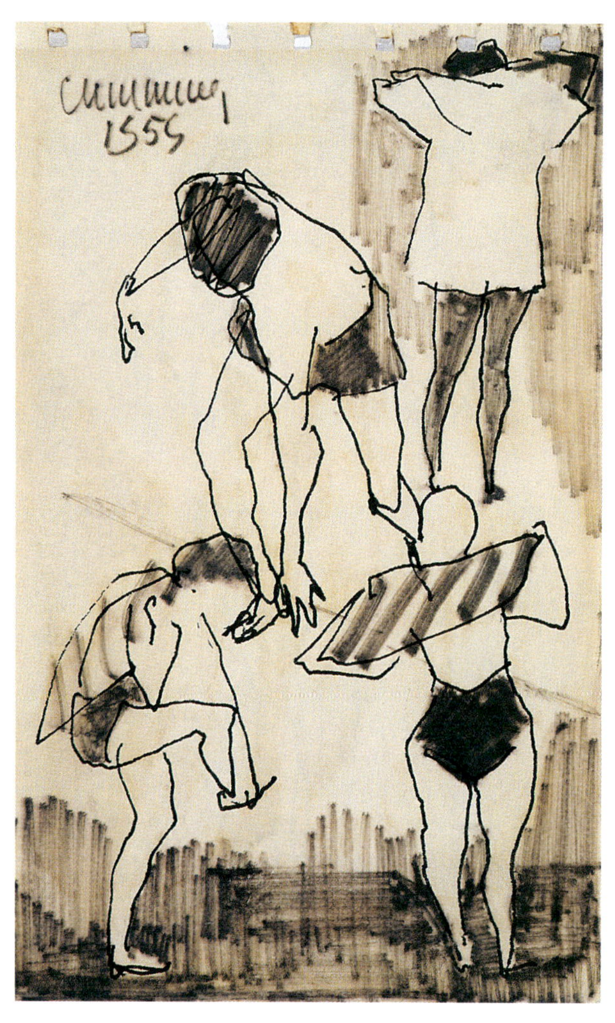

PLATE 12
Swimmers, 1959
Ink on paper
Unframed: 7 3/8 x 4 3/4
Henry Art Gallery, University of Washington 2004.122
Gift from the Estates of Dorothee and Mitchell Taylor Bowie

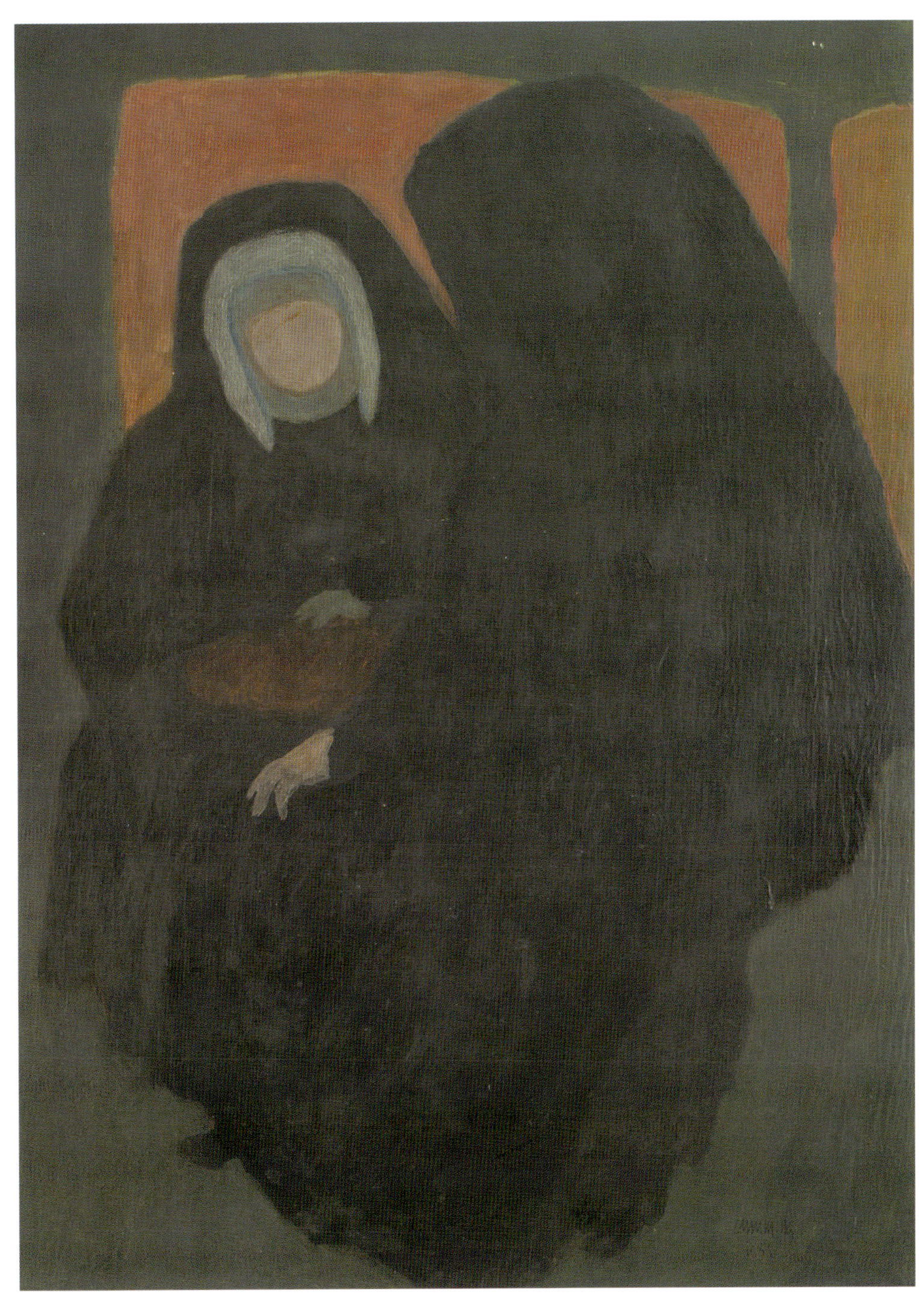

PLATE 13
The Roots of Heaven, 1959
Oil and tempera on board
29 ½ x 22 ½
Private collection, Philadelphia

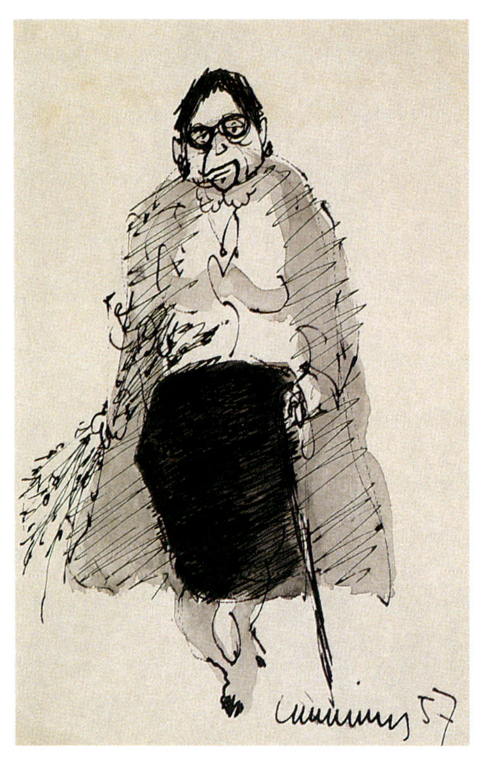

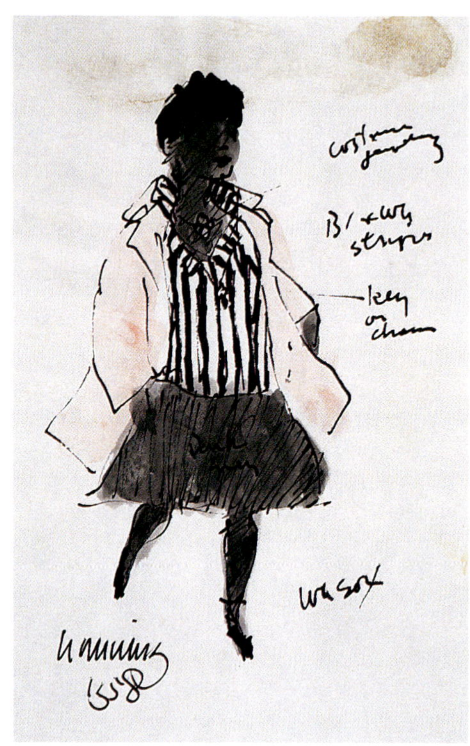

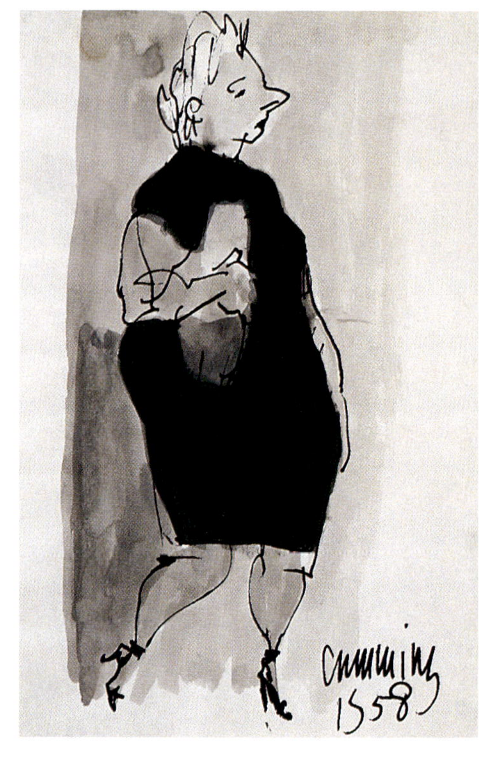

PLATES 14–19 (from left to right)
Woman Wearing Glasses in Coat with Umbrella, 1957
Ink on paper
9 x 6

Woman in Pink Coat, 1958
Ink and watercolor
8 1/4 x 5 1/2

Woman in Dark Dress Carrying Purse, 1958
Ink on paper
8 3/8 x 5 1/8

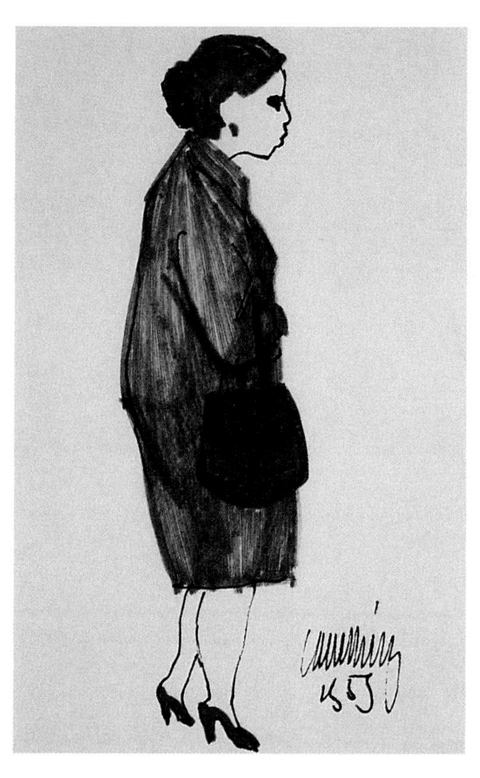

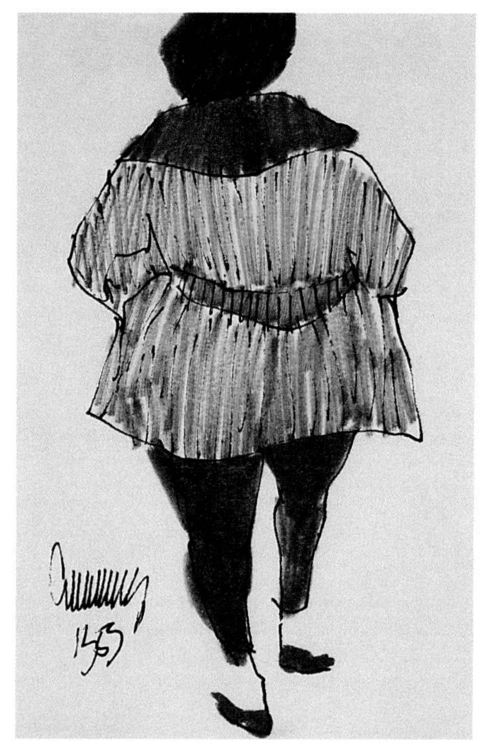

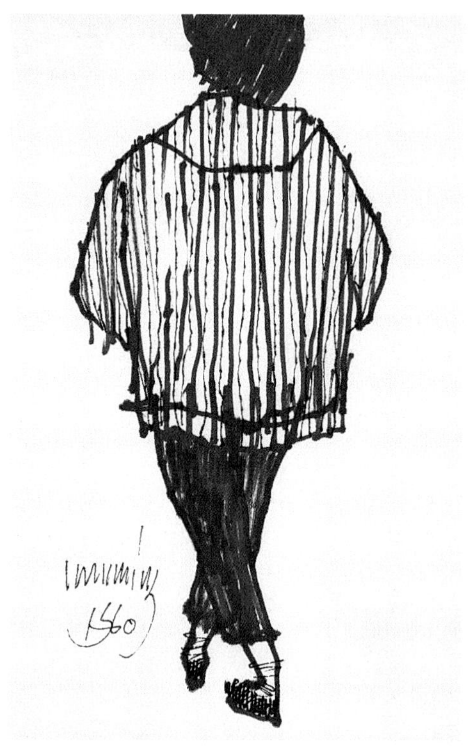

Woman with Bun in Full-length Profile Carrying Purse, 1959
Ink on paper
7 1/2 x 4 3/4

Back of Woman in Belted, Collared Coat, 1959
Inks on paper
7 5/8 x 4 3/4

Back of Woman with Striped Coat, 1960
Inks on paper
10 x 7

Collection of Martin Selig

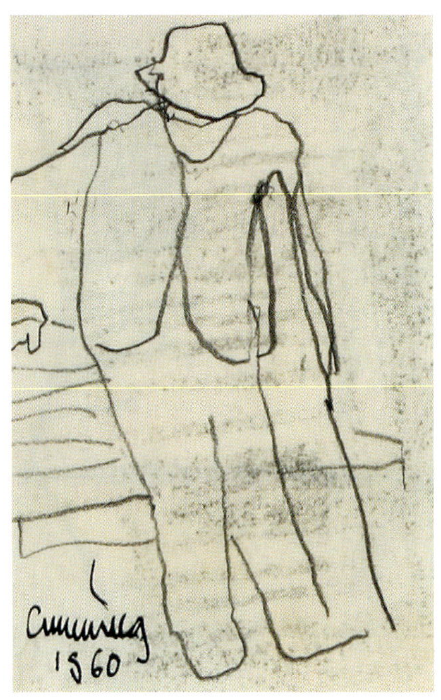

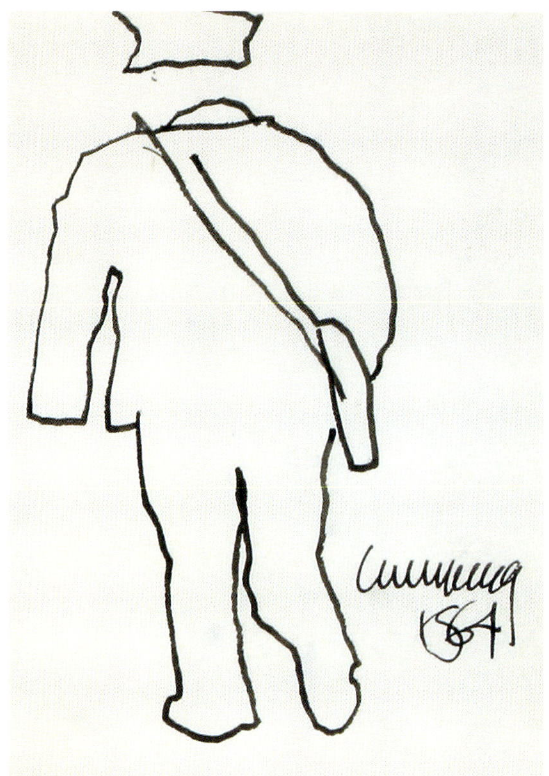

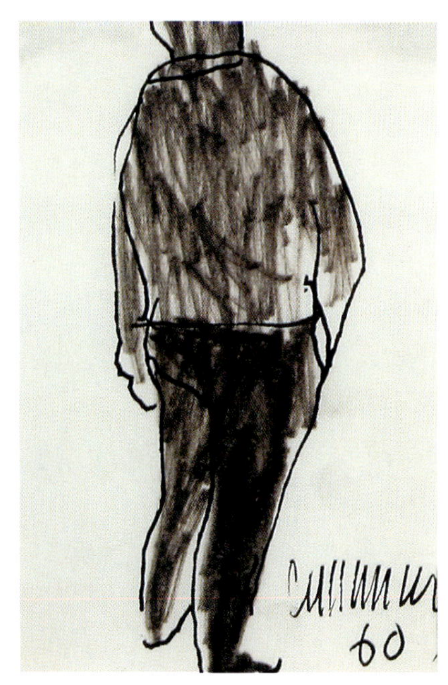

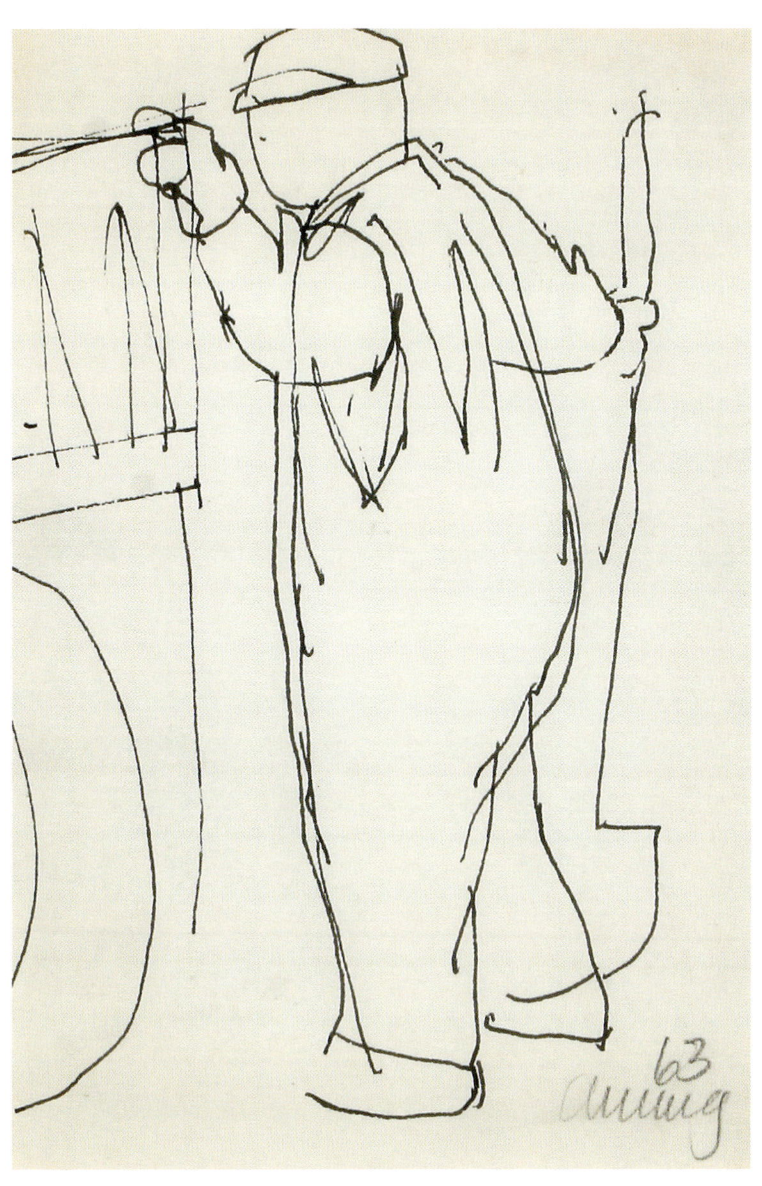

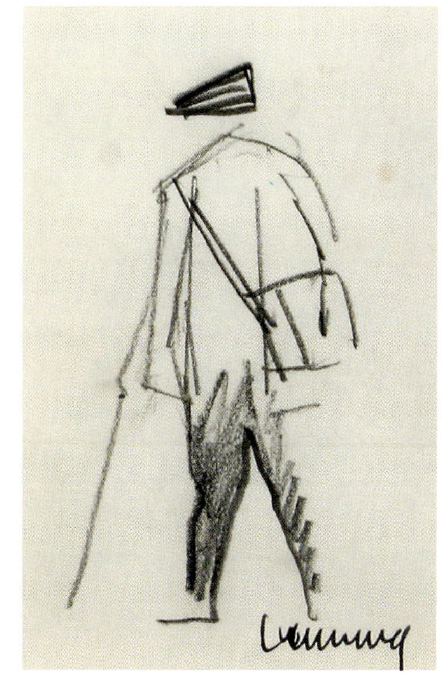

PLATE 20–24
Five Working Men, 1960-64
Mixed media on paper
20 1/4 x 24
Private collection, Seattle

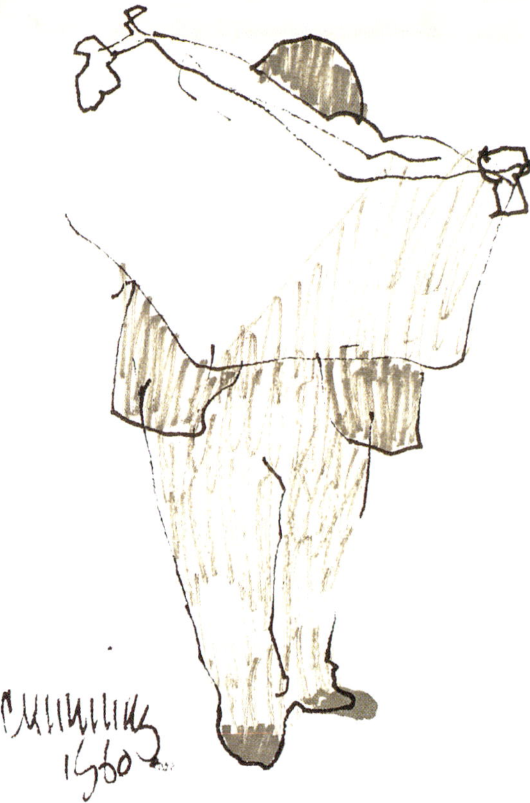

PLATE 25 (above)
Untitled (Man Carrying Boxes), 1960
Umber ink on page of German medical text
Unframed: 10½ x 7
Museum of Northwest Art 1992.014.001
Bequest of James Faber

PLATE 26 (right)
Untitled (Man Reading Newspaper), 1960
Ink and felt tip pen on paper
12¼ x 9¾
Museum of Northwest Art 2004.039.004
Blair and Lucille Kirk Collection

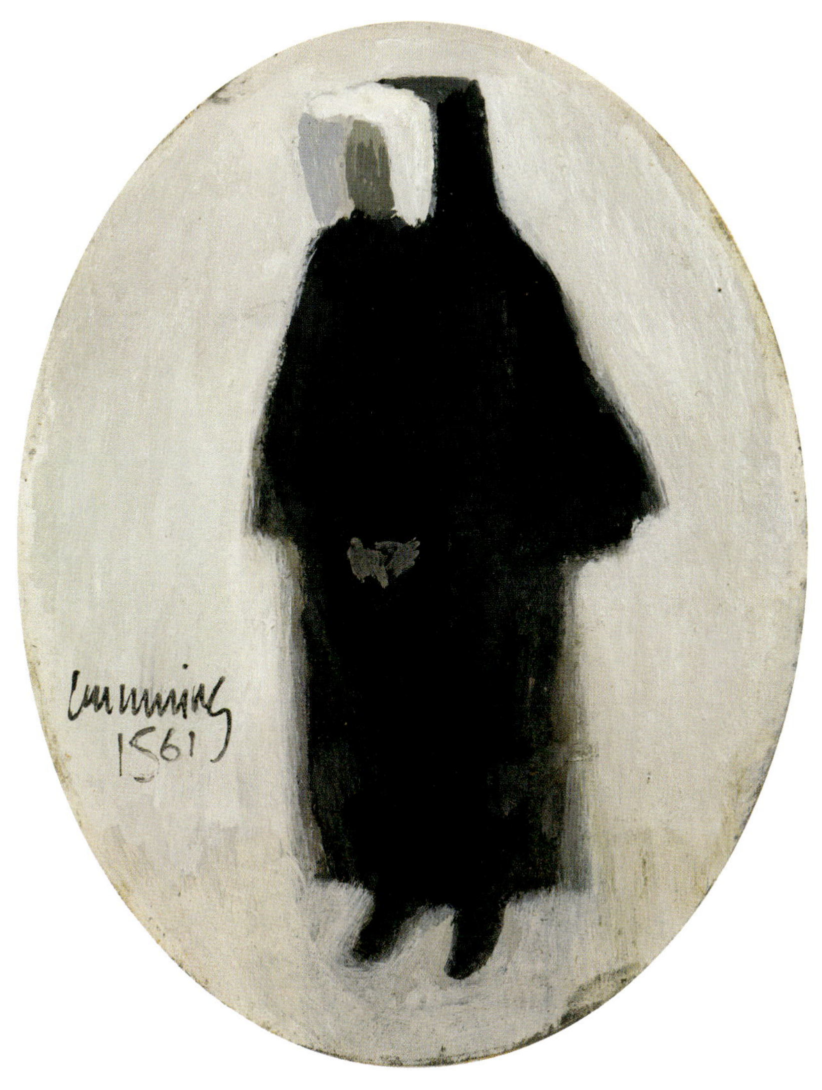

PLATE 27
The Little Nun, 1961
Ink and wash on paper
13 1/2 x 10 1/2
Whatcom Museum of History & Art,
Bellingham, Washington
Gift of Virginia Wright Fund 1976.48.7

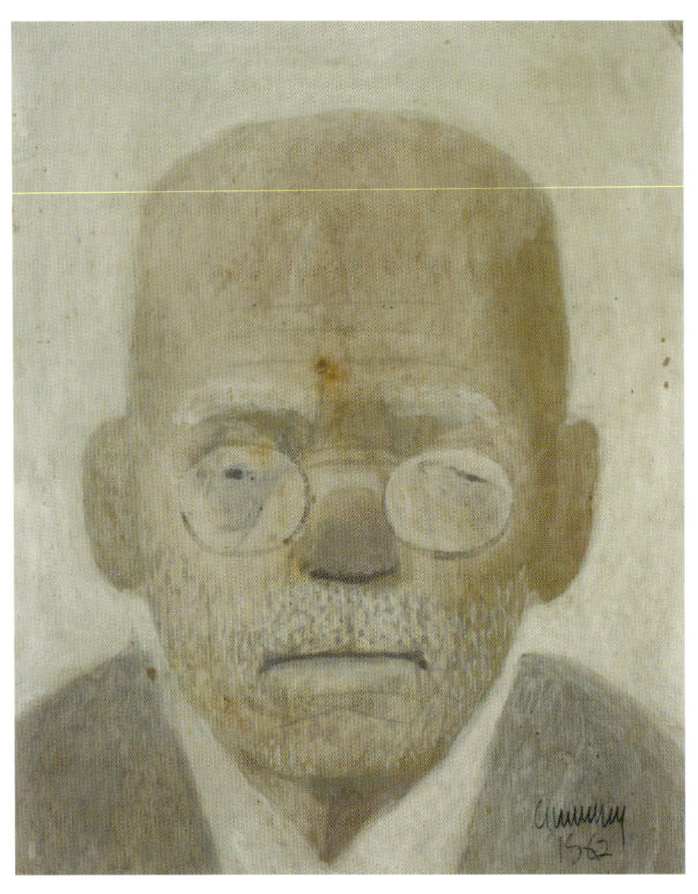

PLATE 28
Old Joe (Issei Merchant), 1962
Colored pencil on cardboard
14 x 10
Collection of the artist

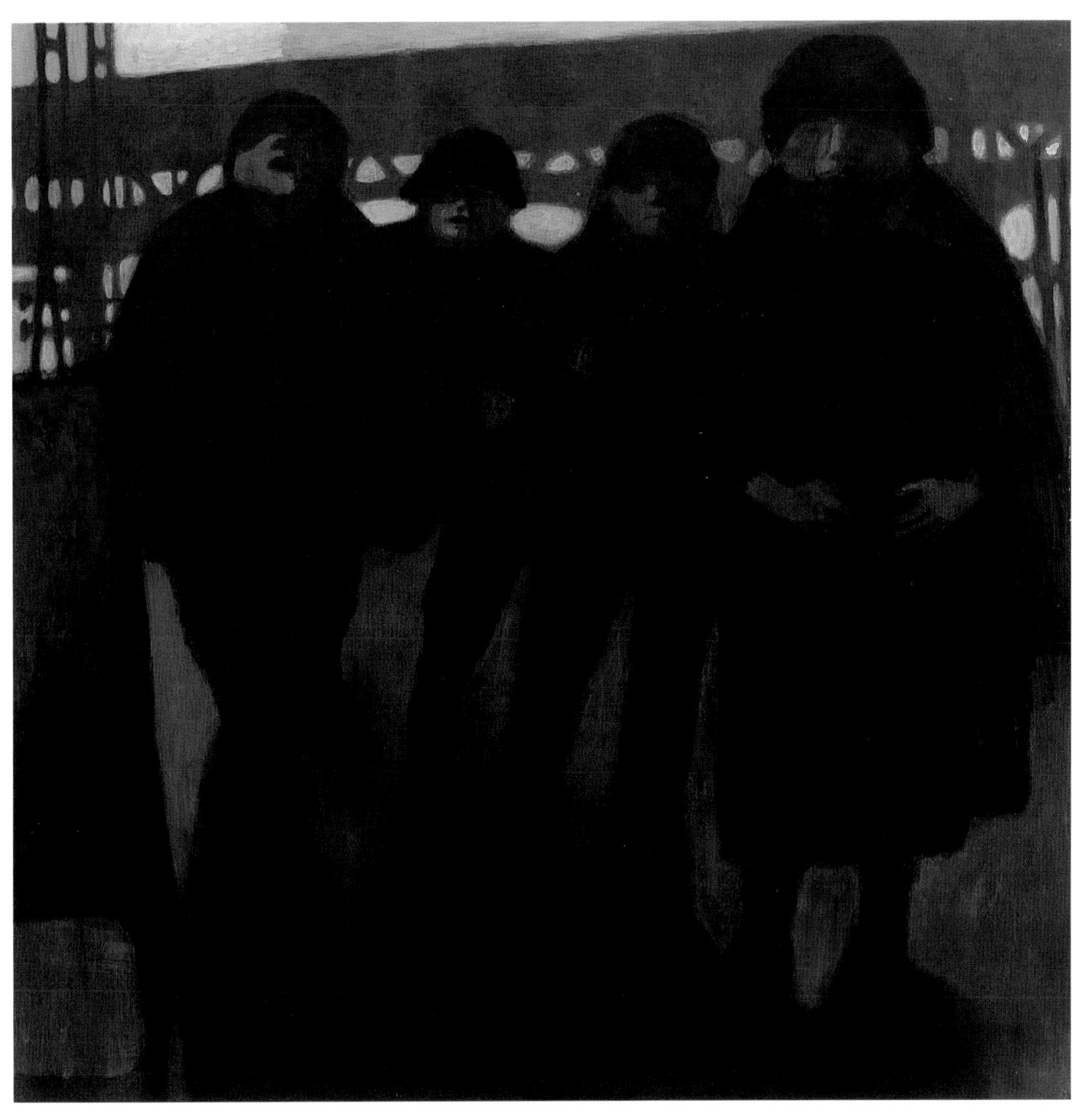

PLATE 29
Journey to the End of Night, 1962
Tempera on masonite
48 x 48
Henry Art Gallery, University of Washington 2004.121
Gift from the Estates of Dorothee and Mitchell Taylor Bowie

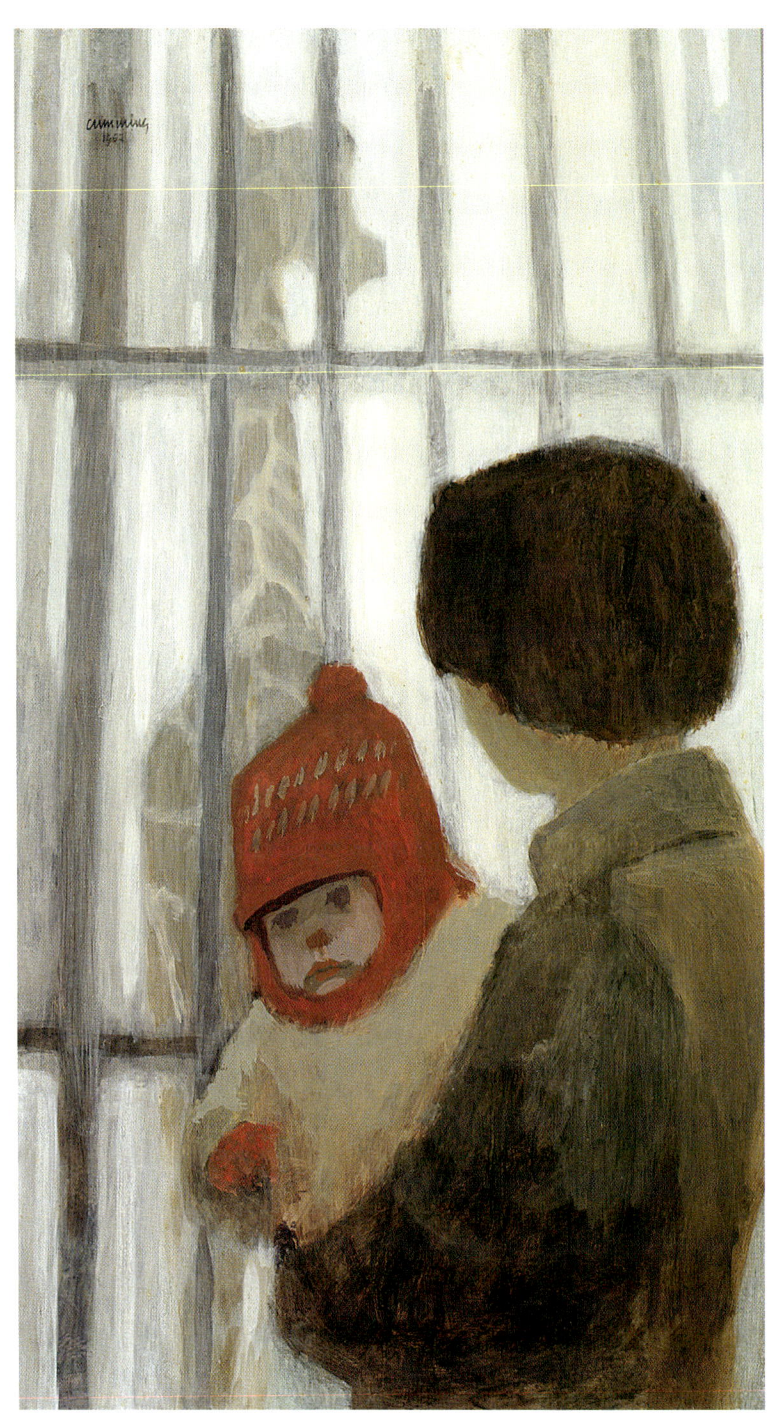

PLATE 30
Mother and Child at the Zoo, 1962
Oil and tempera on panel
47 x 30
Mr. and Mrs. John Behnke Collection

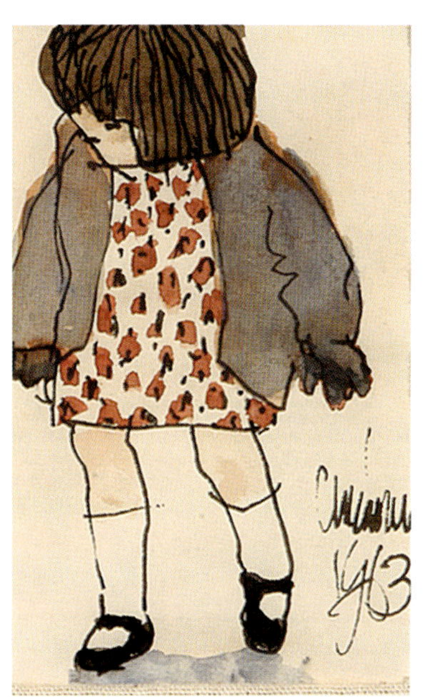

PLATE 31
Little Girl, 1963
Ink and pencil on paper
$4\frac{1}{2} \times 5\frac{1}{2}$
Collection of Philip and Mary Serka

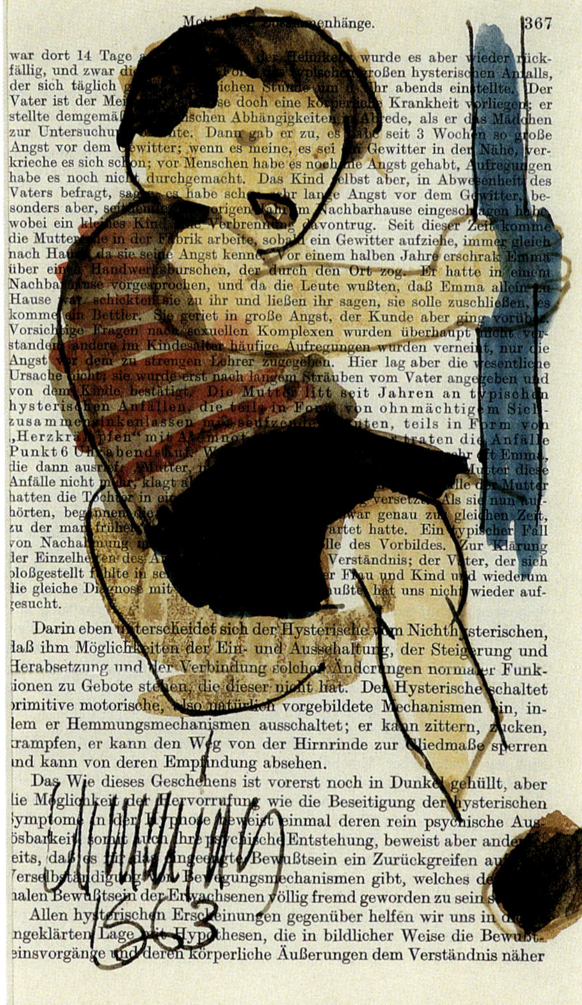

PLATE 32 (above)
Boy on Merry-Go-Round, 1963
Paint on German-language book paper
12 x 8 1/2
Mr. and Mrs. John Behnke Collection

PLATE 33 (right)
Untitled (Little Nun), c. 1963
Bronze
7 1/4 x 3 x 3
Museum of Northwest Art 2004.138.073
Blair and Lucille Kirk Collection

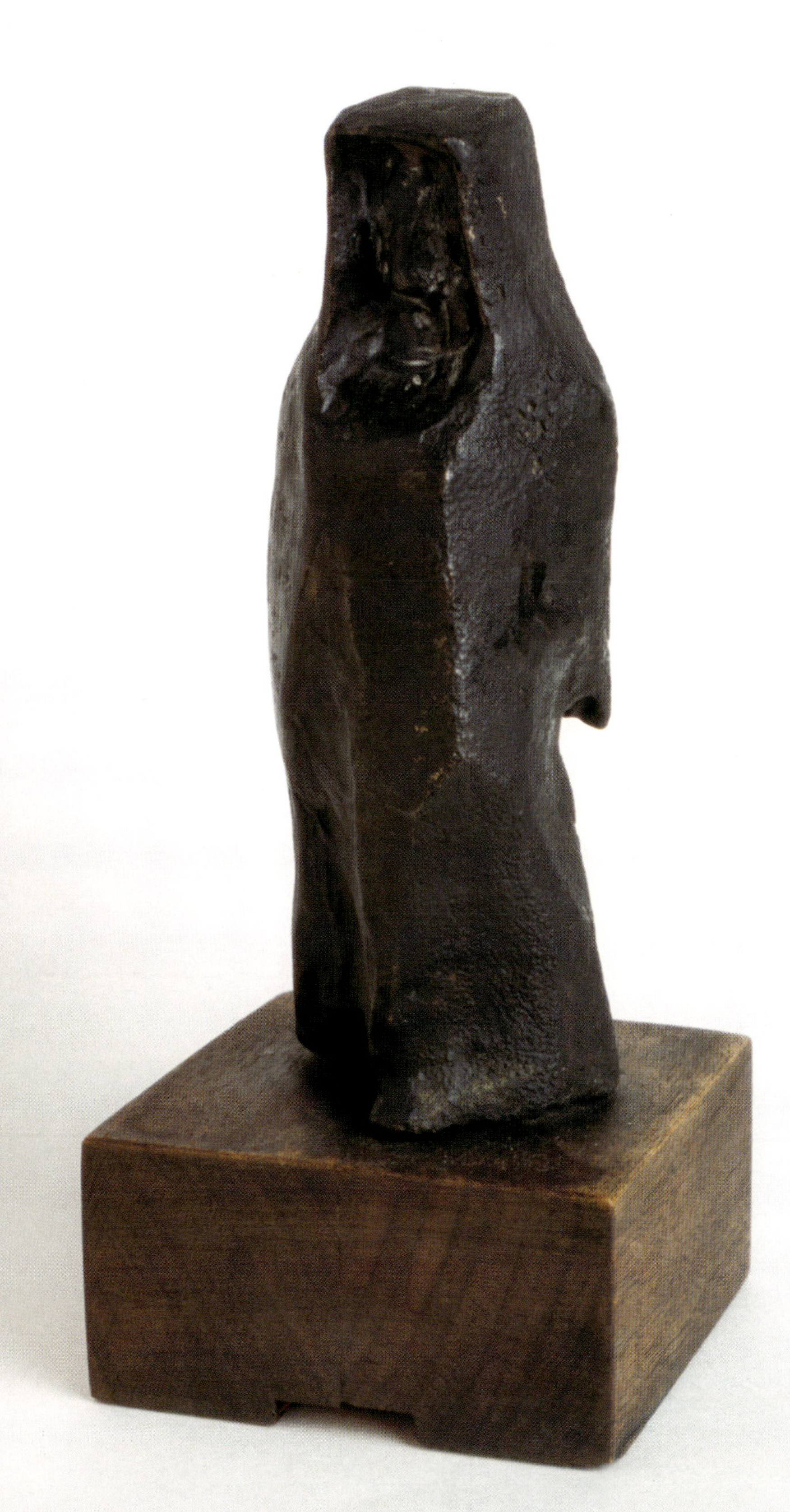

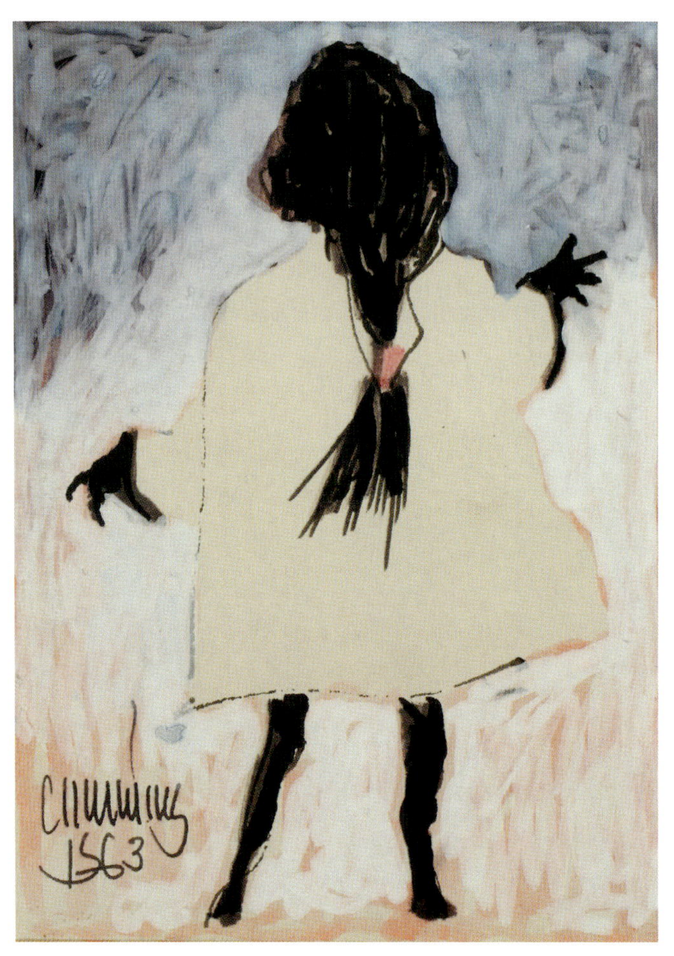

PLATE 34
Figure, 1963
Ink and tempera on paper
10 1/2 x 8 1/2
Collection of the artist

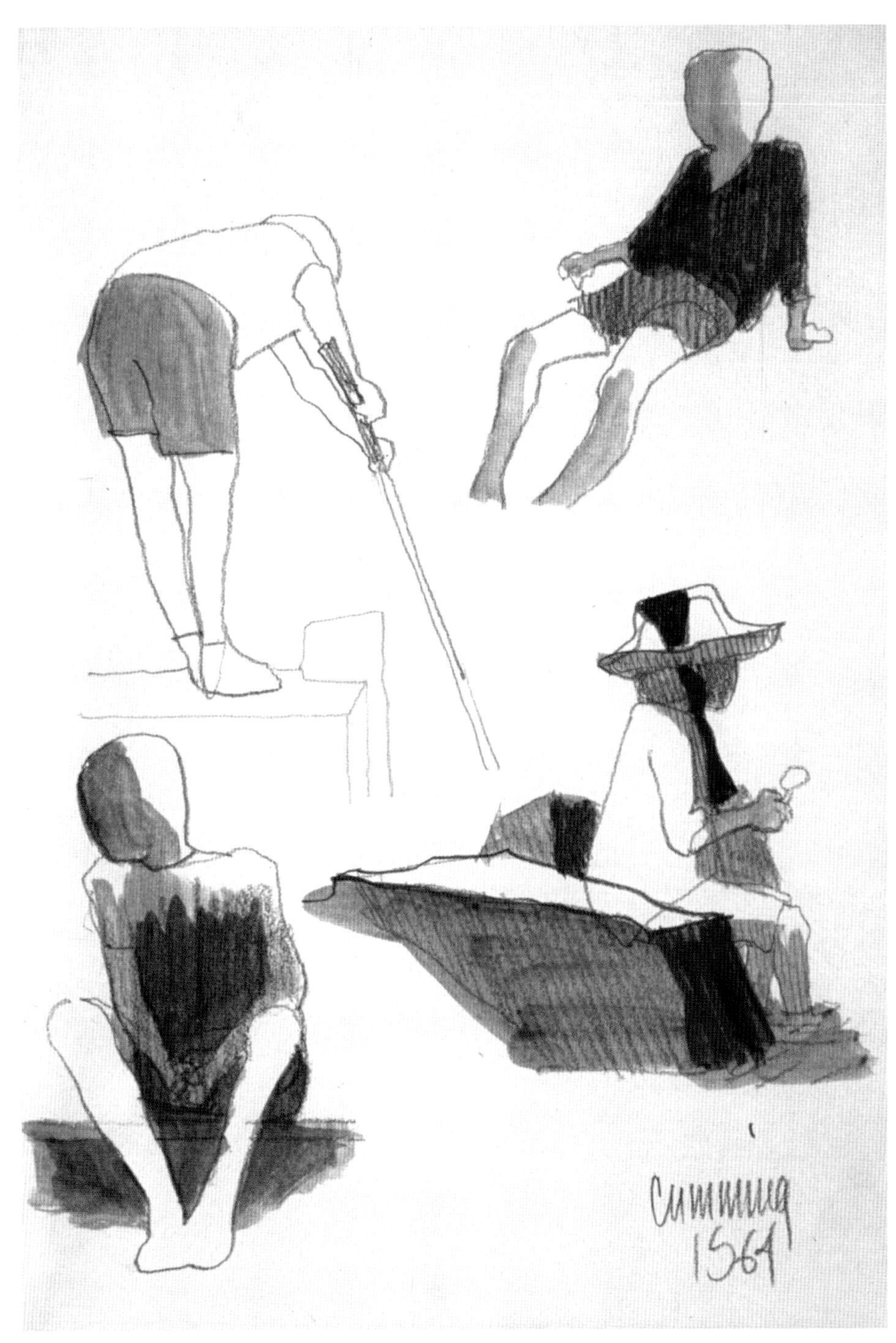

PLATE 35
Sketchbook Study: Beach Figures, 1964
Graphite and polymer on paper
Unframed: 20 x 16
Museum of Northwest Art 2003.126.013
Gift of Dr. David and Beverly Christie

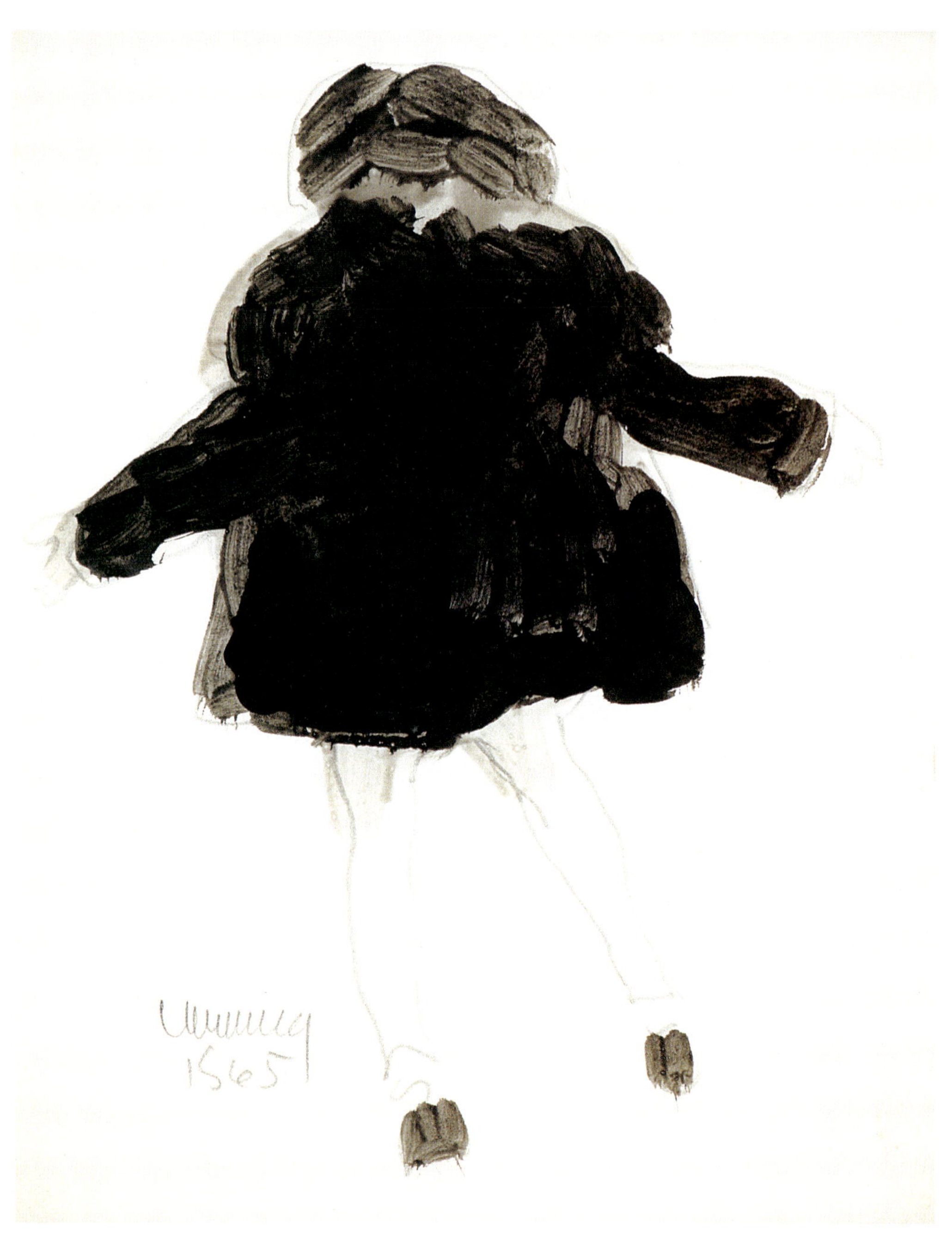

PLATE 36
Girl with Outstretched Arms, 1965
Mixed media on paper
19 x 16½
Mr. and Mrs. John Behnke Collection

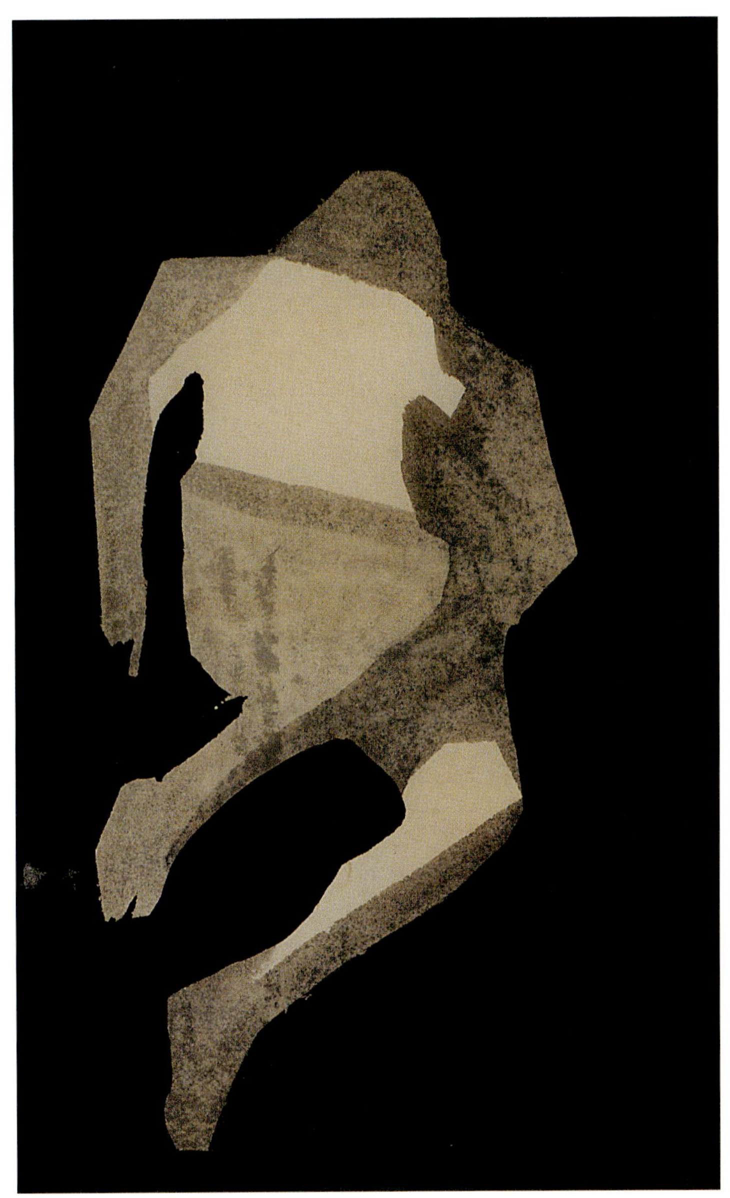

PLATE 37
Nude, 1966
Ink on paper
10 1/4 x 6
Mr. and Mrs. Devitt Barnett

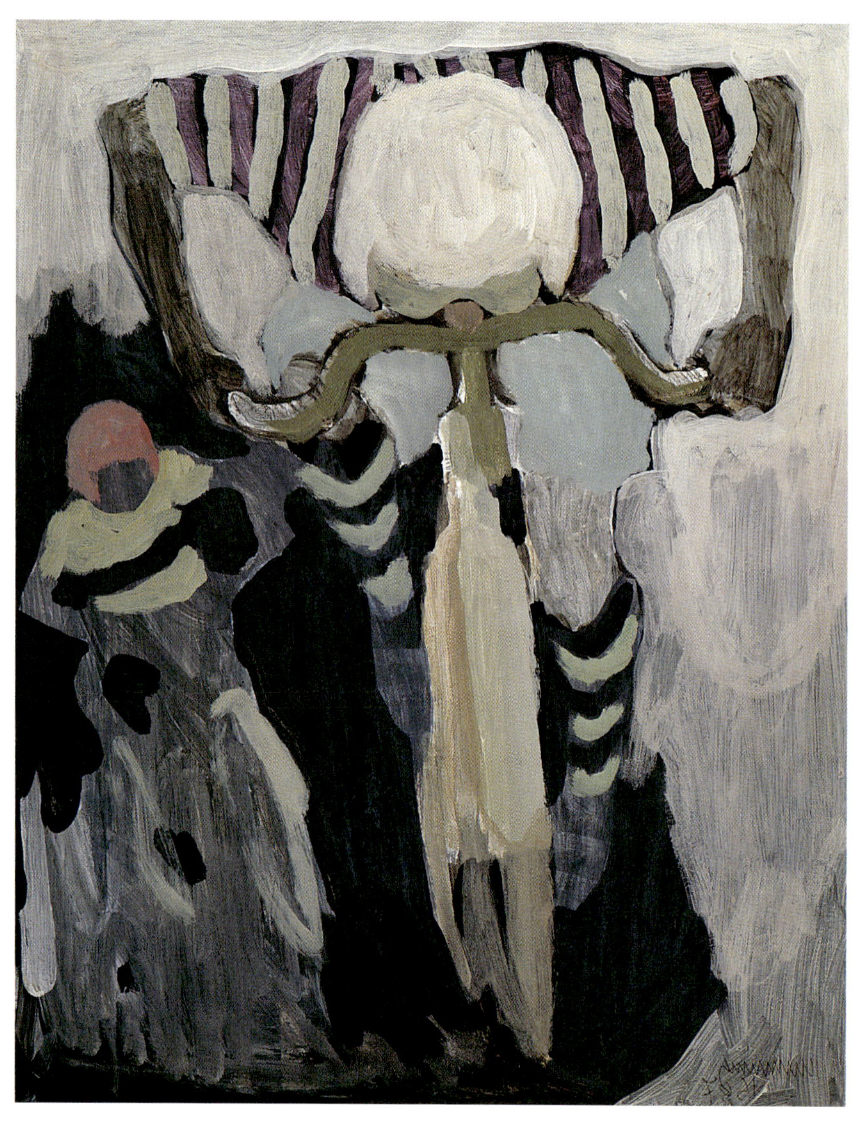

PLATE 38
Cyclists, 1967
Oil and tempera on masonite
25 x 23
Collection of Fredda and Steven Goldfarb

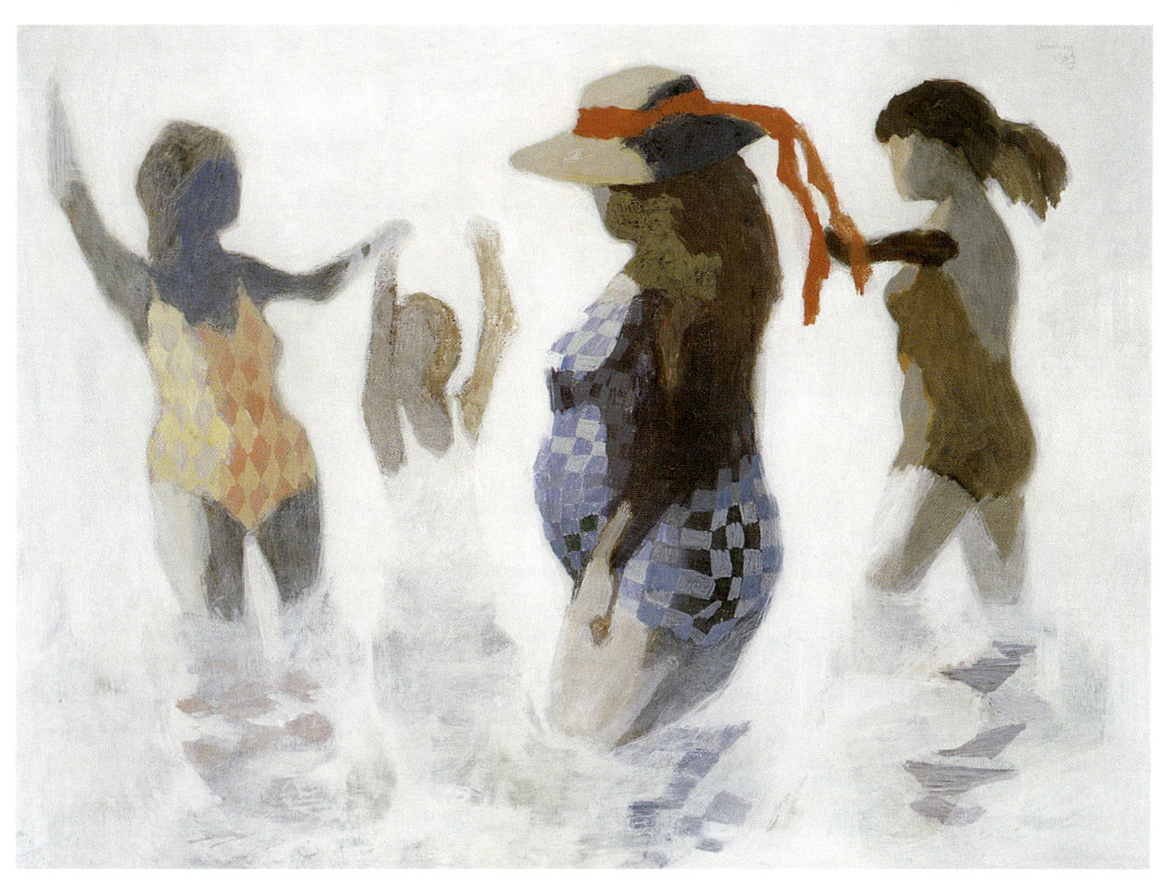

PLATE 39
The Trojan Women, 1967
Oil on masonite
36 x 48
Collection of Lucy and Herb Pruzan

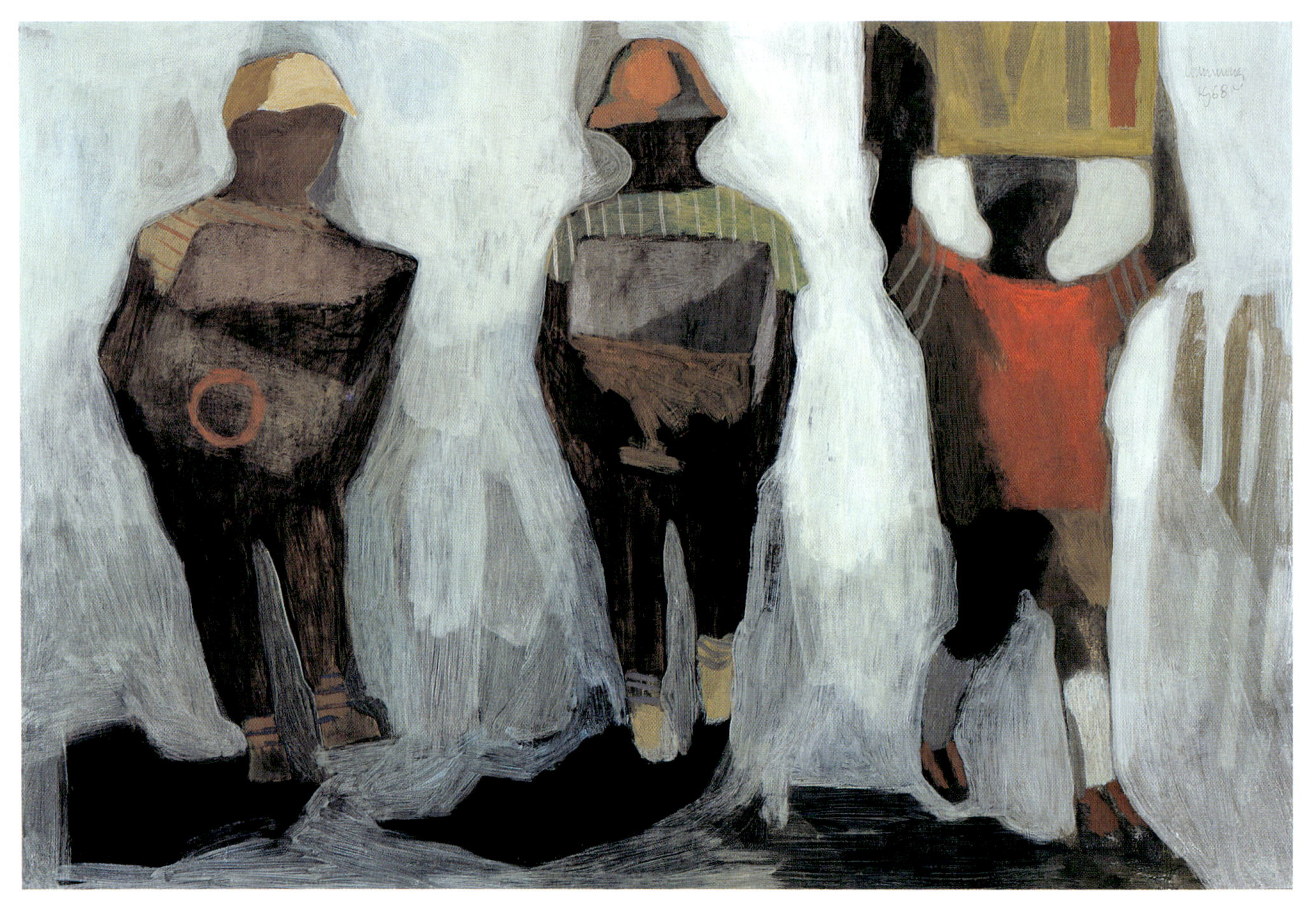

PLATE 40
Three Kids, 1968
Oil on masonite
22 x 36
Portland Art Museum 86.705
Gift of Sandra Stone Peters

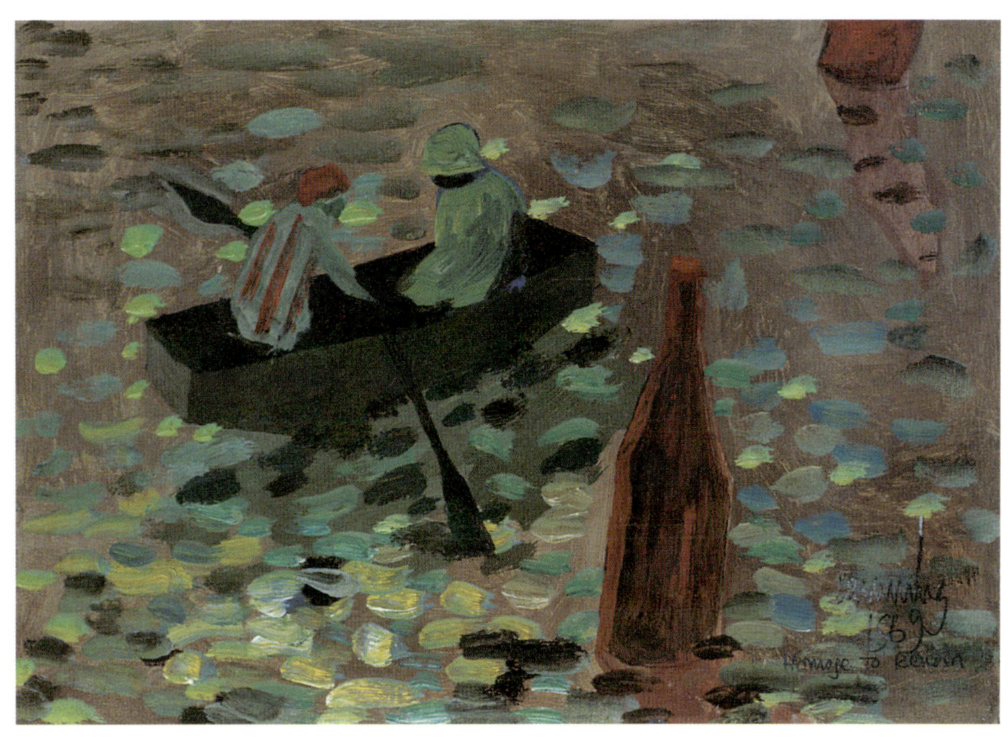

PLATE 41
Homage to Renoir, 1969
Oil and tempera on board
17 x 20 1/2
Private collection, Seattle

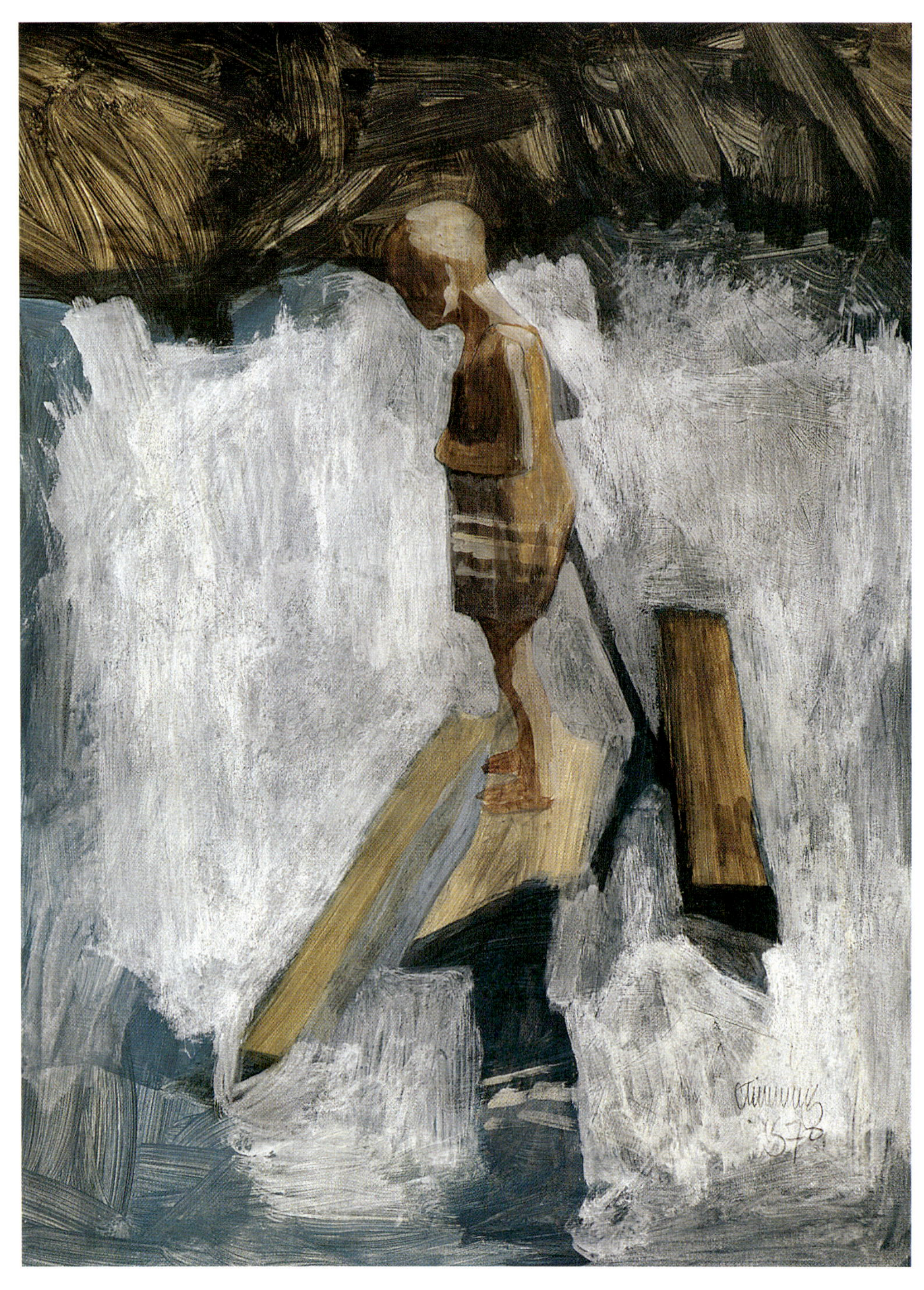

PLATE 42
Boy on Dock, 1970
Oil and tempera on board
25 x 19
Collection of Mr. and Mrs. Alvin Goldfarb

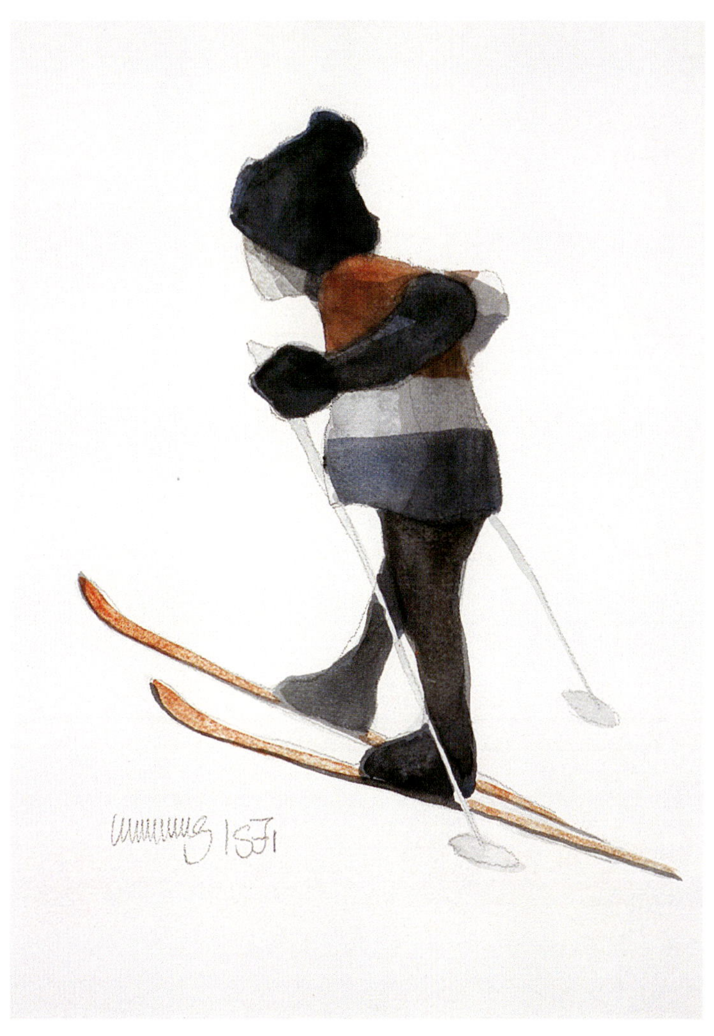

PLATE 43
Young Skier, 1971
Watercolor on paper
14 x 21
Museum of Northwest Art 2004.142.02
The Catterall Collection

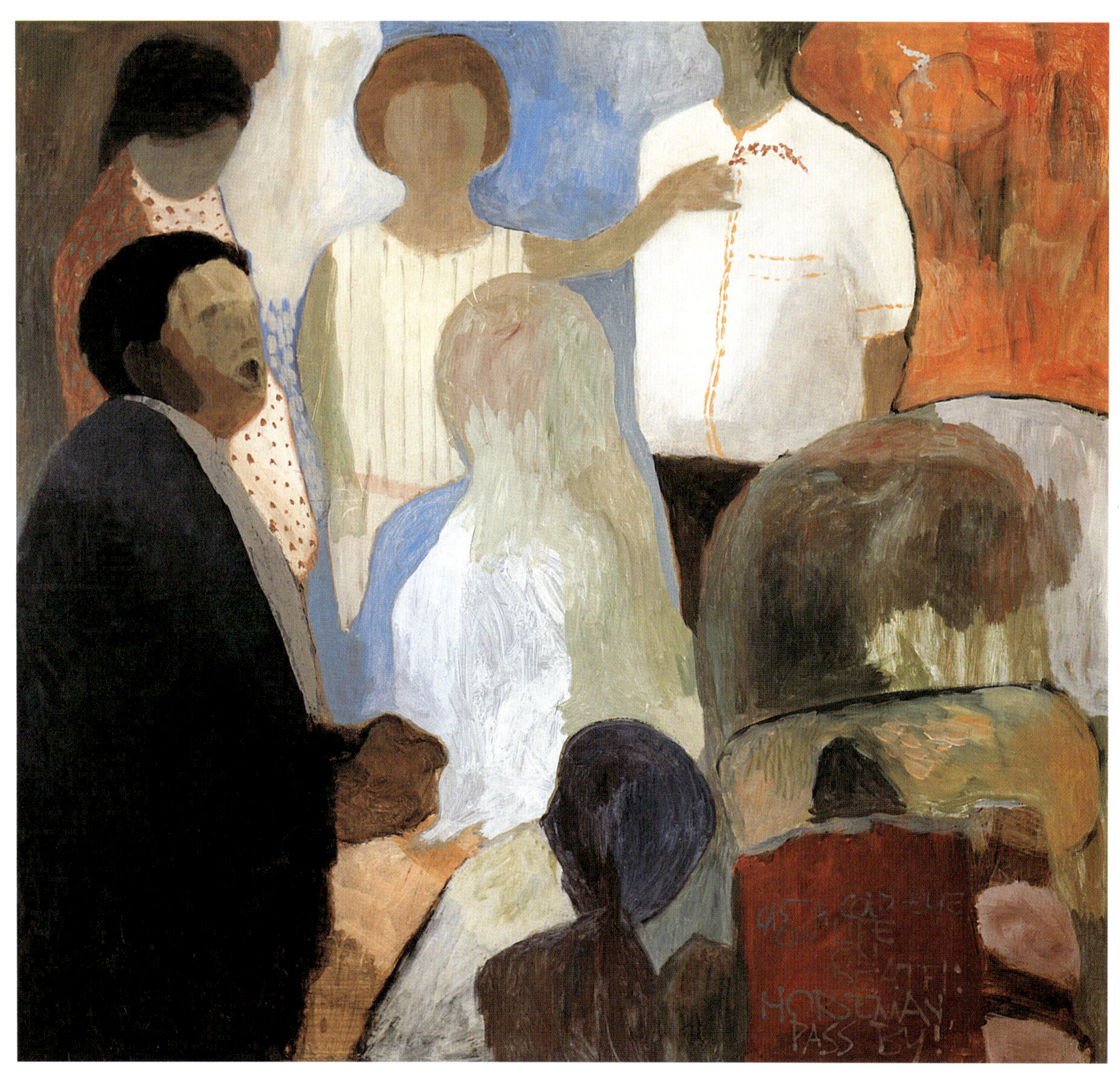

PLATE 44
Cast a Cold Eye, 1973
Oil and tempera on masonite
48 x 48
Collection of the artist

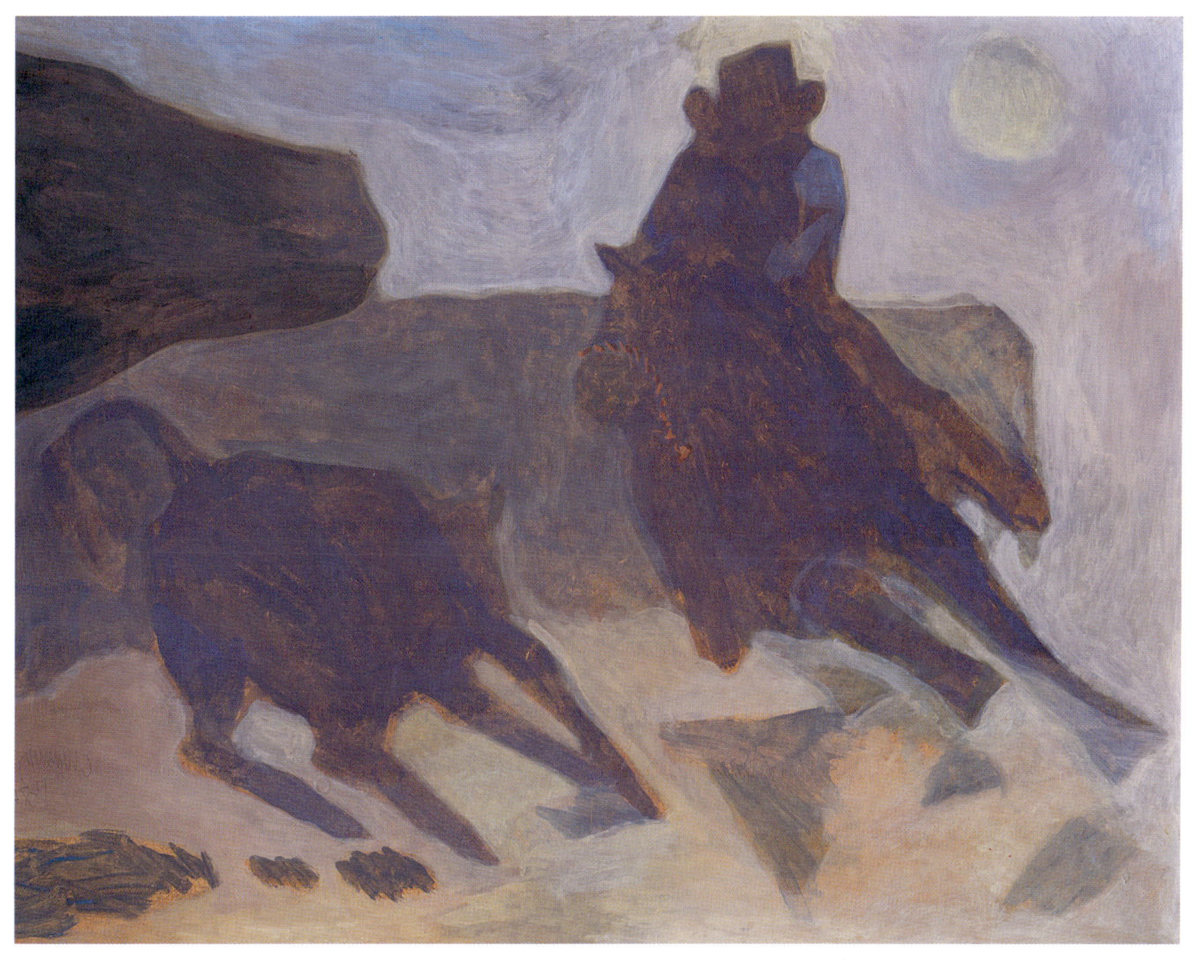

PLATE 45
Rope Them In, 1974
Oil and tempera on board
35 1/2 x 48
The Estate of Edward M. Winskill

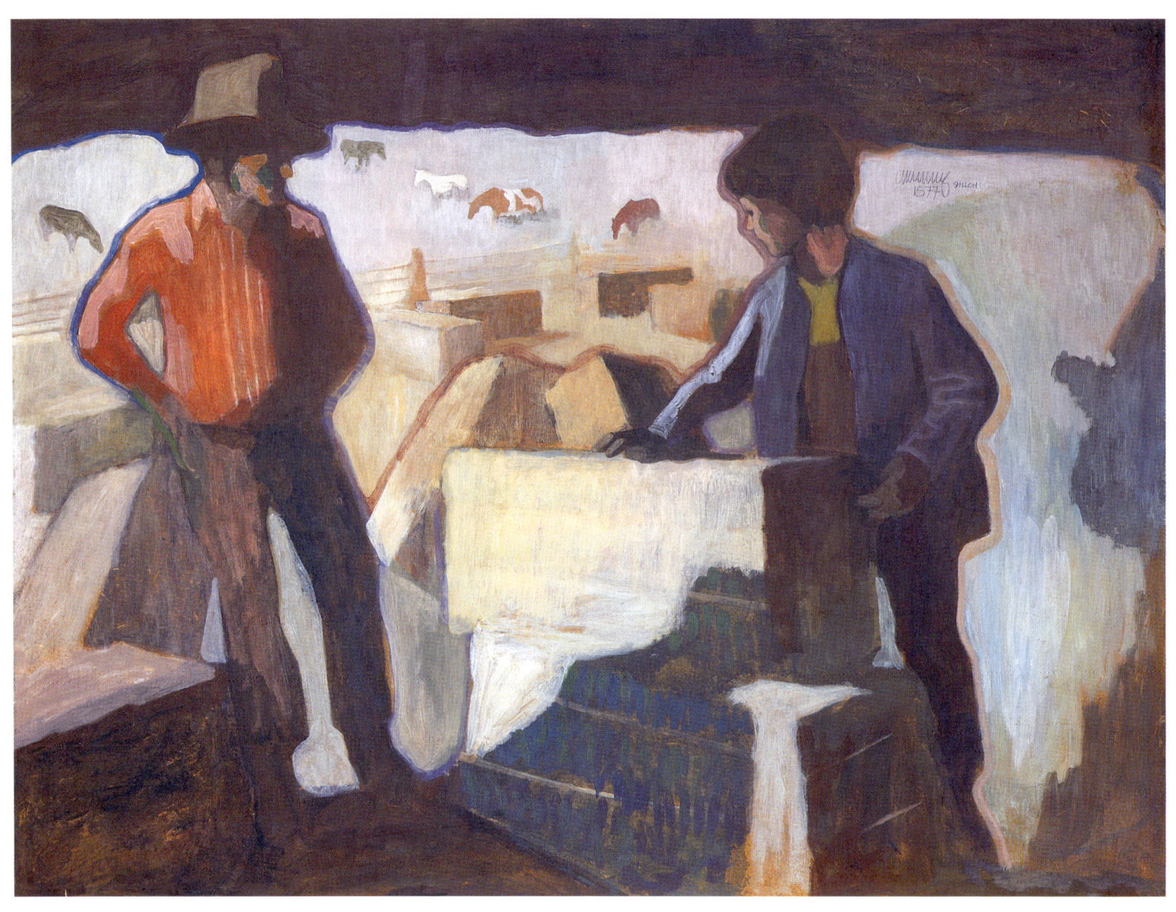

PLATE 46 (above)
Conversation in the Hayfield, 1977
Oil and tempera on board
36 x 48
The Estate of Edward M. Winskill

PLATE 47 (right)
Crucifixion, 1980
Bronze
13 x 7 x 8
Collection of the artist

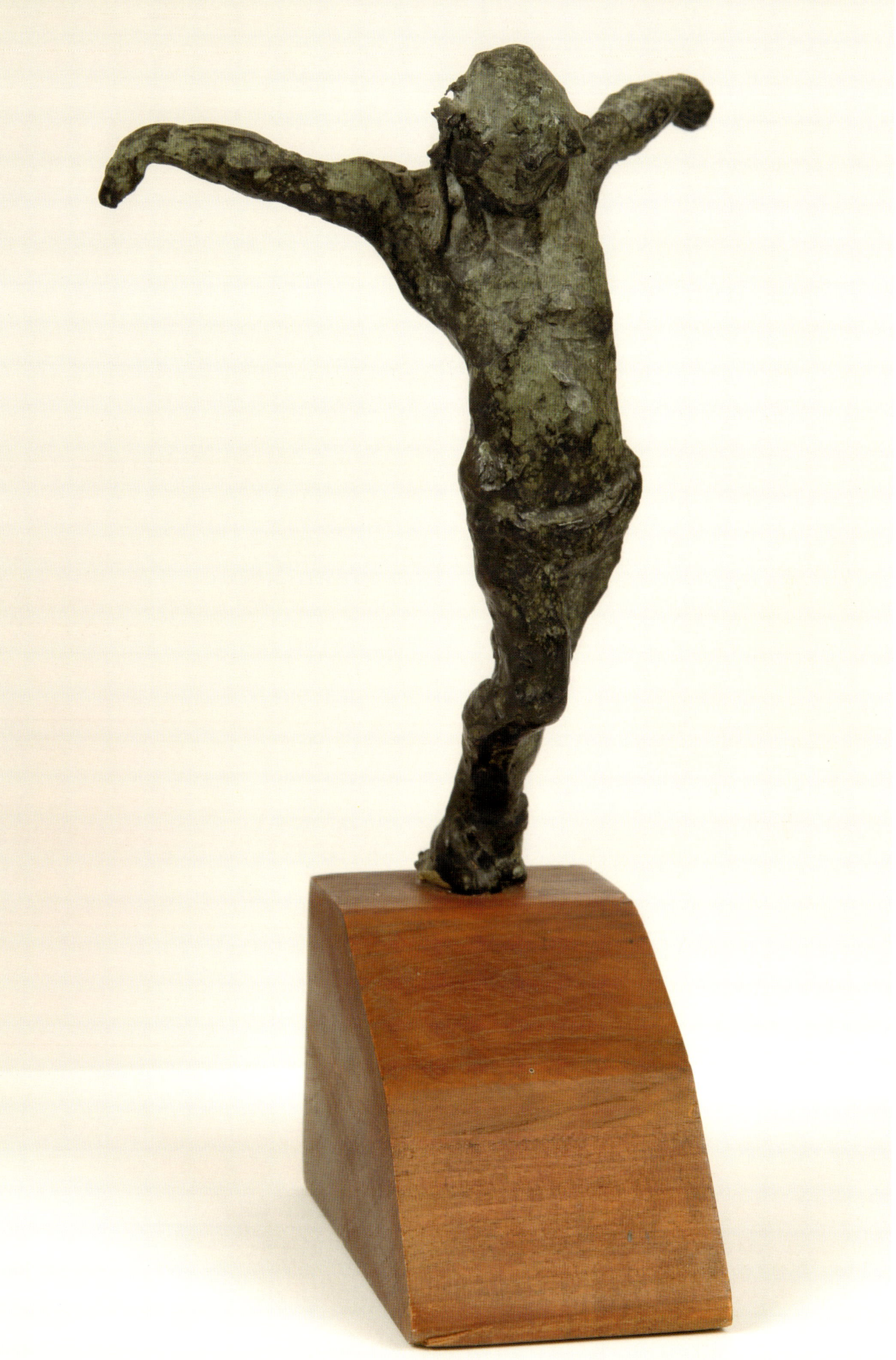

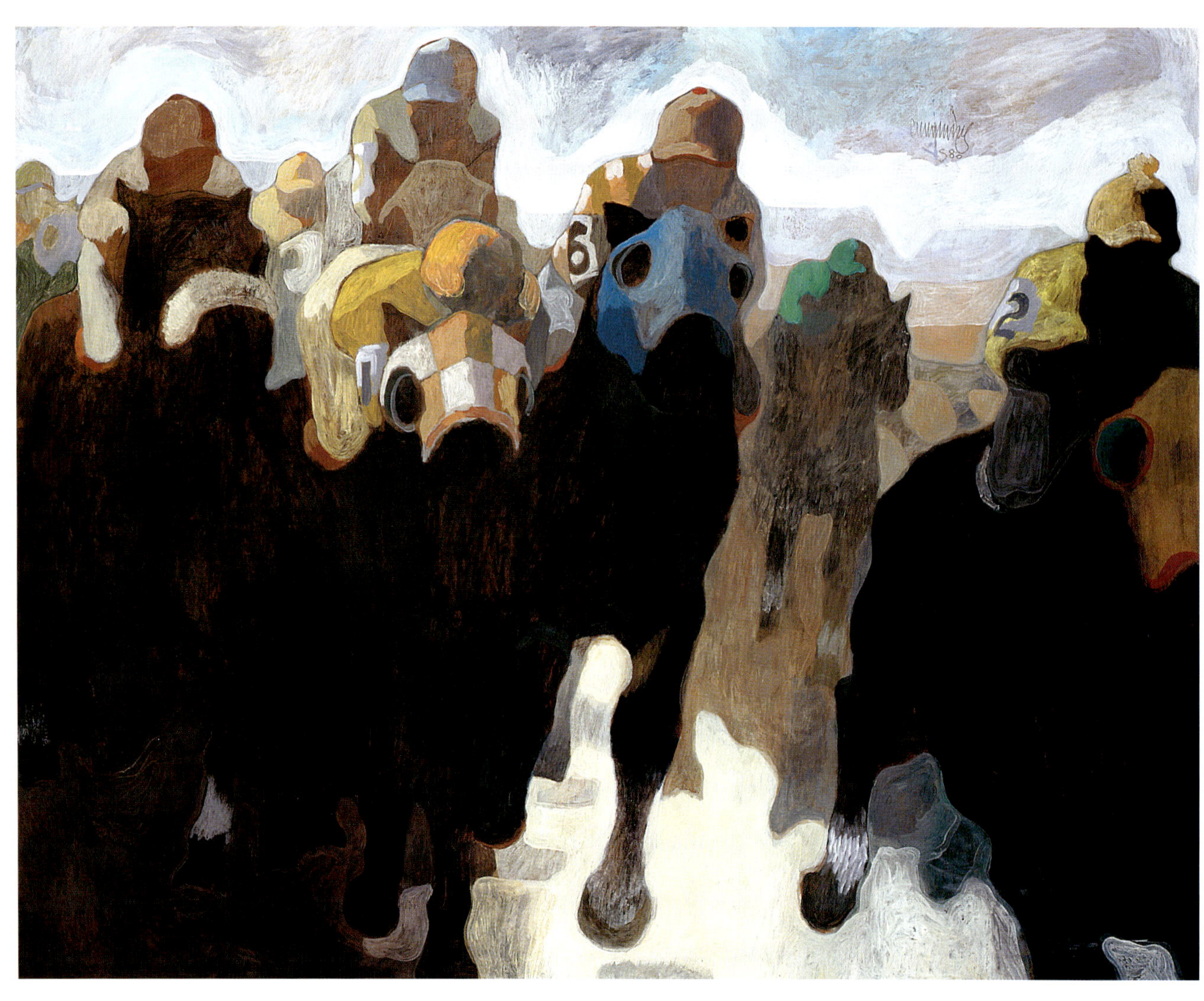

PLATE 48
Stretch Run I, 1980
Oil and tempera on masonite
49 1/2 x 62
The Alhadeff Family, Longacres Collection

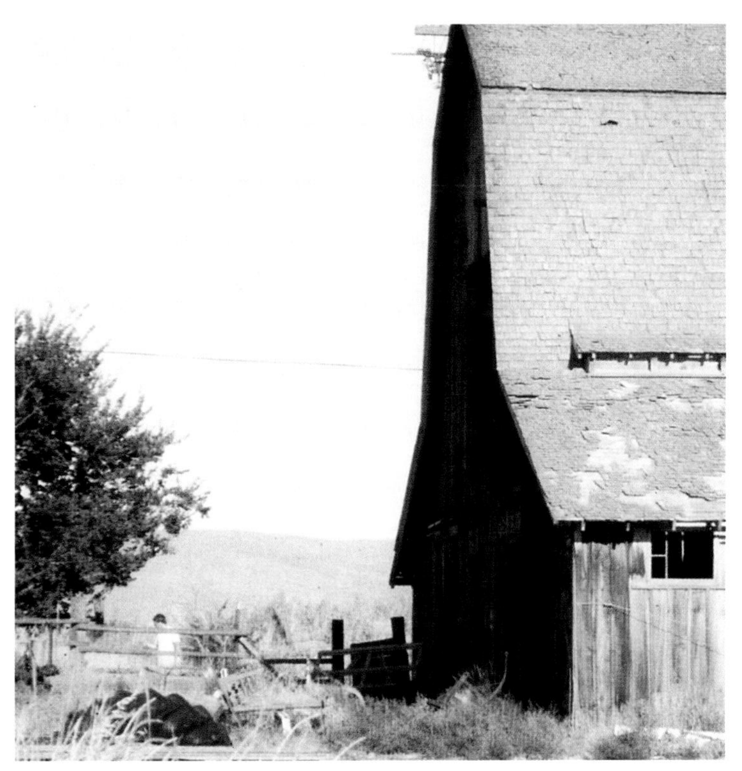

PLATE 49
Old Barn, c. 1980
Polaroid print photograph
3½ x 4
Collection of the artist

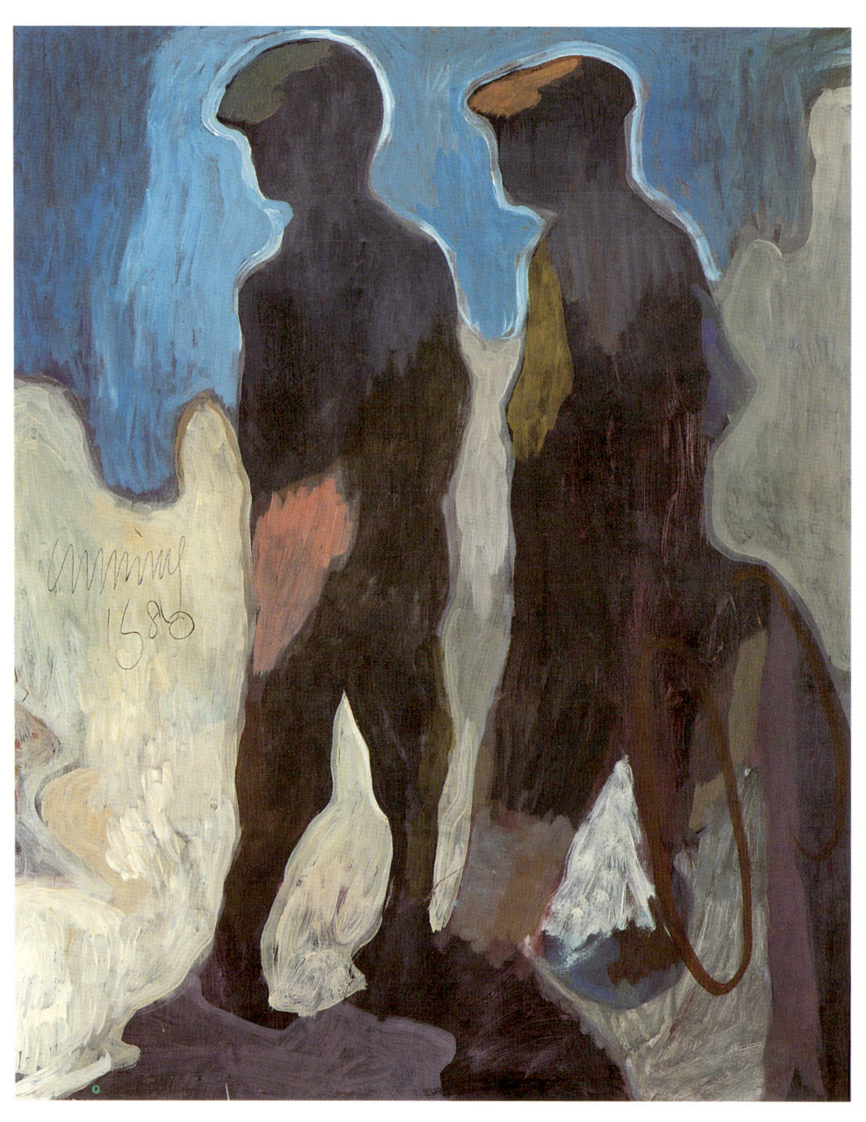

PLATE 50
The Watchers, 1980
Oil and tempera on board
34 7/8 x 29
Collection of Sheraton Seattle Hotel and Towers

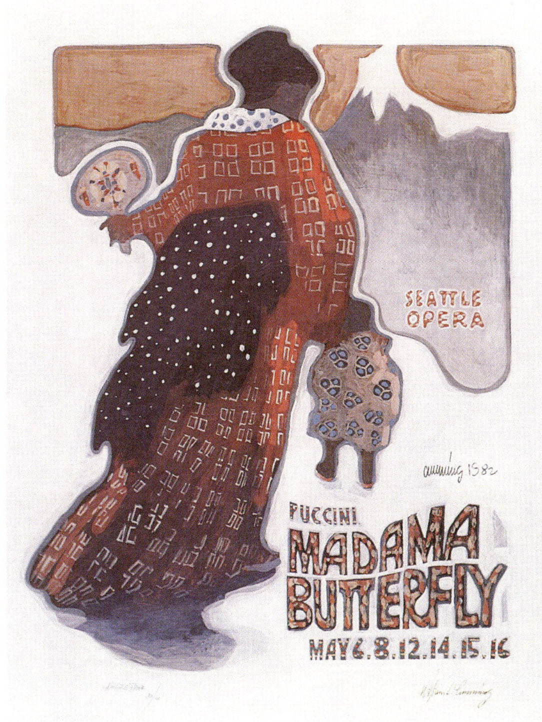

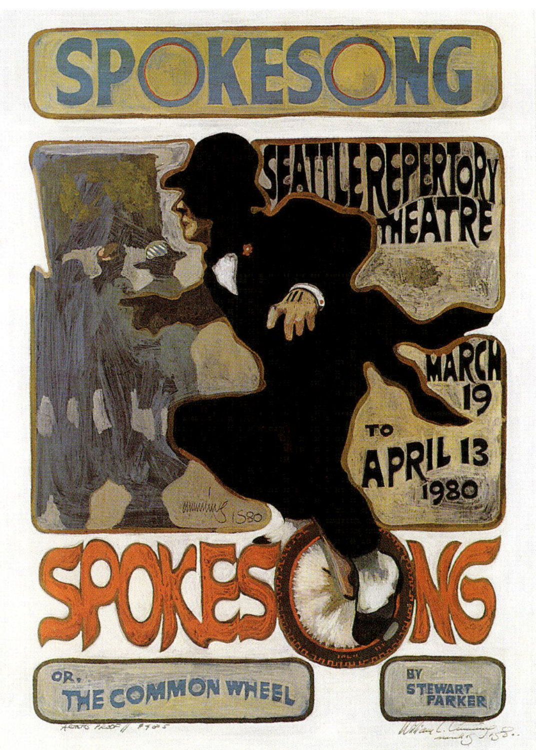

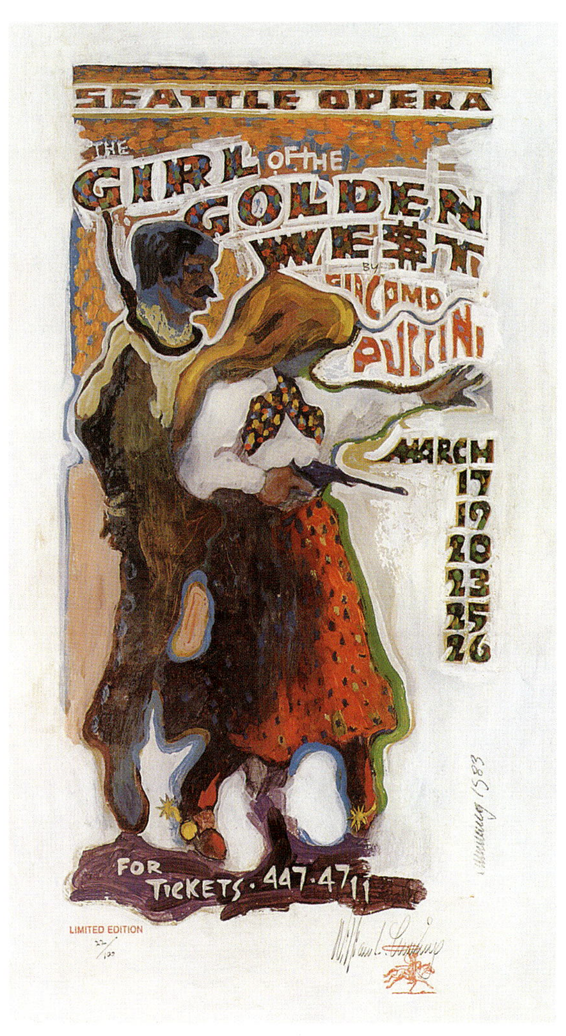

PLATE 51 (top left)
Madama Butterfly, 1982
Color lithograph poster, limited edition
37 x 23

PLATE 52 (top right)
Spokesong, 1985
Color lithograph poster, limited edition
37 x 23

PLATE 53 (right)
Girl of the Golden West, 1982
Color lithograph poster, limited edition
37 x 23

Mr. and Mrs. John Behnke Collection

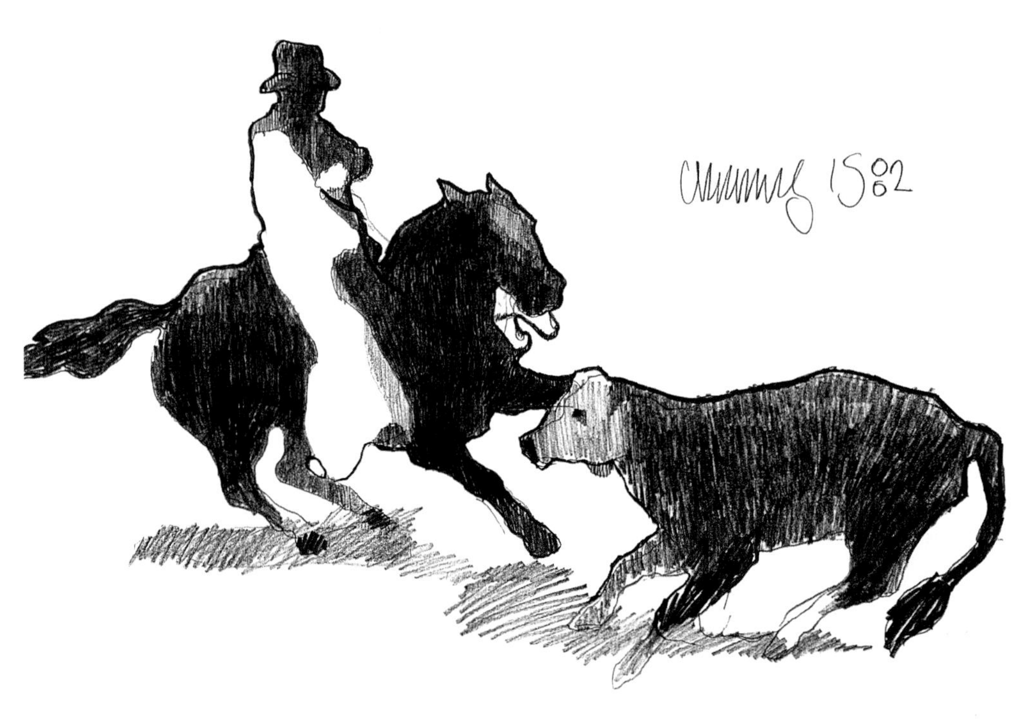

PLATE 54
Rider on Horseback with Cattle, 1982
Pencil on paper
19 x 25
Mr. and Mrs. John Behnke Collection

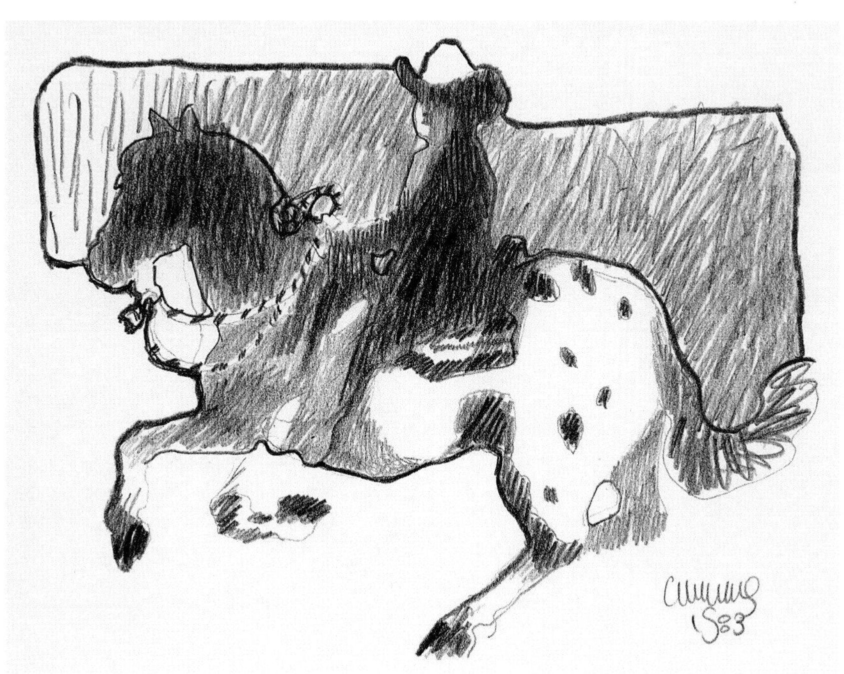

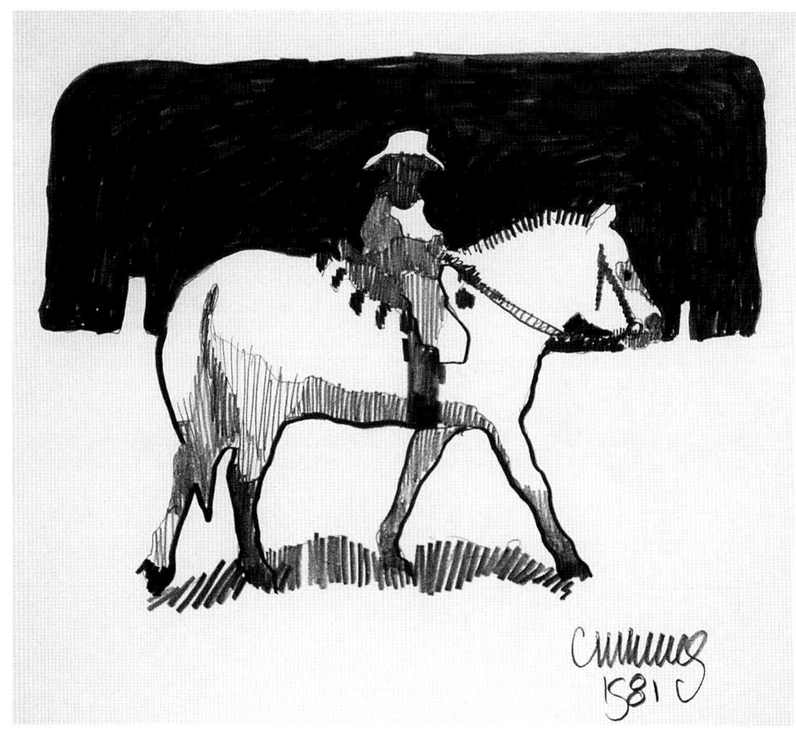

PLATE 55 (top)
Figure on Horseback Galloping, 1983
Pencil on paper
14½ x 17
Mr. and Mrs. John Behnke Collection

PLATE 56 (right)
Figure on Horseback, 1981
Pencil on paper
17 x 16
Mr. and Mrs. John Behnke Collection

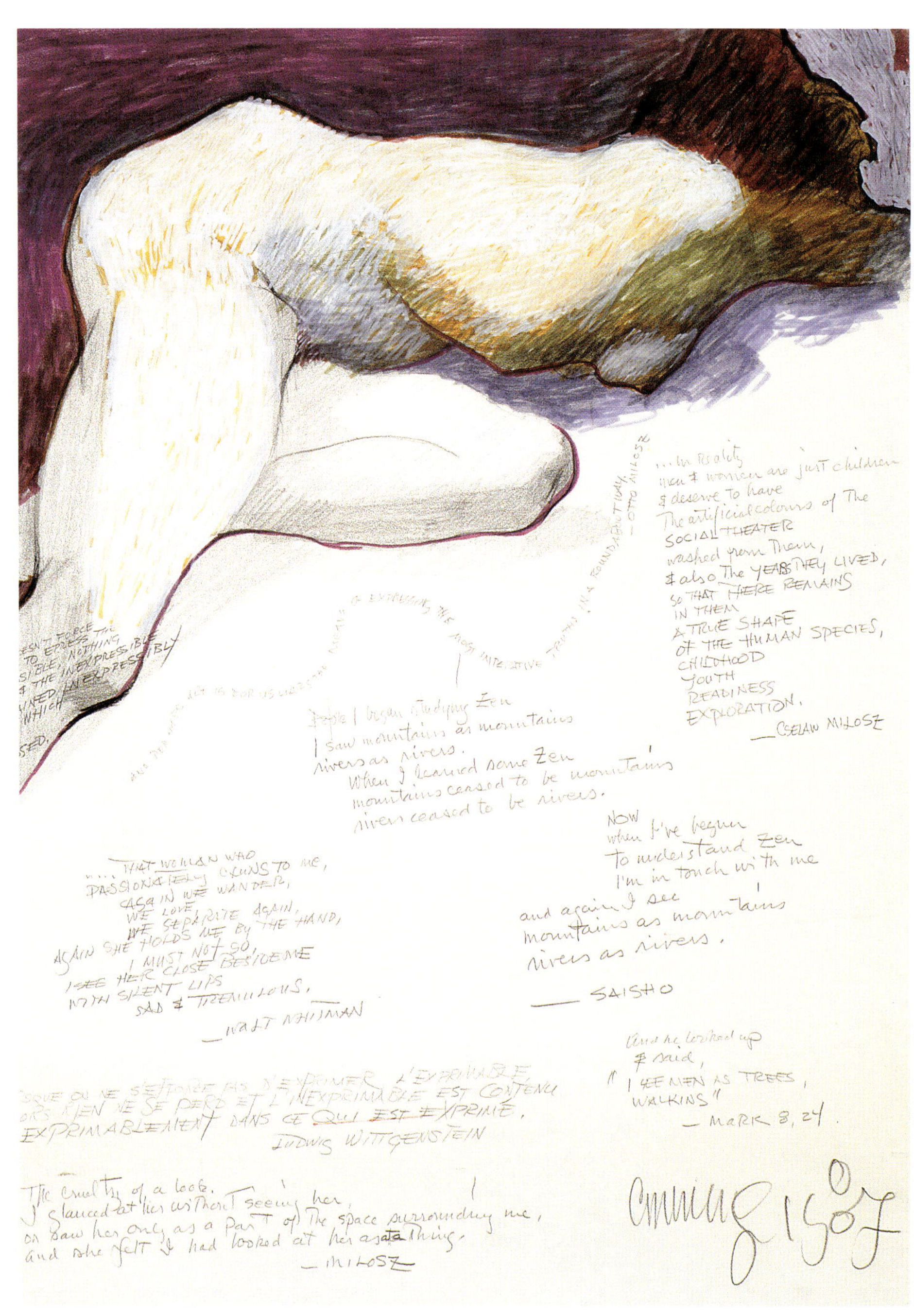

PLATE 57

Reclining Nude with Poetry Excerpts, 1987

Mixed media on paper

29 3/4 x 22

Collection of the artist

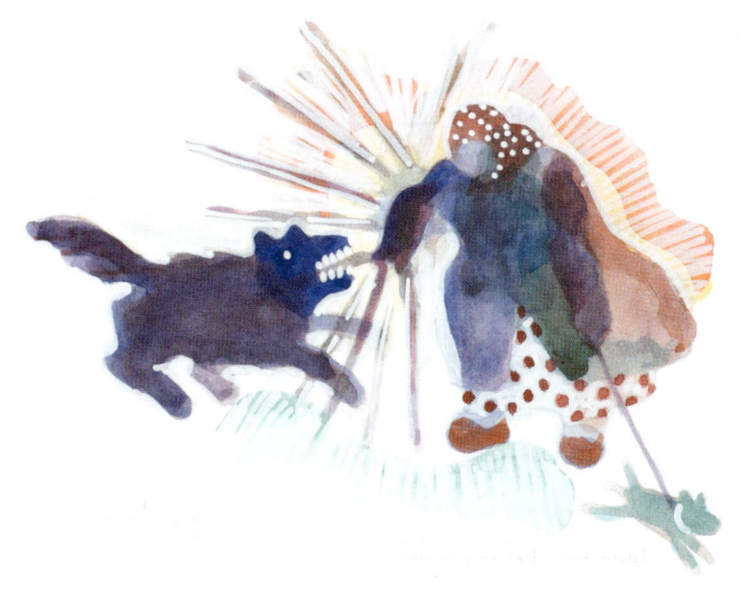

PLATE 58
Old Lady with Barking Dog, 1989
Watercolor on illustration board
9 x 10
Collection of Annette Bauman

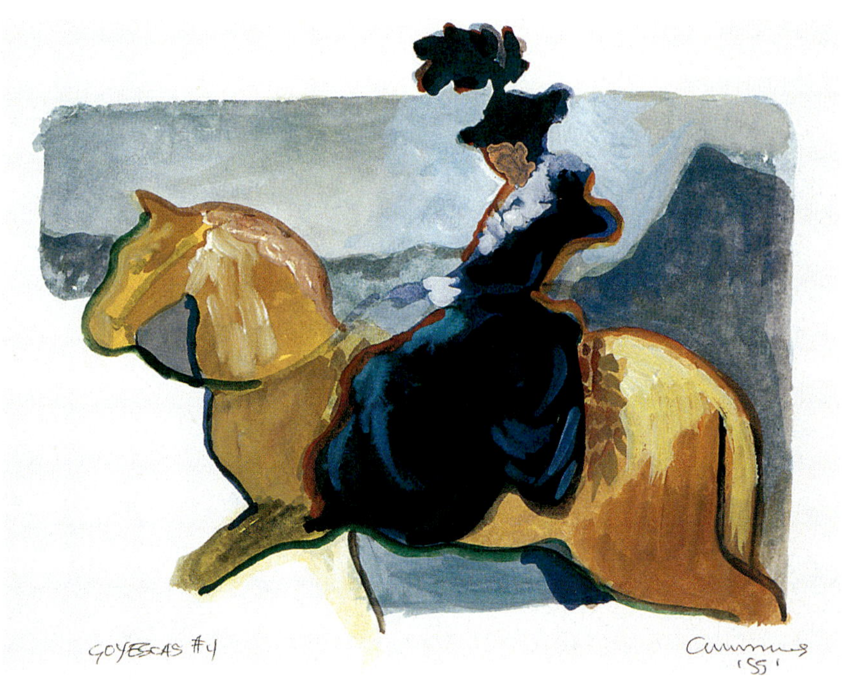

PLATE 59
Goyescas #1 (After Goya), 1991
Oil and tempera on card
18 x 19
Collection of the artist

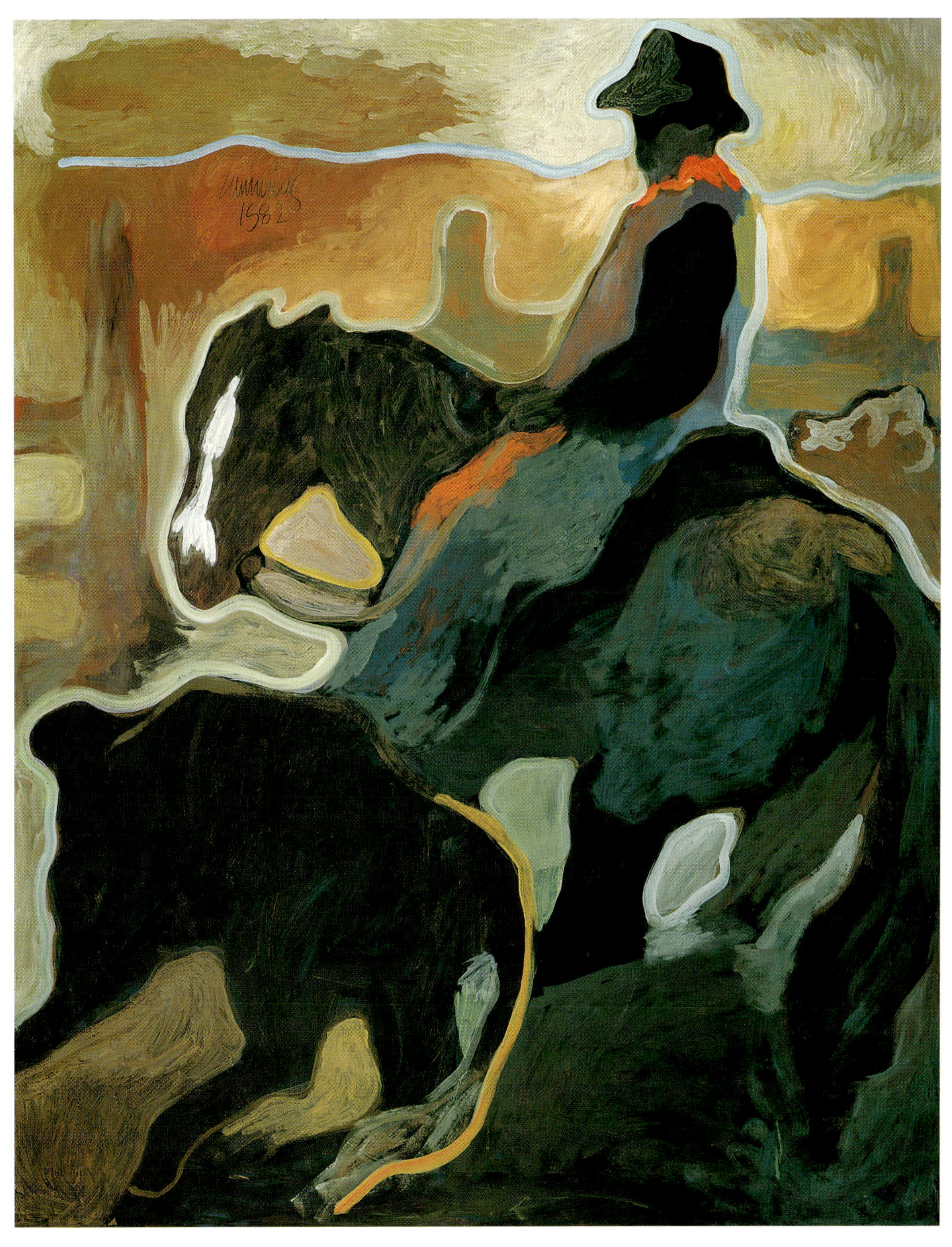

PLATE 60
Cowboy, 1992
Oil and tempera on masonite
54 1/2 x 42 1/2
SAFECO Insurance Companies

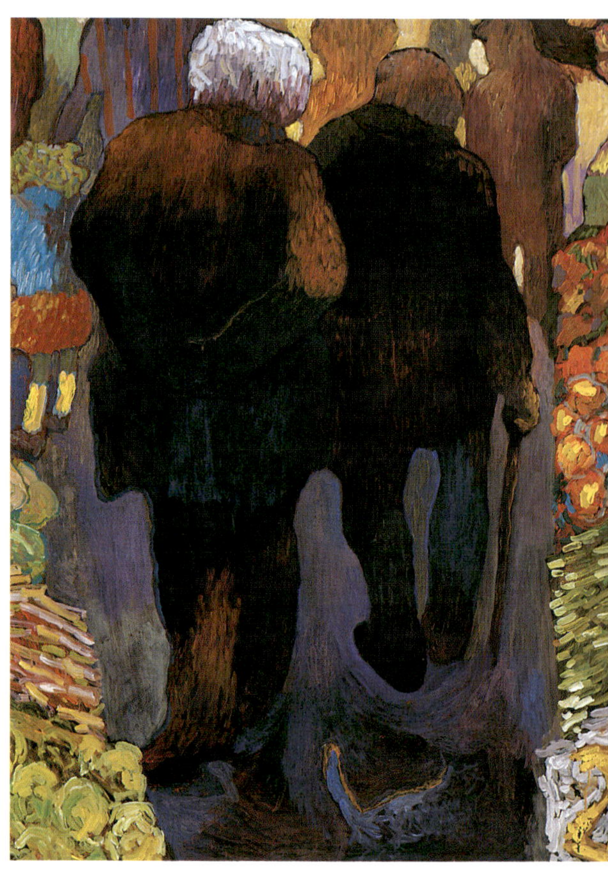

PLATE 61
Triptych, 1992
Oil and tempera on three masonite panels
55 x 42, 55 x 55, 55 x 42
4 Culture and King County Public
Art Collection

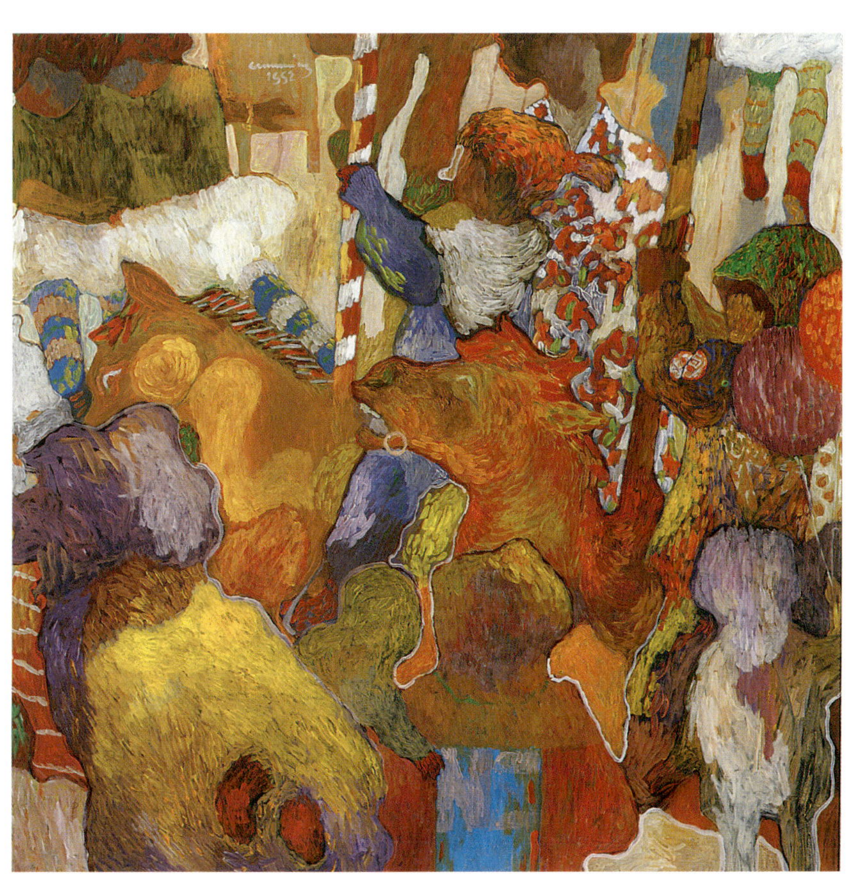

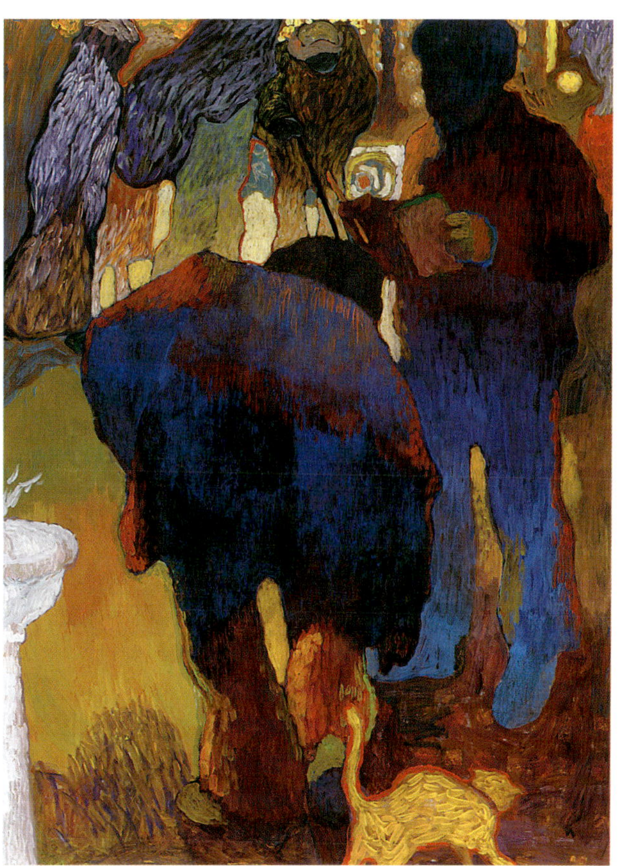

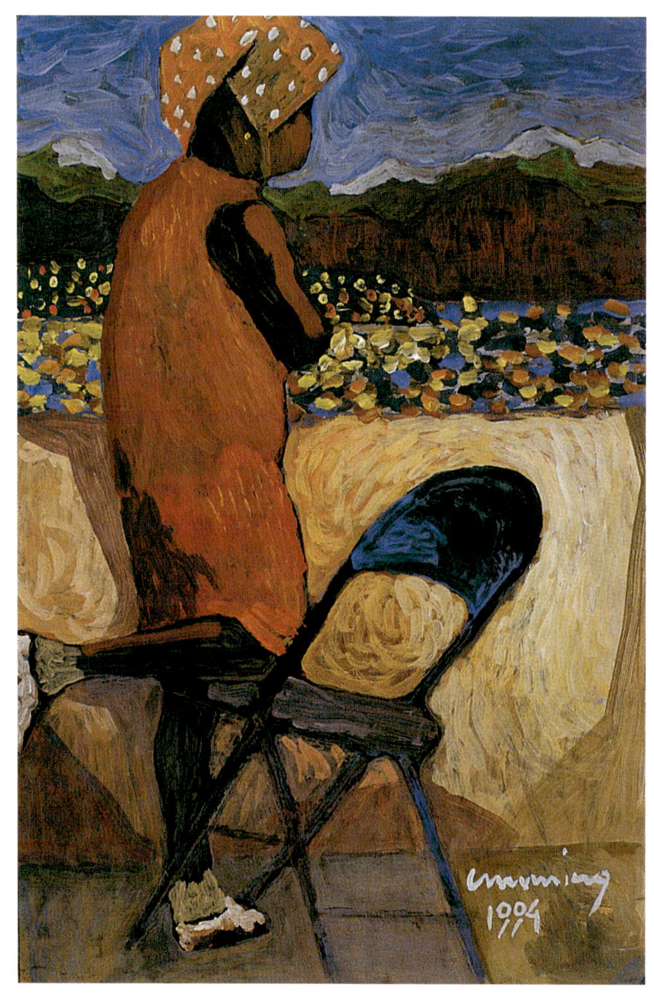

PLATE 62
Reverie, 1994
Oil and tempera on masonite
27 x 21
Mr. and Mrs. Devitt Barnett

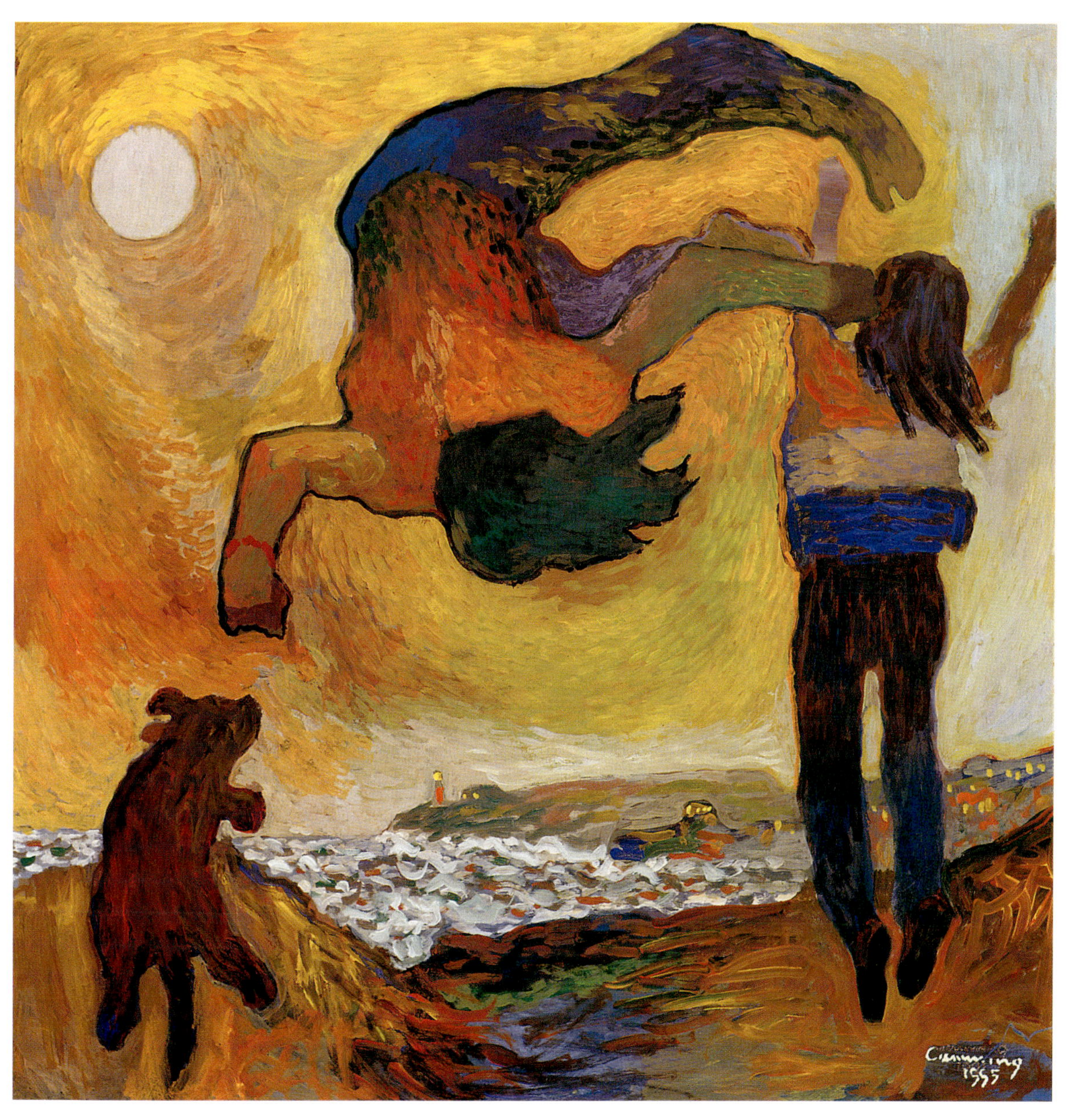

PLATE 63
Acrobat at Golden Gardens, 1995
Oil and tempera on masonite
46 x 45 ½
Private collection of Cairncross & Hempelmann, P.S.

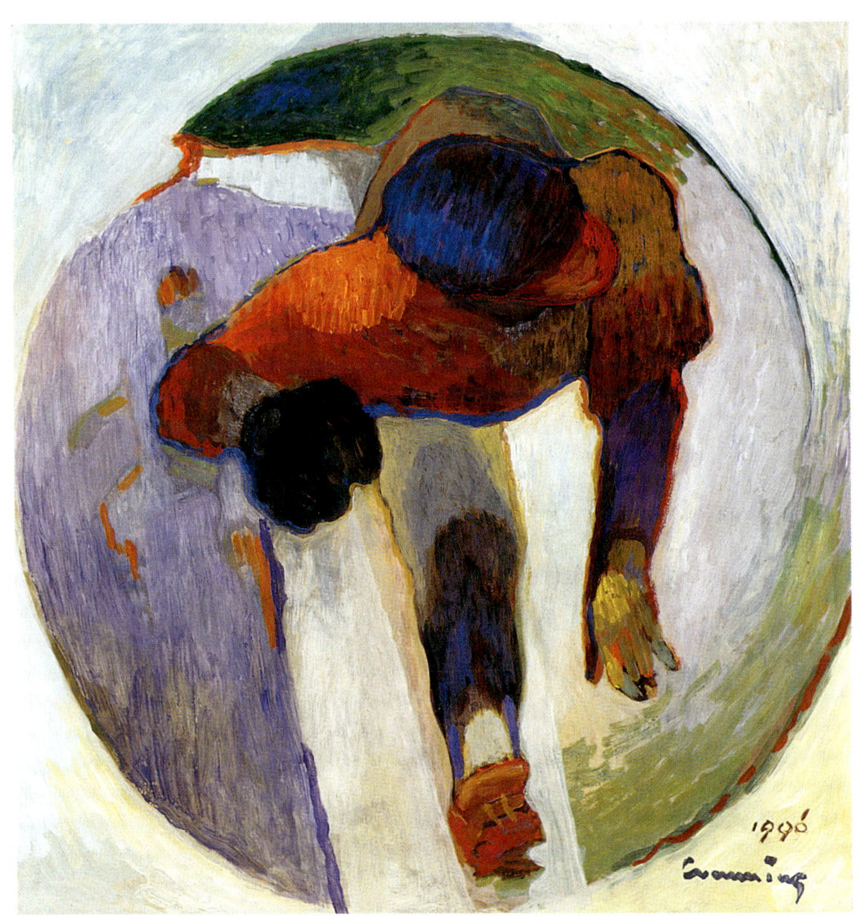

PLATE 64 (above)
Left-Handed Baseball Pitcher, 1996
Oil and tempera on masonite
30 1/2 x 30 1/2
Collection of Dr. and Mrs. Chester Woodside

PLATE 65 (right)
Old Man in the Market, 1995
Bronze
12 h.
Collection of Lucy and Herb Pruzan

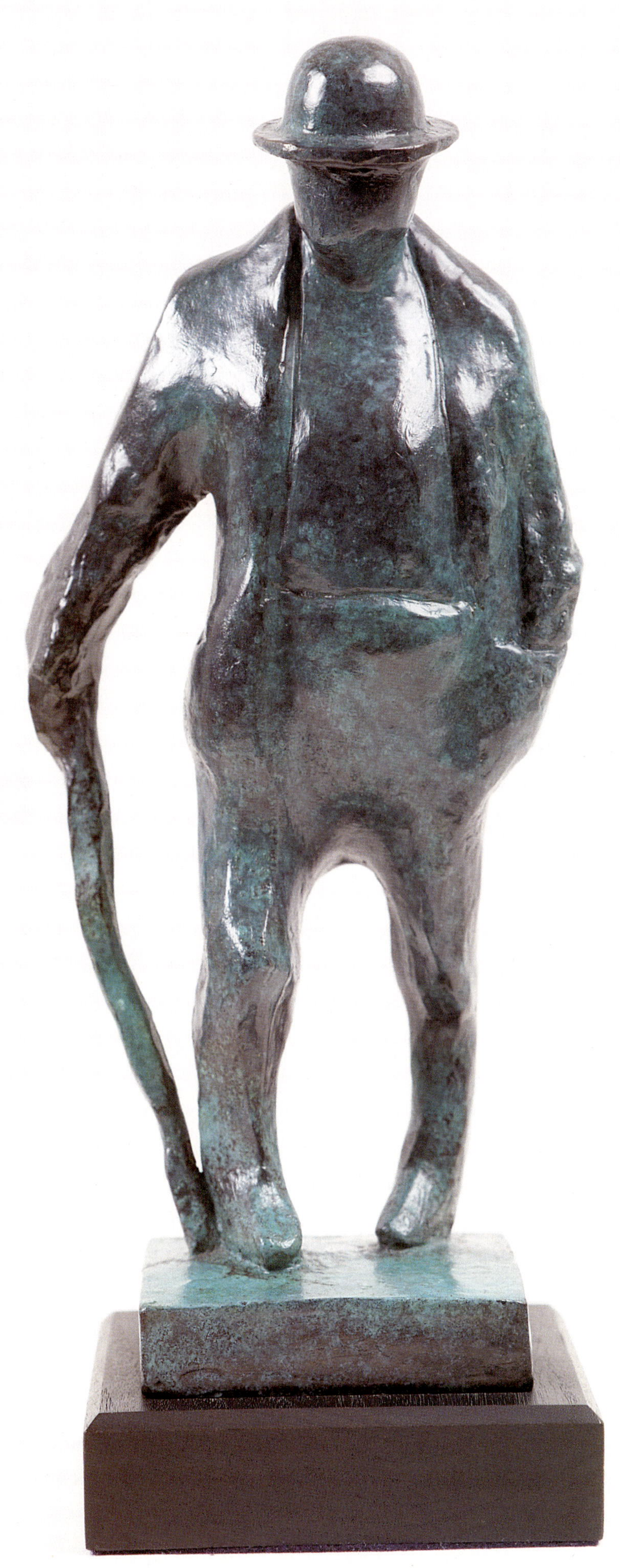

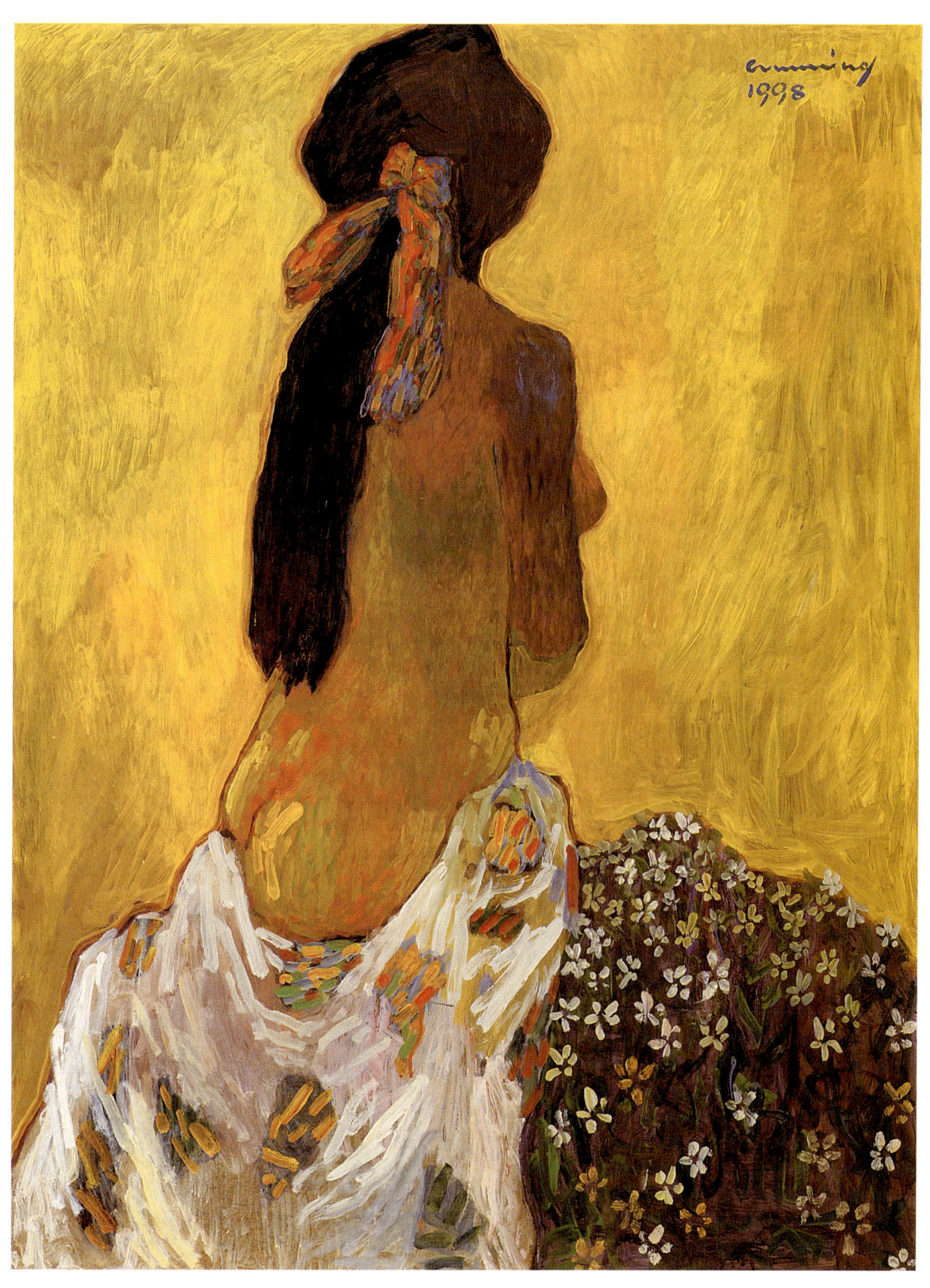

PLATE 66
Dream, 1998
Oil and tempera on masonite
54 1/2 x 42 1/2
Collection of the artist

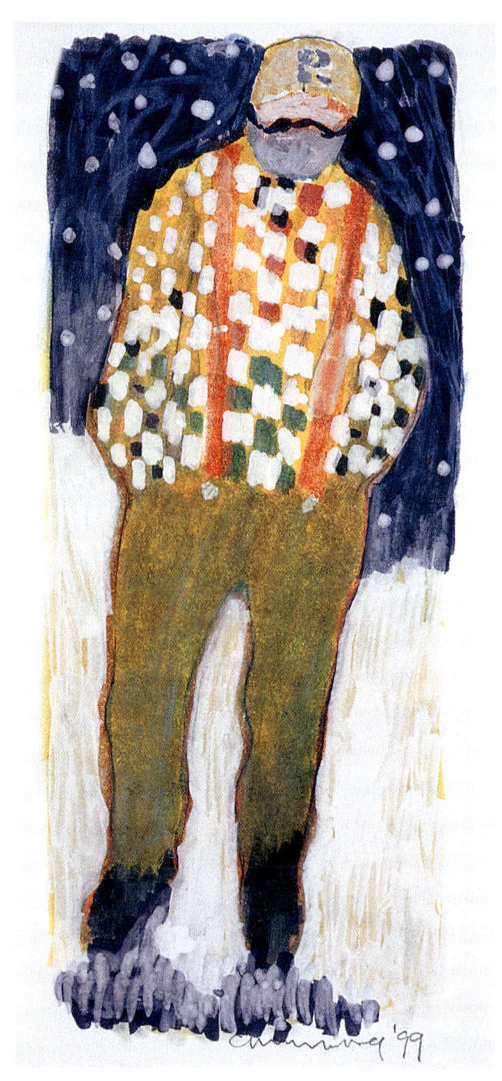

PLATE 67
Checkered Shirt, 1999
Mixed media on paper
17 ½ x 12
Courtesy of Gordon Woodside /
John Braseth Gallery

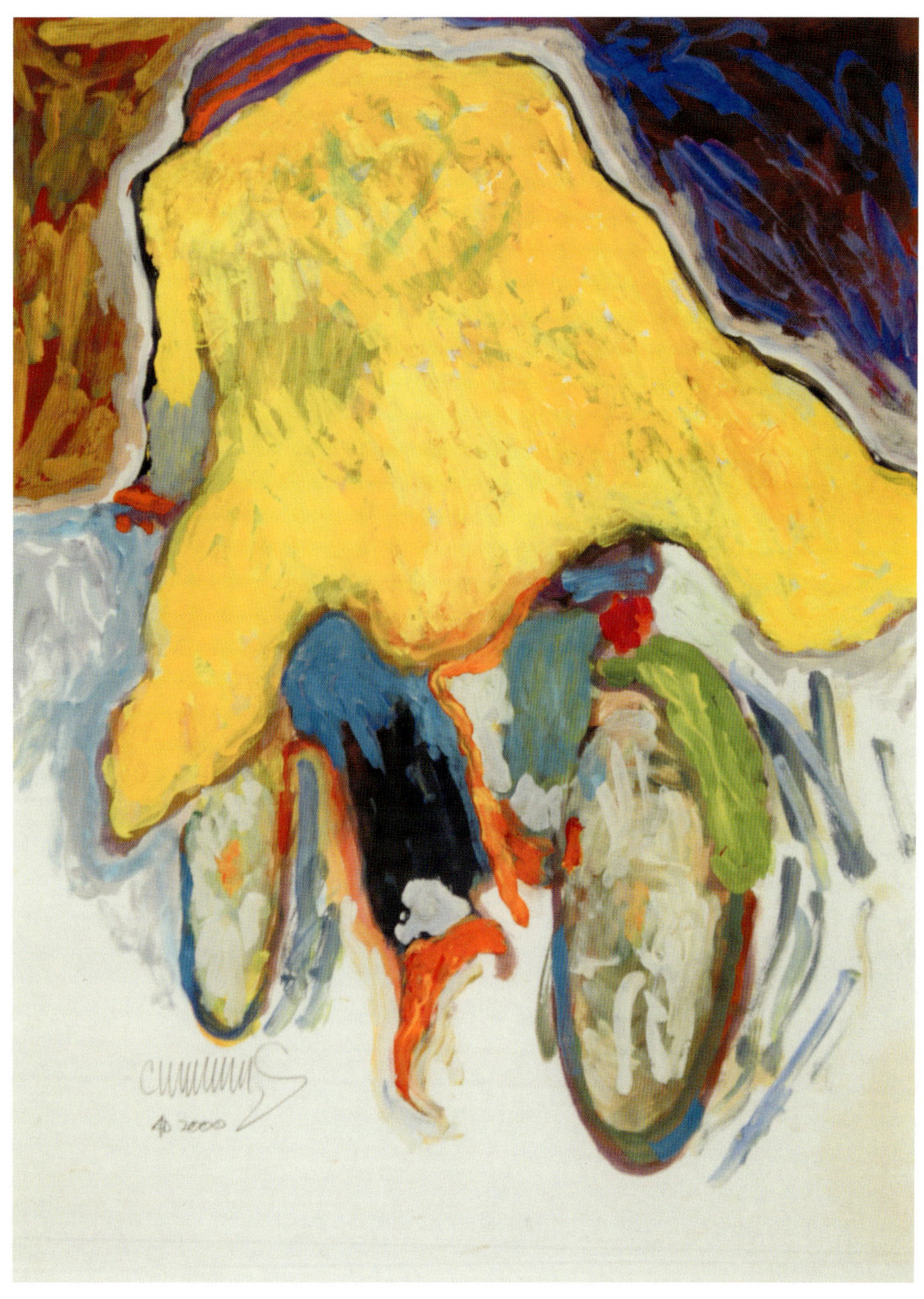

PLATE 68
Man on a Bike, 2000
Mixed media on paper
33 1/2 x 27 1/4
Collection of Sandy and Ron Ryder

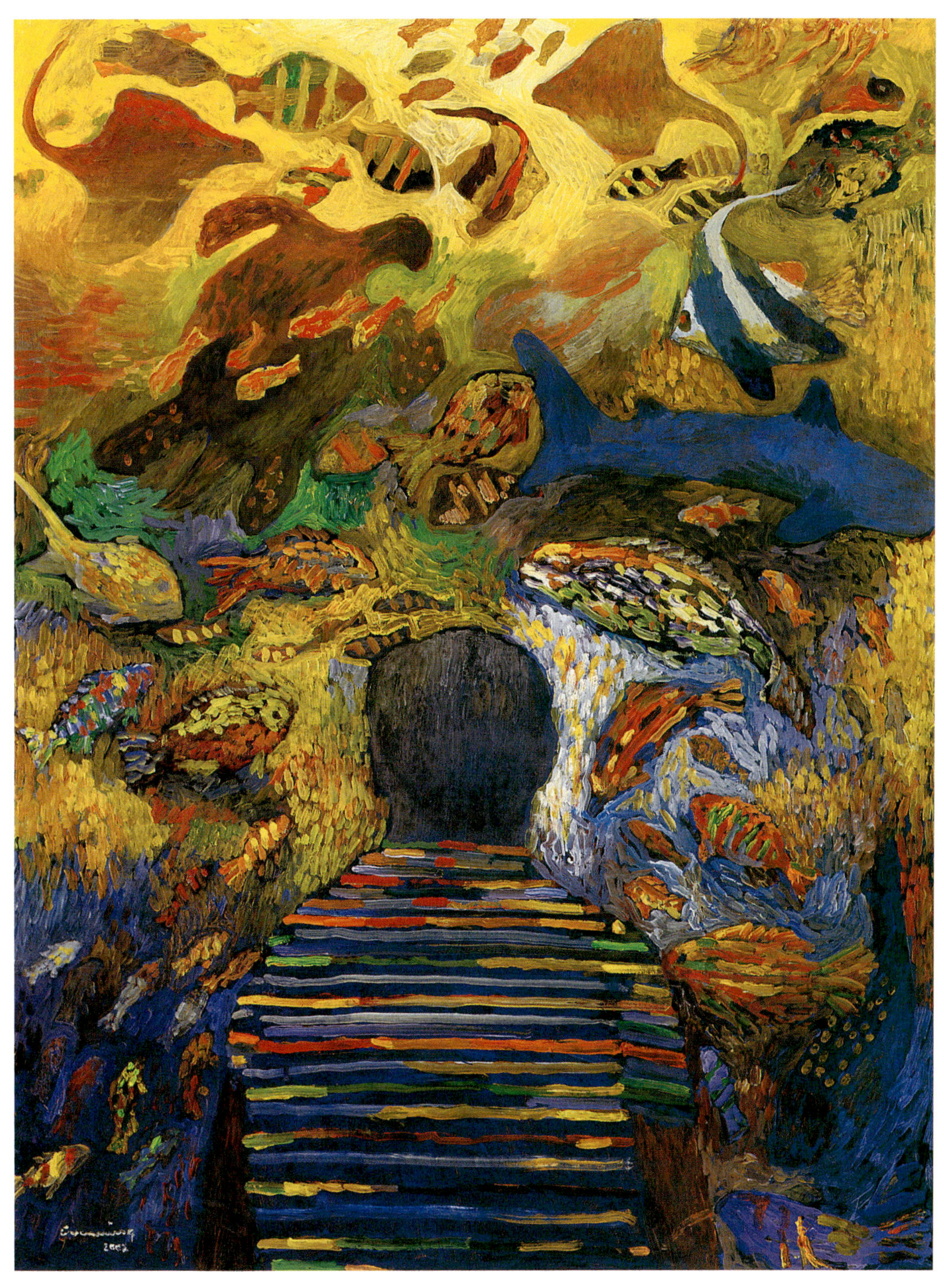

PLATE 69
Carlos and the Fishes, 2001
Oil and tempera on board
55 x 43
Steve Clayton Collection

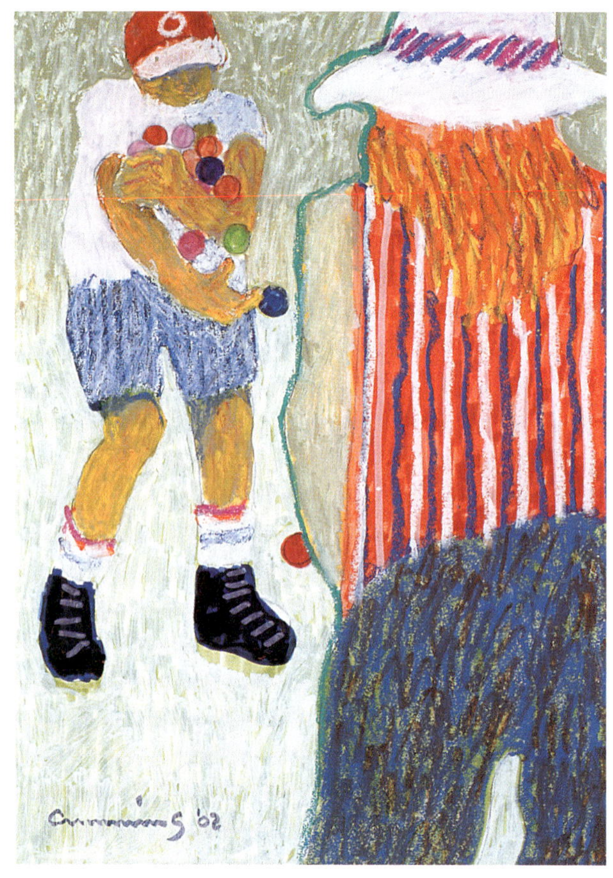

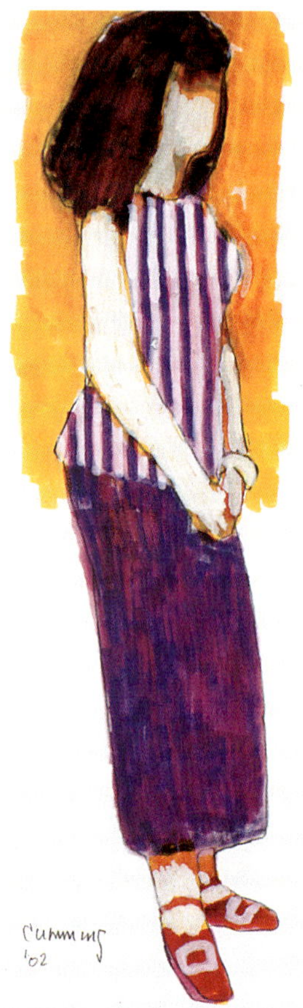

PLATE 70 (above)
Juggler, 2002
Tempera on paper
23 x 18
Collection of the artist; courtesy of Gordon Woodside / John Braseth Gallery

PLATE 71 (right)
Pose, 2002
Mixed media on paper
22 x $14\frac{1}{2}$
Collection of the artist; courtesy of Gordon Woodside / John Braseth Gallery

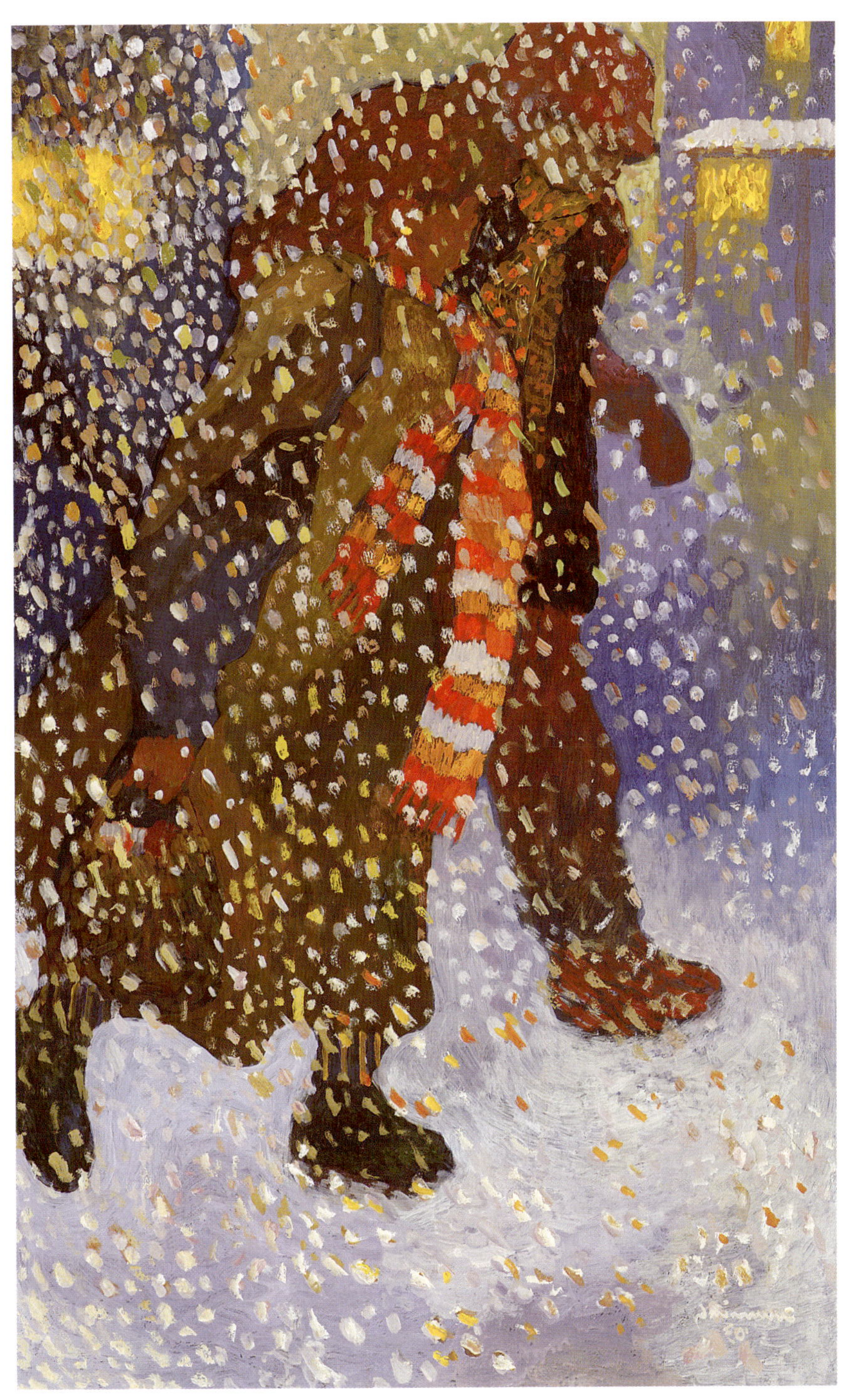

PLATE 72
Evening Snow, 2003
Oil and tempera on board
56 x 38
Collection of Douglas and Ann Williams

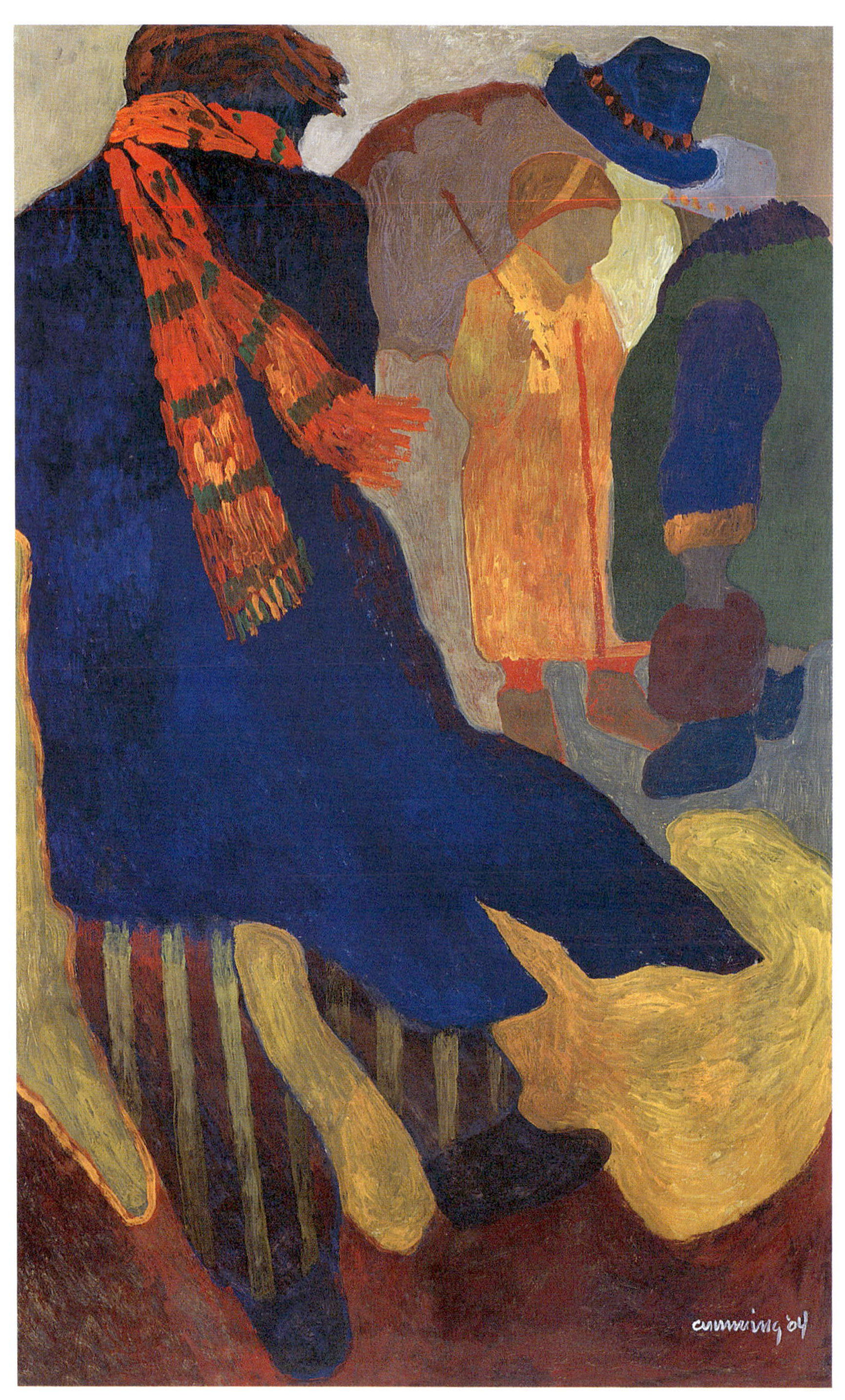

PLATE 73
Windy, 2004
Oil and tempera on masonite
56 x 38
Collection of the artist; courtesy of
Gordon Woodside / John Braseth Gallery

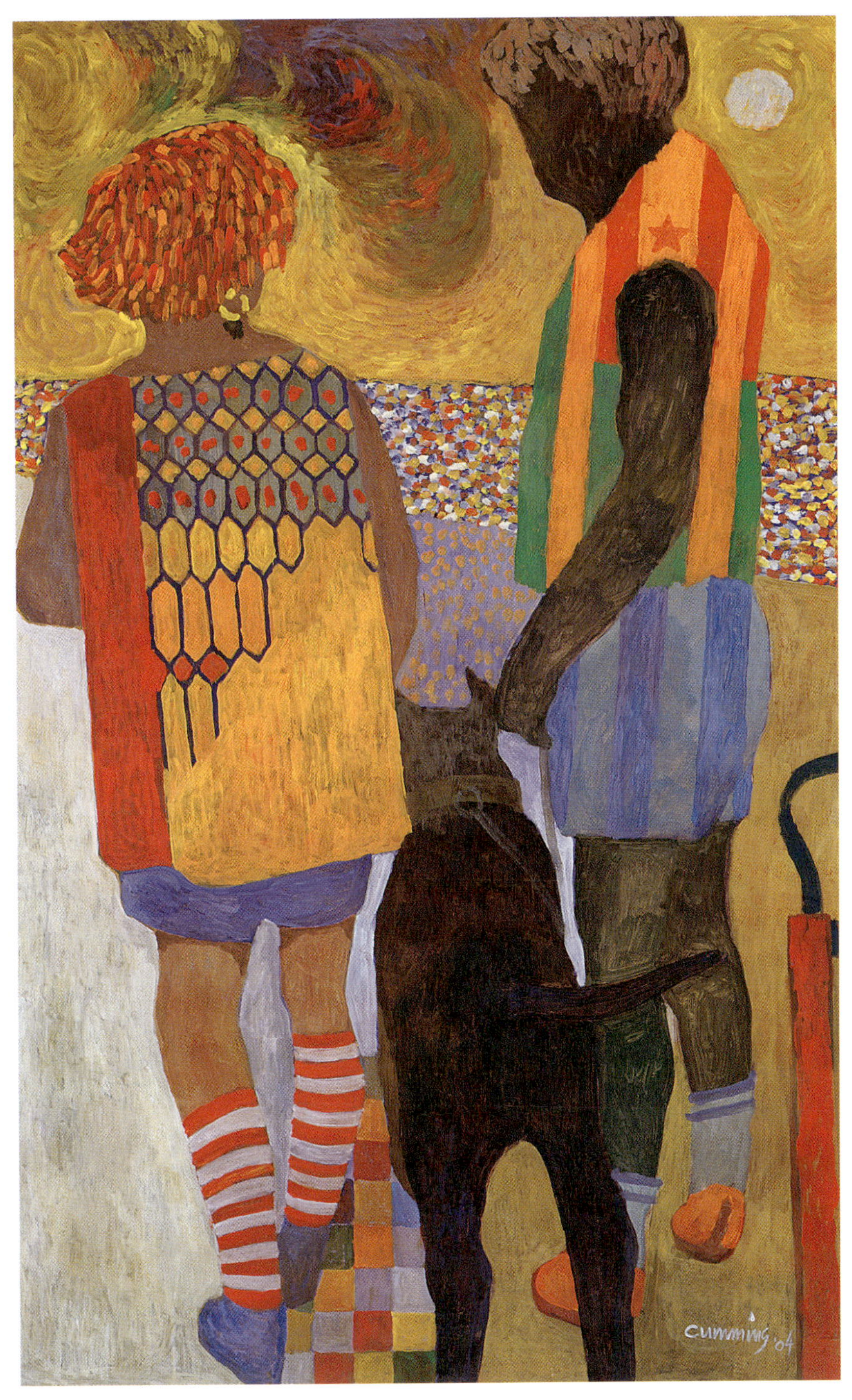

PLATE 74
At the Park, 2004
Oil and tempera on masonite
56¼ x 38
Collection of the artist; courtesy of
Gordon Woodside / John Braseth Gallery

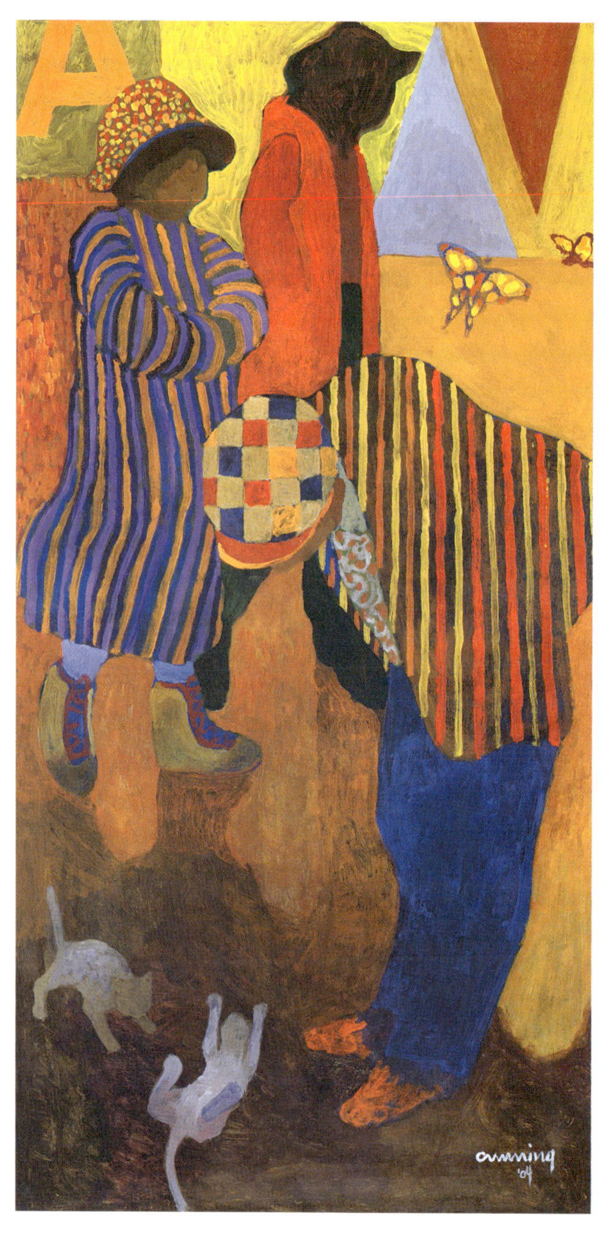

PLATE 75
Red Shoes, 2004
Oil and tempera on masonite
56 ¼ x 32
Private collection, Seattle

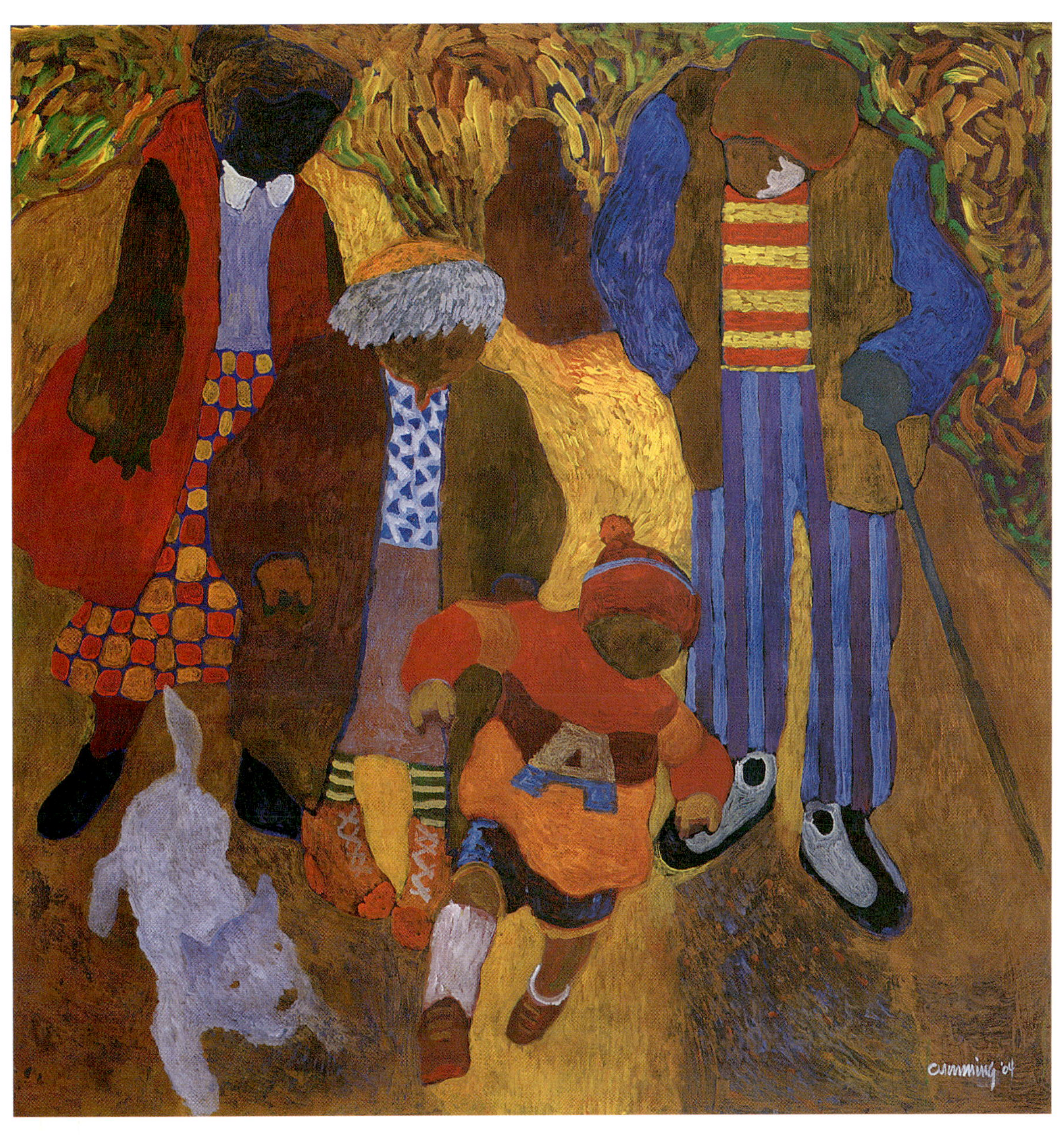

PLATE 76
Generations, 2004
Oil and tempera on masonite
$56\frac{1}{4}$ x $56\frac{1}{4}$
Collection of the artist; courtesy of
Gordon Woodside / John Braseth Gallery

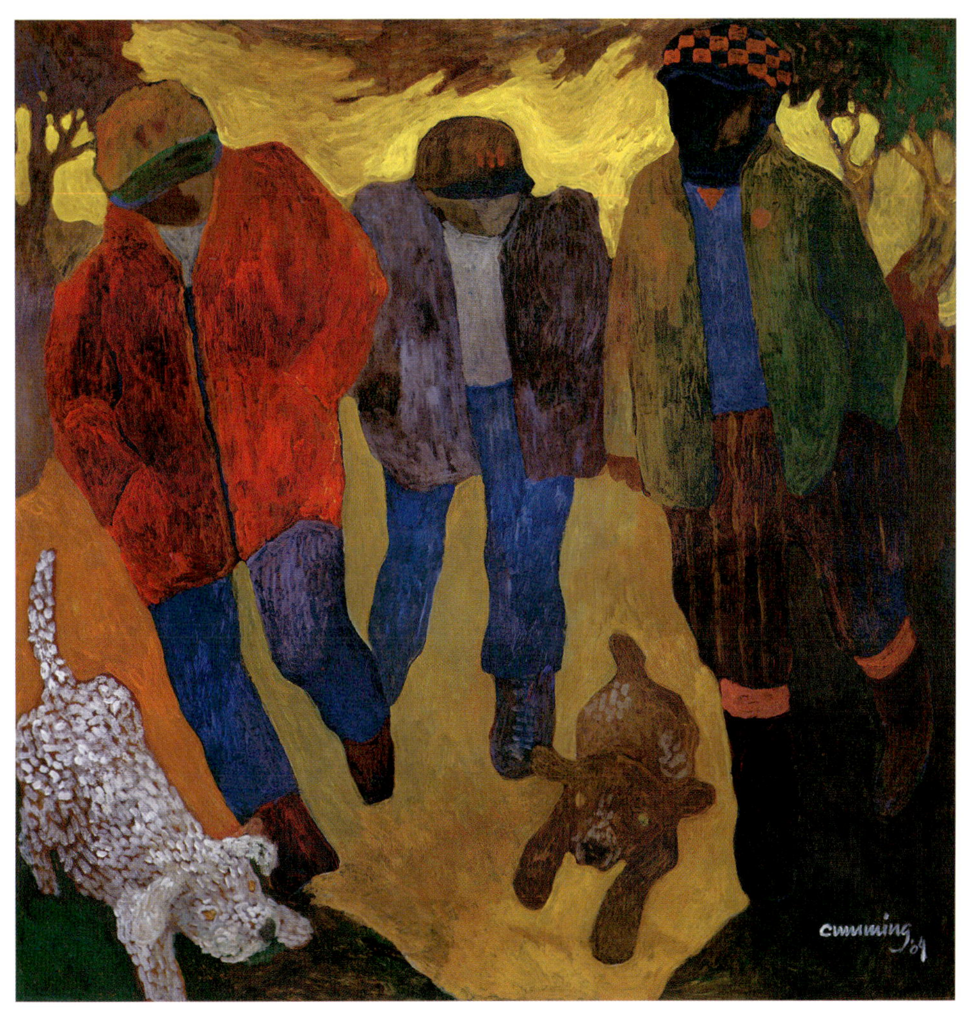

PLATE 77
Walk in the Neighborhood, 2004
Oil and tempera on masonite
44 x 44
Collection of the artist; courtesy of
Gordon Woodside / John Braseth Gallery

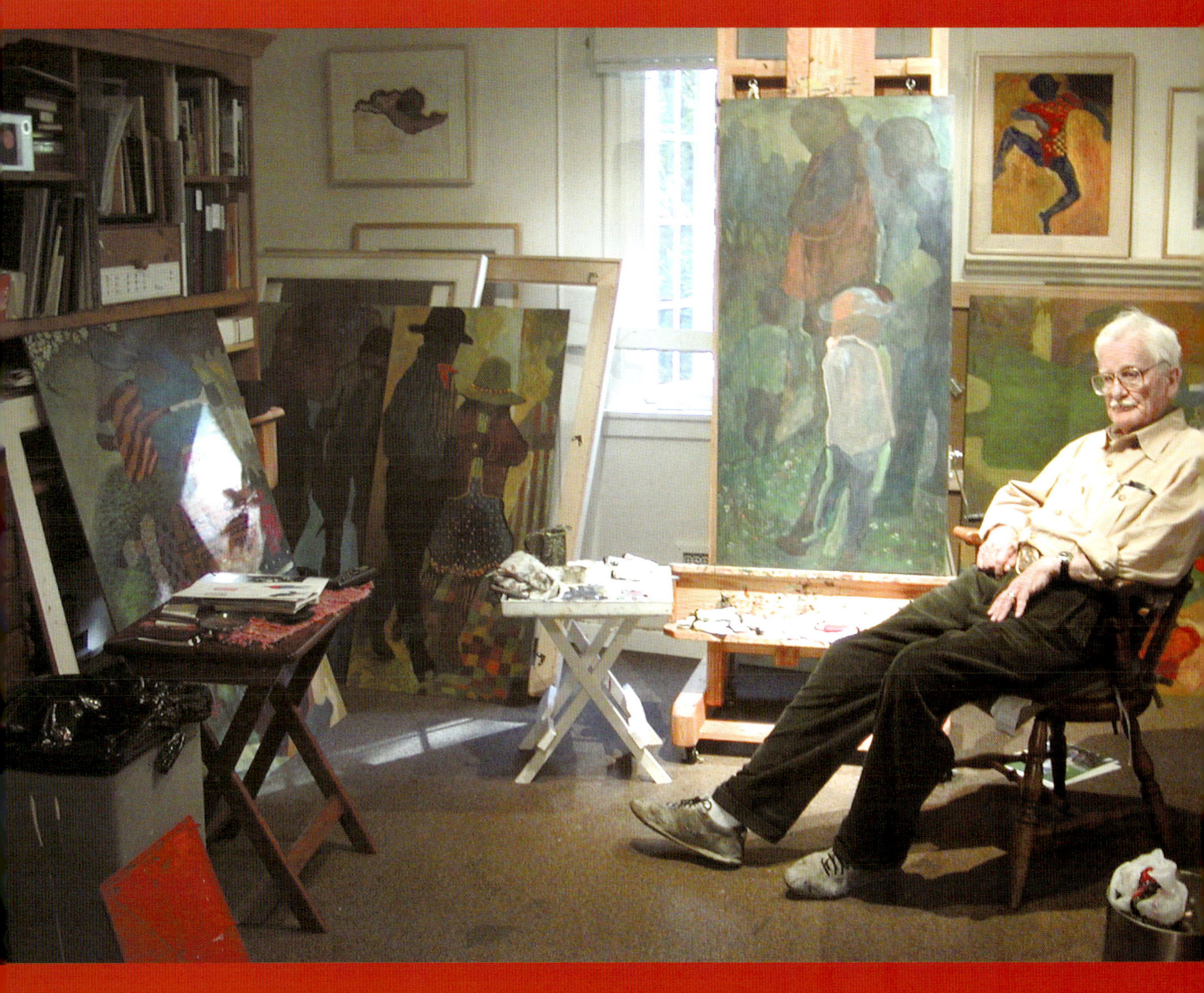

CHRONOLOGY, EXHIBITIONS, AND COLLECTIONS

Biography

Born William Lee Cumming, March 24, 1917, to parents James Rutherford Cumming (1882–1959) and mother, Helen Dorcas Edmiston (1892–1942). Brother to siblings James Francis Cumming (1910–34) and Sarah Elizabeth Cumming (1923–88). Married to Virginia Werst, 1938–39; Virginia Hoyt, 1941–45; Dorothy Elaine Sorenson Loft (1925–72), 1947–55; Clyde Carter (1919–86), 1958–60; Roxanne Johnston, 1961–64; Suzanne Kruger, 1965–84; Dena Lee, 1987–present. Children: Kevin James Woods (b. 1941); Phillip Cumming Arnautoff (b. 1947); Claudia Ann Cumming (b. 1949); Karen Irene Cumming (b. 1950); and Hugh Edmiston Cumming (b. 1961).

Education

Creston Grade School, Portland, Oregon, 1922–24

Tukwila Grade School, Tukwila, Washington, 1924–28

International Correspondence School, 1927

Valedictorian, Foster High School, Tukwila, Washington, 1934

Northwest Academy of Art, Seattle, 1934–35

National Youth Administration, U.S. Government, 1934–36

Works Progress Administration, U.S. Government, 1936–38

Federal Art Project, U.S. Government, 1938–39

Burnley School of Professional Art, studies with Nikolas Damascus, 1948

Teaching Experience

Burnley School of Art, Seattle [1953–], 1961–81

Cornish College of the Arts, 1962–85

Art Institute of Seattle, 1982–present

Awards and Honors

1991 King County Arts Commission Honors Award, Seattle

1965 First Prize, Cellar Gallery open exhibition

1964 First Prize, Cellar Gallery open exhibition

1963 Purchase recommendation, "49th Annual Exhibition of Northwest Artists," Seattle Art Museum

1962 First Prize, "Third Annual Exhibition of Religious Painting and Sculpture," Seattle University Art League

Honorable Mention, Pacific Northwest Arts and Crafts Fair

1961 Honorable Mention, "Puget Sound Area Exhibition," Charles and Emma Frye Art Museum

1960 Honorable Mention, Pacific Northwest Arts and Crafts Fair

First Prize, "Puget Sound Area Exhibition," Charles and Emma Frye Art Museum

Purchase Prize, "Puget Sound Invitational," Charles and Emma Frye Art Museum

1959 Honorable Mention, Pacific Northwest Arts and Crafts Fair

1958 Purchase Prize, Pacific Northwest Arts and Crafts Fair

1947 Honorable Mention and Purchase, "33rd Annual Exhibition of Northwest Artists," Seattle Art Museum

1946 Music and Art Foundation Purchase Prize in Watercolor, Tempera or Gouache, "32nd Annual Exhibition of Northwest Artists," Seattle Art Museum

1942 Honorable Mention in Watercolor, Tempera or Gouache, "28th Annual Exhibition of Northwest Artists," Seattle Art Museum

1940 Seattle Art Museum Purchase Prize in Watercolor, "26th Annual Exhibition of Northwest Artists," Seattle Art Museum

(facing page)
William Cumming in his studio, Lake Forest Park, Washington, 2003

Selected Solo Exhibitions

2005 "William Cumming: The Image of Consequence," Charles and Emma Frye Art Museum, Seattle

Gordon Woodside/John Braseth Gallery, Seattle

2004 Gordon Woodside/John Braseth Gallery

2002 Gordon Woodside/John Braseth Gallery

2001 Gordon Woodside/John Braseth Gallery

2000 Gordon Woodside/John Braseth Gallery

1998 Gordon Woodside/John Braseth Gallery

1996 Gordon Woodside/John Braseth Gallery

1995 Gordon Woodside/John Braseth Gallery

1994 Gordon Woodside/John Braseth Gallery

1993 Gordon Woodside/John Braseth Gallery

1992 Art Institute of Seattle

1991 Gordon Woodside/John Braseth Gallery

1988 Gordon Woodside/John Braseth Gallery

1987 Gordon Woodside/John Braseth Gallery

1985 Gordon Woodside/John Braseth Gallery

1984 Gordon Woodside/John Braseth Gallery

1983 "William Cumming," Bellevue Art Museum, Bellevue, Washington

1982 Foster/White Gallery, Seattle

1981 Foster/White Gallery

1979 Polly Friedlander Gallery, Seattle

1977 Polly Friedlander Gallery

1975 Polly Friedlander Gallery

1974 Polly Friedlander Gallery

1973 Polly Friedlander Gallery

1972 The Bon Marché National Gallery, Seattle

1971 Polly Friedlander Gallery

Gordon Woodside Gallery, Seattle

1970 Gordon Woodside Gallery

1969 Gordon Woodside Gallery

1968 Gordon Woodside Gallery

1967 Gordon Woodside Gallery

1965 Gordon Woodside Gallery

Image Gallery, Portland, Oregon

1964 Scott Galleries, Seattle

Image Gallery, Portland, Oregon

1963 University Unitarian Church Fine Arts Gallery, Seattle

PANACA Gallery, Bellevue, Washington

1961 Pacific Northwest Arts and Crafts Fair, Bellevue, Washington

Seattle Art Museum

1941 Seattle Art Museum

Selected Group Exhibitions

2001 "Northwest Views: Selections from the SAFECO Collection," Charles and Emma Frye Art Museum, Seattle

2000 "Northwest Masters: Paintings from the Cairncross Collection," Sun Valley Center for the Arts, Sun Valley, Idaho

"Bumberbiennale: Painting 2000," Bumbershoot visual arts exhibition, Olympic Room, Seattle Center, Matthew Kangas, curator

"What It Meant to Be Modern: Seattle Art at Mid-Century," Henry Art Gallery, University of Washington, Sheryl Conkelton and Laura Landau, curators

1980 "William Cumming/Nancy Johnson," Foster/White Gallery

1979 "Northwest Traditions," Seattle Art Museum, Charles Cowles and Sarah Clark, curators

1976 "Burnley Faculty Show," Charles and Emma Frye Art Museum

1974 "Art of the Pacific Northwest: From the 1930s to the Present," National Collection of Fine Arts, Smithsonian Institution, Washington, D.C., Martha Kingsbury and Rachael Griffin, curators

1970 "Burnley School of Professional Art Exhibit by Faculty," Charles and Emma Frye Art Museum

1966 Portland Art Museum, Portland, Oregon

"Governor's Invitational," State Capital Museum, Olympia, Washington

"52nd Annual Exhibition of Northwest Artists," Seattle Art Museum

1965 "Governor's Invitational," State Capital Museum, Olympia, Washington

1964 Pacific Northwest Arts and Crafts Fair, Bellevue, Washington

"50th Annual Exhibition of Northwest Artists," Seattle Art Museum

1963 "Fifth Annual Puget Sound Area Exhibition," Charles and Emma Frye Art Museum, Roland Hurd, juror

"Ninth Annual West Coast Oil Paintings," Charles and Emma Frye Art Museum, Ebba Rapp McLauchlan, juror

"Invitational," Henry Art Gallery, University of Washington, T. Gervais Reed, curator

Pacific Northwest Arts and Crafts Fair, Bellevue

"49th Annual Exhibition of Northwest Artists," Seattle Art Museum

1962 "Puget Sound Area Exhibition," Charles and Emma Frye Art Museum

"Eighth Annual West Coast Oil Paintings Exhibition," Charles and Emma Frye Art Museum, Ernest Norling and Arne Jensen, jurors

"Northwest Art Today," Century 21 Exposition, Inc., Seattle World's Fair Exhibition Hall, Millard R. Rogers, curator

"Invitational," Henry Art Gallery, University of Washington, T. Gervais Reed, curator

Pacific Northwest Arts and Crafts Fair, Bellevue

"48th Annual Exhibition of Northwest Artists," Seattle Art Museum

1961 "Third Puget Sound Area Exhibition," Charles and Emma Frye Art Museum

"Seventh Annual West Coast Oil Painting Exhibition," Charles and Emma Frye Art Museum, Fletcher Martin, juror

"Invitational," Henry Art Gallery, University of Washington, T. Gervais Reed, curator

Pacific Northwest Arts and Crafts Fair, Bellevue

"47th Annual Exhibition of Northwest Artists," Seattle Art Museum

1960 "Puget Sound Invitational," Charles and Emma Frye Art Museum

"Puget Sound Area Exhibition," Charles and Emma Frye Art Museum, Lisel Salzer, Arne Jensen, and Ernest Norling, jurors

Pacific Northwest Arts and Crafts Fair, Bellevue

"46th Annual Exhibition of Northwest Artists," Seattle Art Museum

"Invitational," Henry Art Gallery, University of Washington

1959 "First Annual Puget Sound Area Exhibition," Charles and Emma Frye Art Museum, Percy Manser, Ebba Rapp McLauchlan, and Roy Terry, jurors

Pacific Northwest Arts and Crafts Fair, Bellevue

"Invitational," Henry Art Gallery, University of Washington

1958 Pacific Northwest Arts and Crafts Fair, Bellevue

1956 "Governor's Invitational," State Capital Museum, Olympia, Washington, Richard E. Fuller, curator

"Washington State Governor's Invitational," Kobe Municipal Art Museum, Kobe, Japan, Richard E. Fuller, curator

1948 "34th Annual Exhibition of Northwest Artists," Seattle Art Museum, Carl Morris, Rudolph Bundas, Everett DuPen, and Opal Fleckenstein, jurors

1947 "33rd Annual Exhibition of Northwest Artists," Seattle Art Museum, David McCosh, Guy Irving Anderson, Andrew Hofmeister, and Roy Terry, jurors

1946 "32nd Annual Exhibition of Northwest Artists," Seattle Art Museum, William Givler, Dale Goss, Harris K. Prior, and Elizabeth Willis, jurors

1944 "30th Annual Exhibition of Northwest Artists," Seattle Art Museum, Worth Griffin, James FitzGerald, Halley Savery, and Bernard Geiser, jurors

1943 "29th Annual Exhibition of Northwest Artists," Seattle Art Museum

1942 "28th Annual Exhibition of Northwest Artists," Seattle Art Museum, Franz Brasz, Frederick Adams, Jean Johanson, and Ambrose Patterson, jurors

1941 "27th Annual Exhibition of Northwest Artists," Seattle Art Museum

1940 "26th Annual Exhibition of Northwest Artists," Seattle Art Museum, Robert Tyler Davis, Margaret Camfferman, George Laisner, and Carl Morris, jurors

1939 "25th Annual Exhibition of Northwest Artists," Seattle Art Museum, David McCosh, Franz Baum, Worth Griffin, and Mark Tobey, jurors

1938 "24th Annual Exhibition of Northwest Artists," Seattle Art Museum

Selected Public Collections

A. E. I. Music
The Alhadeff Family, Longacres Collection
Amgen, Inc.
Archives of Northwest Art
Bank of America
Betts, Patterson and Mines, P.S.
Birmingham, Thorson and Barnett, P.S.
The Boeing Company, Chicago, Illinois
Cairncross and Hempelmann, P.S.
Cancer Consultants, Ketchum, Idaho
Centris
Charles and Emma Frye Art Museum
Foster High School, Tukwila, Washington
Henry Art Gallery, University of Washington
Lowell Elementary School, Seattle Public Schools
Mayor's Office of Arts & Cultural Affairs, City of Seattle
Merrill Lynch
Minor and James Medical
Moore Financial, Boise, Idaho
Museum of Northwest Art
Northshore Senior Center
Northwest Museum of Arts & Culture
PACCAR, Inc.
Peasley Ross and Co.
People's Bank, Lynden, Washington
The Polyclinic
Portland Art Museum
Preston, Gates and Ellis, L.L.P.
Providence Hospital
Raisbeck Engineering
SAFECO Insurance Companies
Seattle Art Museum
Seattle Tennis Club
Sheraton Seattle Hotel and Towers
Swedish Medical Center
Tacoma Art Museum
University of Washington Allen Library Manuscripts Collection
US Bank
Westin Hotel
Whatcom Museum of History & Art

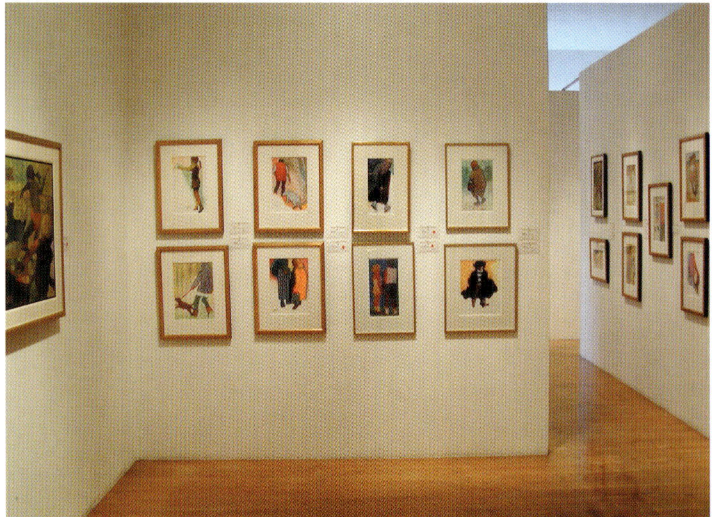

Installation, "William Cumming," Gordon Woodside/John Braseth Gallery exhibition, Seattle, 2002.

CHECKLIST OF THE EXHIBITION

Height precedes width precedes depth.
All dimensions are in inches; all artworks are framed unless otherwise noted.

Untitled (Female Figure), 1935
Gouache on paper
17 1/4 x 11
Collection of B. T. Callahan
FIG. 7

Near Twelfth and Yesler, 1938
Gouache on board
9 x 13
Collection of B. T. Callahan
FIG. 2

Two-Story House, 1938
Tempera on board
17 3/4 x 22
Private collection, Seattle
PLATE 1

Lubin Petric, 1938
[and *William Cumming* by Lubin Petric, 1938]
Ink on paper
21 1/2 x 29 1/2
Collection of the artist

Untitled #1 (Worker Series), 1939
Ink and watercolor on brown paper
7 3/4 x 10 1/2
Courtesy of Mr. and Mrs. Robert M. Sarkis

Skidroad Group, c. 1940
Tempera on board
Unframed: 14 7/8 x 19 5/8
Seattle Art Museum 41.45
Eugene Fuller Memorial Collection
PLATE 4

Untitled (Man Reaching for Cigarette), c. 1940
Tempera on board
Unframed: 10 1/4 x 15
Museum of Northwest Art 1999.59.011
Bequest of James Odlin
PLATE 2

Worker Lifting a Rock, 1940
Tempera on board
27 3/4 x 37 1/2
Seattle Art Museum 40.71
Seattle Art Museum Purchase Prize in Watercolor
FIG. 17

Worker Resting, 1941
Tempera on board
Unframed: 15 x 19 3/4
Seattle Art Museum 41.44
Eugene Fuller Memorial Collection
PLATE 3

Black Man in Overcoat, 1943
Ink and watercolor on paper
6 1/4 x 3 1/2
Collection of B. T. Callahan
PLATE 7

Policeman and Citizen #1, 1943
Ink and watercolor on paper
6 1/4 x 3 1/2
Collection of B. T. Callahan
FIG. 12

Policeman and Citizen #2, 1943
Ink and watercolor on paper
3 1/2 x 6 1/4
Collection of B. T. Callahan

Reclining Homeless Person, 1943
Ink and watercolor on paper
6 1/4 x 3 1/2
Collection of B. T. Callahan
FIG. 10

Two Homeless Men, c. 1943
Ink and watercolor on paper
6 1/4 x 3 1/2
Collection of B. T. Callahan
FIG. 11

Working Girl #1, 1943
Ink and watercolor on paper
6 1/4 x 3 1/2
Collection of B. T. Callahan
FIG. 18

Working Girl with John, 1943
Ink and watercolor on paper
6 1/4 x 3 1/2
Collection of B. T. Callahan
PLATE 6

Working Girl #3, 1943
Ink and watercolor on paper
6 1/4 x 3 1/2
Collection of B. T. Callahan
PLATE 5

Working Girl #4, 1943
Ink and watercolor on paper
6 1/4 x 3 1/2
Collection of B. T. Callahan

Workman, 1943
Gouache on board
20 x 15
Collection of B. T. Callahan
FIG. 1

Spokane Backyard, 1943
Gouache on composition board
14 1/2 x 17 1/2
Collection of the Northwest Museum of Arts & Culture, 3921.1
Eastern Washington State Historical Society, Spokane
Gift of Glenn and Judith Mason and Museum Purchase
Works from the Heart Acquisition Fund, 1999
FIG. 20

Two Loggers, 1944
Tempera on board
23 3/8 x 15 1/2
Seattle Art Museum 46.207
32nd Annual Exhibition of Northwest Artists Purchase Prize
Music and Art Foundation
FIG. 15

Planting the Flare, 1945
Gouache on board
30 1/2 x 25 1/8
Seattle Art Museum 47.156
Eugene Fuller Memorial Collection
PLATE 8

Cyclist, 1955
Oil on panel
40 x 27 1/2
Tom Robbins, La Conner
FIG. 19

Untitled (Female Figure—Bending Over), 1956
Ink and wash on paper
Unframed: 5 3/4 x 4
Museum of Northwest Art
2004.138.102
Blair and Lucille Kirk Collection
FIG. 23

Untitled (Female Figure—Hand Touching Floor), c.1956
Ink and gouache on paper
Unframed: 5 3/4 x 4
Museum of Northwest Art
2004.138.101
Blair and Lucille Kirk Collection
FIG. 24

Untitled (Female Figure—Arms at Sides), c. 1956
Ink and gouache on paper
Unframed: 5 3/4 x 4
Museum of Northwest Art
2004.138.104
Blair and Lucille Kirk Collection
FIG. 27

Woman with Earrings, 1957
Ink on paper
21 1/2 x 17
Collection of Martin Selig
PLATE 9

Woman Wearing Glasses in Coat with Umbrella, 1957
Ink on paper
9 x 6
Collection of Martin Selig
PLATE 14

Woman in Dark Dress Carrying Purse, 1958
Ink on paper
8 3/8 x 5 1/8
Collection of Martin Selig
PLATE 16

Woman in Pink Coat, 1958
Ink and watercolor
8 1/4 x 5 1/2
Collection of Martin Selig
PLATE 15

Woman with Bun in Full-length Profile Carrying Purse, 1959
Ink on paper
7 1/2 x 4 3/4
Collection of Martin Selig
PLATE 17

The Child, l958
Oil on masonite
37 5/8 x 17 3/8
Tacoma Art Museum 1998.26.21
Gift of Bellevue Art Museum
PLATE 11

Nude, 1958
Ink and wash on paper
14 1/4 x 16 1/4
Whatcom Museum of History & Art, Bellingham, Washington
Gift of Virginia Wright Fund, 1976.48.6
PLATE 10

Back of Woman in Belted, Collared Coat, 1959
Inks on paper
7 5/8 x 4 3/4
Collection of Martin Selig
PLATE 18

Boy on Stilts, 1959
Oil and tempera on board
65 x 23 1/2
Collection of Fredda and Steven Goldfarb
FIG. 29

Swimmers, 1959
Ink on paper
Unframed: 7 3/8 x 4 3/4
Henry Art Gallery, University of Washington 2004.122
Gift from the Estates of Dorothee and Mitchell Taylor Bowie
PLATE 12

Woman with Striped Top in Coat with Pants, 1959
Inks on paper
8 x 4 3/4
Collection of Martin Selig

Untitled (Running Female Figure), 1959
Ink and wash on paper
Unframed: 5 3/4 x 4
Museum of Northwest Art
2004.138.015
Blair and Lucille Kirk Collection
FIG. 25

Untitled (Seated Female Figure), 1959
Ink and wash on paper
Unframed: 5 3/4 x 4
Museum of Northwest Art
2004.138.100
Blair and Lucille Kirk Collection
FIG. 26

Untitled (Crouching Female Figure), 1959
Ink and wash on paper
Unframed: 5 3/4 x 4
Museum of Northwest Art
2004.138.103
Blair and Lucille Kirk Collection
FIG. 28

Back of Woman with Striped Coat, 1960
Inks on paper
10 x 7
Collection of Martin Selig
PLATE 19

Five Working Men, 1960-64
Mixed media on paper
20 1/4 x 24
Private collection, Seattle
PLATES 20–24

The Sisters, 1960
Oil and tempera on masonite
36 x 48
Collection of Philip and Mary Serka
FIG. 30

Two Girls, 1960
Oil and tempera on board
34 1/2 x 22 1/4
Charles and Emma Frye Art Museum
1960.014
Purchase Prize from First Invitational Exhibition by Puget Sound Artists

Untitled (Man Carrying Boxes), 1960
Umber ink on page of German medical text
Unframed: 10 1/2 x 7
Museum of Northwest Art
1992.014.001
Bequest of James Faber
PLATE 25

Untitled (Man Reading Newspaper), 1960
Ink and felt tip pen on paper
12 1/4 x 9 3/4
Museum of Northwest Art
2004.039.004
Blair and Lucille Kirk Collection
PLATE 26

The Little Nun, 1961
Ink and wash on paper
13 1/2 x 10 1/2
Whatcom Museum of History & Art, Bellingham, Washington
Gift of Virginia Wright Fund, 1976.48.7
PLATE 27

Journey to the End of Night, 1962
Tempera on masonite
48 x 48
Henry Art Gallery, University of Washington 2004.121
Gift from the Estates of Dorothee and Mitchell Taylor Bowie
PLATE 29

Mother and Child at the Zoo, 1962
Oil and tempera on panel
47 x 30
Mr. and Mrs. John Behnke Collection
PLATE 30

Old Joe (Issei Merchant), 1962
Colored pencil on cardboard
14 x 10
Collection of the artist
PLATE 28

Untitled (Girl Walking with Dog), 1962
Tempera on cardboard
Unframed: 14 1/2 x 10
Henry Art Gallery, University of Washington 2004.123
Gift from the Estates of Dorothee and Mitchell Taylor Bowie

Boy on Merry-Go-Round, 1963
Paint on German-language book paper
12 x 8 1/2
Mr. and Mrs. John Behnke Collection
PLATE 32

Figure, 1963
Ink and tempera on paper
10 1/2 x 8 1/2
Collection of the artist
PLATE 34

Girl, 1963
Bronze
4 h.
Private collection, Bellevue

Little Girl, 1963
Ink and pencil on paper
4 1/2 x 5 1/2
Collection of Philip and Mary Serka
PLATE 31

Untitled (Little Nun), c. 1963
Bronze
7 1/4 x 3 x 3
Museum of Northwest Art
2004.138.073
Blair and Lucille Kirk Collection
PLATE 33

Sketchbook Study: Beach Figures, 1964
Graphite and polymer on paper
Unframed: 20 x 16
Museum of Northwest Art
2003.126.013
Gift of Dr. David and Beverly Christie
PLATE 35

Drinking Fountain, 1965
Graphite on paper
12 1/2 x 9 3/4
Courtesy of Gordon Woodside / John Braseth Gallery

Girl with Outstretched Arms, 1965
Mixed media on paper
19 x 16 1/2
Mr. and Mrs. John Behnke Collection
PLATE 36

Bag Lady, Jan. 11, 1966, 1966
Ink on newsprint
36 x 24
Lowell Elementary School
Seattle Public Schools

Nude, 1966
Ink on paper
10 1/4 x 6
Mr. and Mrs. Devitt Barnett
PLATE 37

Untitled (Hatted Man with Polka-dot Shirt), 1966
Pencil and watercolor on paper
Unframed: 5 1/4 x 3 1/2
Museum of Northwest Art
2004.039.001
Gift of Simon and Carol Ottenberg

Cyclists, 1967
Oil and tempera on masonite
25 x 23
Collection of Fredda and Steven Goldfarb
PLATE 38

The Trojan Women, 1967
Oil on masonite
36 x 48
Collection of Lucy and Herb Pruzan
PLATE 39

Three Kids, 1968
Oil on masonite
22 x 36
Portland Art Museum 86.705
Gift of Sandra Stone Peters
PLATE 40

Homage to Renoir, 1969
Oil and tempera on board
17 x 20 1/2
Private collection, Seattle
PLATE 41

Little Boy on Parade, 1969
Ink and pencil on paper
17 1/2 x 15
Courtesy of Gordon Woodside / John Braseth Gallery
FIG. 35

Boy on Dock, 1970
Oil and tempera on board
25 x 19
Collection of Mr. and Mrs. Alvin Goldfarb
PLATE 42

Three Boys, 1970
Oil and tempera on board
21 x 15 3/4
City of Seattle, Mayor's Office of Arts & Cultural Affairs
Portable Works Collection CL03.003
FIG. 5

Young Skier, 1971
Watercolor on paper
14 x 21
Museum of Northwest Art 2004.142.02
The Catterall Collection
PLATE 43

Cast a Cold Eye, 1973
Oil and tempera on masonite
48 x 48
Collection of the artist
PLATE 44

Cutting Horse II, 1974
Oil and tempera on masonite
14 3/4 x 19 3/4
Courtesy of Mr. and Mrs. Robert M. Sarkis
FIG. 6

Rope Them In, 1974
Oil and tempera on board
35 1/2 x 48
The Estate of Edward M. Winskill
PLATE 45

Driving Cattle, 1975
Oil and tempera on board
20 x 27
City of Seattle, Seattle City Light 1% for Art CL76.009
FIG. 36

Poco Bueno Cutting, 1975
Oil and tempera on board
17 x 20
City of Seattle, Mayor's Office of Arts & Cultural Affairs
Portable Works Collection CL76.010

Snapshot—Boy with Dog 1922, 1976
Oil and tempera on board
20 1/2 x 16 3/4
Private collection, Bellevue
FIG. 39

Conversation in the Hayfield, 1977
Oil and tempera on board
36 x 48
The Estate of Edward M. Winskill
PLATE 46

Structural Steel Shop, 1978
Oil and tempera on masonite quadriptych
48 x 120
Preston, Gates and Ellis, L.L.P.
FIG. 40

Crucifixion, 1980
Bronze
13 x 7 x 8
Collection of the artist
PLATE 47

Cutting Horse, 1980
Oil and tempera on masonite
49 x 36 3/4
SAFECO Insurance Companies

Poet at Big Sur (Homage to Robinson Jeffers), 1980
Oil and tempera on board
35 1/2 x 35 1/2
Charles and Emma Frye Art Museum MA(G)585
Anonymous Gift

Stretch Run I, 1980
Oil and tempera on masonite
49 1/2 x 62
The Alhadeff Family, Longacres Collection
PLATE 48

The Watchers, 1980
Oil and tempera on board
34 7/8 x 29
Collection of Sheraton Seattle Hotel and Towers
PLATE 50

Cutting the Cow, 1981
Oil and tempera on masonite
41 3/4 x 52 1/2
SAFECO Insurance Companies

Figure on Horseback, 1981
Pencil on paper
17 x 16
Mr. and Mrs. John Behnke Collection
PLATE 56

Madama Butterfly, 1982
Color lithograph poster, limited edition
37 x 23
Mr. and Mrs. John Behnke Collection
PLATE 51

Inherit the Wind, 1982
Color lithograph poster, limited edition
36 x 28
Mr. and Mrs. John Behnke Collection

Rider on Horseback with Cattle, 1982
Pencil on paper
19 x 25
Mr. and Mrs. John Behnke Collection
PLATE 54

Girl of the Golden West, 1982
Color lithograph poster, limited edition
37 x 23
Mr. and Mrs. John Behnke Collection
PLATE 53

Figure on Horseback Galloping, 1983
Pencil on paper
14 1/2 x 17
Mr. and Mrs. John Behnke Collection
PLATE 55

Chinese Horse, 1984
Mixed media on paper
Unframed: 11 1/2 x 7
Museum of Northwest Art
1987.018.002
Gift of Art Hupy

Return of Odysseus (Tribute to Nikos Kazantzakis), 1984
Oil and tempera on board
47 1/2 x 59 1/2
Museum of Northwest Art
1992.027.001
Gift of Marshall and Helen Hatch
FIG. 48

My Garden, 1984
Oil and tempera on board
36 x 48
Collection of Swedish Medical Center
FIG. 46

Belshazzar's Feast, 1985–88
Oil and tempera on masonite
52 x 100
Collection of the artist; courtesy of Gordon Woodside / John Braseth Gallery
FIG. 49

Spokesong, 1985
Color lithograph poster, limited edition
37 x 23
Mr. and Mrs. John Behnke Collection
PLATE 52

Reclining Nude with Poetry Excerpts, 1987
Mixed media on paper
29 3/4 x 22
Collection of the artist
PLATE 57

Self-Portrait, 1988
Oil and tempera on masonite
36 3/4 x 24
Collection of Dr. and Mrs. Chester Woodside
FIG. 43

Watercolor Number 11, 1988
Watercolor on paper
21 x 17
Collection of Dr. and Mrs. Chester Woodside

Girl with Bracelet and High Heels, 1989
Watercolor and pencil on paper
18 3/4 x 16 3/4
Collection of the artist

Old Lady with Barking Dog, 1989
Watercolor on illustration board
9 x 10
Collection of Annette Bauman
PLATE 58

Goyescas #1 (After Goya), 1991
Oil and tempera on card
18 x 19
Collection of the artist
PLATE 59

Cowboy, 1992
Oil and tempera on masonite
54 1/2 x 42 1/2
SAFECO Insurance Companies
PLATE 60

Triptych, 1992
Oil and tempera on three masonite panels
55 x 42, 55 x 55, 55 x 42
4 Culture and King County Public Art Collection
King County Arts Commission Honors Award
PLATE 61

Reverie, 1994
Oil and tempera on masonite
27 x 21
Mr. and Mrs. Devitt Barnett
PLATE 62

Acrobat at Golden Gardens, 1995
Oil and tempera on masonite
46 x 45 1/2
Private collection of Cairncross & Hempelmann, P.S.
PLATE 63

Old Man in the Market, 1995
Bronze
12 h.
Collection of Lucy and Herb Pruzan
PLATE 65

Left-Handed Baseball Pitcher, 1996
Oil and tempera on masonite
30 1/2 x 30 1/2
Collection of Dr. and Mrs. Chester Woodside
PLATE 64

Dream, 1998
Oil and tempera on masonite
54 1/2 x 42 1/2
Collection of the artist
PLATE 66

Dream, 1998
Oil and tempera on masonite
55 x 43
Private collection, Bellevue
FIG. 44

Checkered Shirt, 1999
Mixed media on paper
17 1/2 x 12
Courtesy of Gordon Woodside / John Braseth Gallery
PLATE 67

Man on a Bike, 2000
Mixed media on paper
33 1/2 x 27 1/4
Collection of Sandy and Ron Ryder
PLATE 68

Untitled (Memory of Muriel), 2000
Oil on canvas
27 1/8 x 21 1/4
Tacoma Art Museum 2000.40
Gift of Gene and Liz Brandzel

A Day at the Beach, 2001
Oil and tempera on board
55 x 55
Collection of Lea Anne and Randy Ottinger

Carlos and the Fishes, 2001
Oil and tempera on board
55 x 43
Steve Clayton Collection
PLATE 69

Girl with Chemise, 2001
Oil and tempera on paper
21 x 12
Mr. and Mrs. John Behnke Collection

Juggler, 2002
Tempera on paper
23 x 18
Collection of the artist; courtesy of Gordon Woodside / John Braseth Gallery
PLATE 70

Pose, 2002
Mixed media on paper
22 x 14 1/2
Collection of the artist; courtesy of Gordon Woodside / John Braseth Gallery
PLATE 71

Two Boys Diving, 2002
Oil and tempera on masonite
23 1/2 x 18 1/2
Private collection, Seattle

Girl in White Dress, 2003
Mixed media on paper
22 1/2 x 16
Collection of the artist; courtesy of Gordon Woodside / John Braseth Gallery

Evening Snow, 2003
Oil and tempera on board
56 x 38
Collection of Douglas and Ann Williams
PLATE 72

At the Park, 2004
Oil and tempera on masonite
56 1/4 x 38
Collection of the artist; courtesy of Gordon Woodside / John Braseth Gallery
PLATE 74

Generations, 2004
Oil and tempera on masonite
56 1/4 x 56 1/4
Collection of the artist; courtesy of Gordon Woodside / John Braseth Gallery
PLATE 76

Red Shoes, 2004
Oil and tempera on masonite
56 1/4 x 32
Private collection, Seattle
PLATE 75

Windy, 2004
Oil and tempera on masonite
56 1/4 x 38
Collection of the artist; courtesy of Gordon Woodside / John Braseth Gallery
PLATE 73

Additional Works

JOSEF SCAYLEA (American, 1913–2004): *William Cumming*, 1963
Black and white silver print photograph
14 x 10.
Collection of William Cumming
Courtesy of Josef Scaylea Photography, LLC

DAVID HOWE (American): *William Cumming*, c. 1980.
Black and white silver print photograph
12 x 10
Collection of William Cumming
FIG. 42

JIM BALL (American, b. 1947): *William Cumming*, 1997
Black and white silver print photograph
10 x 10
Courtesy of Jim Ball Photo

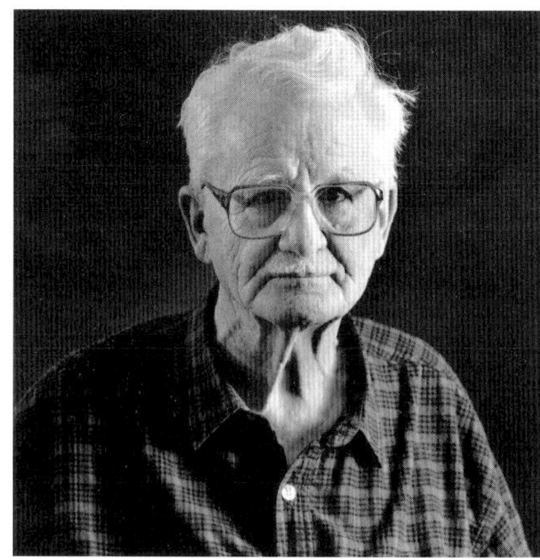

JIM BALL (American, b. 1947): *William Cumming*, 1997. Black and white silver print photograph, 10 x 10.

LENDERS

The Alhadeff Family
Mr. and Mrs. Charles Andonian
Mr. and Mrs. Devitt Barnett
Annette Bauman
Mr. and Mrs. John Behnke
Cairncross & Hempelmann, P.S.
Mr. and Mrs. Brian T. Callahan
Steve Clayton
William and Dena Cumming
4 Culture and King County Public Art Collection
Charles and Emma Frye Art Museum
Marshall and Helen Hatch
Mr. and Mrs. Alvin Goldfarb
Fredda and Steven Goldfarb
Henry Art Gallery, University of Washington
Lowell Elementary School, Seattle Public Schools
The Mayor's Office of Arts & Cultural Affairs, City of Seattle
Museum of Northwest Art
Jeanne-Marie Musto
Northwest Museum of Arts and Culture
Lea Anne and Randy Ottinger
Portland Art Museum
Preston, Gates and Ellis, L.L.P.
Lucy and Herb Pruzan
Tom Robbins
Sandy and Ron Ryder
SAFECO Insurance Companies
Mr. and Mrs. Robert M. Sarkis
Seattle Art Museum
Martin Selig
Sheraton Seattle Hotel and Towers
Philip and Mary Serka
Swedish Medical Center
Tacoma Art Museum
Whatcom Museum of History and Art
Douglas and Ann Williams
The Estate of Edward M. Winskill
Dr. and Mrs. Chester Woodside
Gordon Woodside / John Braseth Gallery

SELECTED BIBLIOGRAPHY

Books and Articles

Ament, Deloris Tarzan. "Art on the Town." *Seattle Times*, November 3, 1988, H5.

———. "William Cumming Shows He's Still a Good Draw." *Seattle Times*, March 8, 1990, F5.

———. "Cumming Show: A Light Touch." *Seattle Times*, March 18, 1993, F2.

———. "Work by Great Northwest Artists is Right at Home in La Conner Museum." *Seattle Times*, May 30, 1993, 9, F8.

———. "William Cumming: 'The Willie Nelson of Northwest Painting.'" In Ament, *Iridescent Light: The Emergence of Northwest Art*. Seattle: University of Washington Press, 2002, 165–81.

Anderson, C. L. "Seattle's Artist 'Of the People.'" *Seattle Times Pictorial*, April 9, 1961, 50–55.

Armstrong, Roma. "Seattle Art Museum Holds Fall Opening and Preview." *Seattle Post-Intelligencer*, October 2, 1947, 8.

Batie, Jean. "Woodside Gallery Has Unusual 'Op.'" *Seattle Times*, July 9, 1967, 40.

———. "Old Lady Missed Bus, But Cumming Didn't." *Seattle Times*, June 14, 1968, 21.

———. "Little Gallery Shows Big Northwest Talent." *Seattle Times*, August 16, 1968, 31.

———. "Cumming's Comments Human as His Art." *Seattle Times*, July 2, 1969, 66.

"Bill Cumming/Finding Himself in the Past." *Seattle Times*, March 14, 1982, G1, 8.

Braun, Suzanne. "The Great Courtroom Hassle that Made History Here: Did He Slander? Did He Plagiarize?" *Seattle Magazine*, March 1965, 6.

Campbell, R. M. "Powerful William Cumming Exhibit." *Seattle Post-Intelligencer*, March 27, 1977, G7.

———. "Northwest School Exhibit Misses Mark." *Seattle Post-Intelligencer*, December 24, 1978, F6.

———. "Realism Is Strength of Cumming's Work." *Seattle Post-Intelligencer*, March 24, 1982, 12.

Conant, Michael. "Era of Great Local Artists Comes Alive." *Seattle Post-Intelligencer*, November 10, 1984, C1.

Conkelton, Sheryl. "What It Meant to Be Modern—An Introduction." In *What It Meant to Be Modern: Seattle Art at Mid-Century*, ed. Sheryl Conkelton, Martha Kingsbury, and Laura Landau. Seattle: Henry Art Gallery, University of Washington, 2000, 8.

Cowles, Charles, and Sarah Clark. *Northwest Traditions*. Seattle: Seattle Art Museum, 1978, 76, 91–92.

Davis, Norman, and Millard B. Rogers. *Northwest Art Today*. Seattle: Century 21 Exposition, Inc., 19, 20.

Duncan, Don. "'Old Pro' Conquers New Artistic Field." *Seattle Times*, June 5, 1968, 50.

Faber, Ann. "People Equal Motion in Cumming Paintings." *Seattle Post-Intelligencer*, September 18, 1960, 15.

———. "Lesson of the Human Figure Taught Well." *Seattle Post-Intelligencer*, March 13, 1961, 10.

———. "Four Reasons for Joy in the Art Museum." *Seattle Post-Intelligencer Sunday Pictorial*, March 26, 1961, 7.

———. "Cumming Influence Felt at Exhibition." *Seattle Post-Intelligencer*, November 9, 1964, 9.

Fish, Byron. "Seattle Has Many Artists Versed in Depicting Sports." *Seattle Times*, November 15, 1963.

Godden, Jean. "At 80, He Still Lives for His Art." *Seattle Times*, March 24, 1997, B1.

———. "A Master at Art and the Gibe." *Seattle Times*, November 19, 2001, B1.

Graves, Jen. "Old-School Perspectives: Artists with Ties to the Celebrated Northwest School and Its 'Mystics' Share Thoughts on This Area's Artistic Identity." *Tacoma News-Tribune*, July 23, 2003, D1.

Hackett, Regina. "Folklore It Is; Definitive Art Tome It's Not." *Seattle Post-Intelligencer*, November 10, 1984, C1, 7.

———. "Bellevue's NW Annual Highlights Rising Artists." *Seattle Post-Intelligencer*, July 28, 1995, 17.

———. "Visions of Baseball Glisten in 'Good Eye.'" *Seattle Post-Intelligencer*, July 2, 1999, 14.

———. "Art a Visual Feast to Celebrate Countdown." *Seattle Post-Intelligencer*, September 7, 1999, 20.
———. "Cornish Honors Northwest Artists—Not an Easy Task." *Seattle Post-Intelligencer*, October 4, 1999, E2.
———. "'Modern' Exhibit Avoids Old Quarrels." *Seattle Post-Intelligencer*, October 26, 1999, C1.
———. "Cumming's Vision Only Grows Sharper with Age." *Seattle Post-Intelligencer*, October 26, 2001, 16.
———. "The Frye at 50: 'Five Decades of Collecting' Chronicles the Museum's Changing Tastes within the Context of Its Mission, Realist Art." *Seattle Post-Intelligencer*, February 8, 2002, E1.
———. "Get an Education from Exhibit of Northwest School Artists." *Seattle Post-Intelligencer*, February 22, 2002, 22.
———. "Cumming's Prolific Output Just Gets Better and Better." *Seattle Post-Intelligencer*, May 7, 2004, 20.
Hawthorn, Maggie. "Wm. Cumming at the Beach." *Seattle Post-Intelligencer,* June 3, 1973, Book World, 9.
Hayman, Sally. "For the Love of Art." *Seattle Post-Intelligencer Northwest Today*, June 23, 1968, 18.
Johnsrud, Byron. "'Big City' Flight Leads to Island Delight." *Seattle Times*, September 4, 1966, 16.
Kangas, Matthew. "Book Review: *Sketchbook: A Memoir of the 1930s and the Northwest School.*" *ArtStars*, May 1985, 5, 12–13.
———. "Cumming at 80: Still a Force in the Art World." *Seattle Times*, February 20, 1998, I20.
———. "Better with Age: William Cumming Follows Up 80th Birthday Show with Exhibit Focusing on Leisure, Relationships." *Seattle Times*, November 19, 1998, 20.
Kelleher, Elise. "Profile of An Artist." *Puget Soundings*, January 1962, 14, 19, 31.
Keziere, Russell. "Individualism Assuming the Form of a Tradition." *Vanguard*, November 1978, 13.
Kingsbury, Martha. "Seattle and the Puget Sound." In *Art of the Pacific Northwest: From the 1930s to the Present,* ed. Adelyn Breeskin et al. Washington, D.C.: National Collection of Fine Arts, Smithsonian Institution, 1974, 39–77.
———. "Northwest Art: The Mid-Century Seen from the End of the Century." In *What It Meant to Be Modern: Seattle Art at Mid-Century*, ed. Sheryl Conkelton, Martha Kingsbury, and Laura Landau. Seattle: Henry Art Gallery, University of Washington, 2000, 26, 32, 34, 39.
Lehmann, Thelma. "William Cumming Paintings on View in Area." *Seattle Post-Intelligencer*, October 16, 1963, 12.
Lunzer, Jean Hudson. "An Artist Oasis Far from City Tumult." *Seattle Post-Intelligencer Northwest Today*, n.d., 10–11.
"Museum Exhibit Brings Out Many Art Lovers." *Seattle Post-Intelligencer*, October 3, 1940, 9.
"Northwest Guide." *Seattle Times*, December 17, 1971, July 20, 1972.
"PANACA Art Class Begins Wednesday." *Bellevue American*, September 16, 1963.
Phillips, Margery R. "Art Works Benefit Room Decor." *Seattle Times*, March 5, 1961, Section 5, 12.
"Puget Sound Exhibition Opens at Frye Museum." *Seattle Times*, March 3, 1963, 36.
"Religious Art Works to Be Shown." *Seattle Times*, December 9, 1962, 10.
Robbins, Tom. "Three Sweet Notes and One Sour." *Seattle Times*, May 19, 1963, 35.
———. "Testy Prophet Hits Stride as Major Painter." *Seattle Times*, October 20, 1963, 33.
———. "Husky Touchdown—A Northwest Artist Covers U.W. Football." *Seattle Times Pictorial Magazine*, October 31, 1965, 4–11.
Rogers, Millard B. *William Cumming*. Seattle: Seattle Art Museum, 1961.
Tarzan, Deloris. "The Cumming Thing: Shadow and Mass." *Seattle Times*, June 3, 1973, D1.
———. "Cumming Mounts Impressive Show." *Seattle Times Tempo*, June 28, 1974, 2.
———. "Artists' Shadows Have No Smile." *Seattle Times*, November 23, 1975, A16.
———. "Cumming Paints Tough Images." *Seattle Times*, March 27, 1977, E2.
———. "'Northwest Traditions' Lively." *Seattle Times*, July 9, 1978, L1.
———. "Bill Cumming—Finding Himself in the Past." *Seattle Times*, March 14, 1982, G1, 8.

———. "Sketches of Seattle: Artist's 'Sketchbook' Replays Bohemian Heyday of 'Northwest School.'" *Seattle Times*, November 11, 1984, G1–2.

———. "Sunlight Bathes Artist's New Works." *Seattle Times*, November 22, 1985, 6.

———. "Masters of Canvas/Gallery Openings Celebrate Two of the Northwest School's Leading Lights." *Seattle Times*, March 4, 1987, C1, 8.

"Today's Youngsters Depicted in Mural." *Seattle Times*, May 20, 1963, 2.

Todd, Anne G. "Displays Will Go To Japan." *Seattle Times*, January 26, 1956, 49.

———. "Little Gallery Shows Work of Six Women and Two Men." *Seattle Times*, April 12, 1959, 27.

———. "Roby Exhibition Stresses Conservative Values." *Seattle Times*, March 12, 1961, 33.

———. "Cumming Views a Few Heroes." *Seattle Times*, November 28, 1965, 14S.

———. "Iconoclasm Works Well for Cumming." *Seattle Times*, June 10, 1967.

Voorhees, John. "Cumming Turns to Painting with Success." *Seattle Times*, June 12, 1970, B7.

———. "Cumming's Colorful 'People' Revisited." *Seattle Times*, May 28, 1971.

"Watercolor Prizewinner at Museum." *Seattle Post-Intelligencer*, October 6, 1940.

Wehr, Wesley. *The Eighth Lively Art: Conversations with Painters, Poets, Musicians and The Wicked Witch of the West*. Seattle: University of Washington Press, 2000, 84.

——— *The Accidental Collector: Art, Fossils, and Friendships*. Seattle: University of Washington Press, 2004, 59–60, 70, 80, 88, 144, 147, 157, 187, 202.

Weiner, Ed. "Northwest Artist Tackles Fashion/William Cumming Brings Fine Art to Couture Runway." *Seattle Times*, August 26, 1981, D1.

Selected Writings by and Interviews with the Artist

Cumming, William. "Art." *Town Crier*, July 23–August 5, 1937, 10; October 13, 1937, 12–13; October 20, 1937, 13.

———. "The Foster-Gates Debate: 'New Look' Revisionism vs. 'Old Look' Revisionism." Unpublished manuscript, July 14, 1957 (later attributed by Cumming to Clara Fraser).

———. Letter of Resignation to the Communist Party of Washington State. Unpublished manuscript, July 14, 1957 (later attributed by Cumming to Clara Fraser).

———. "Cumming at Bay." *Seattle Magazine*, May 1964, 6.

——— "Look Back in Laughter." *Puget Soundings*, January 1965, 16–19; 26–27.

——— "Art Students Need Fundamentals." *Seattle Times*, October 10, 1965, S11.

———. "Fragments of a Journal." *Puget Soundings*, June 1966, 20–25.

———. *Sketchbook: A Memoir of the 1930s and the Northwest School*. Seattle: University of Washington Press, 1984.

———. "Notes Regarding 'Peaceful Coexistence.'" Unpublished manuscript, n.d.

"Talking About Art," Bill Cumming and Bert Garner, tape-recorded radio broadcast interview with Jim Wilkie, KING-FM, transcript, Archives of Northwest Art, Allen Library, University of Washington, October 1966, 45 minutes, Accession 2553, Box VF896.

"Whither Goest Cumming?" Interview with Tom Robbins, *Seattle Magazine*, September 1967, 11–16.

"William Cumming." Tape-recorded interview with Bill Hoppe, Archives of Northwest Art, transcript, Allen Library, University of Washington, August 2, 1972.

"A Conversation with Northwest Artist William Cumming." Interview with Joan Mann, *The Arts—Newsletter of the King County Arts Commission*, March 1979, 5.

"A Man's View—Art and the Artist: An Interview with William Cumming." Interview with Jeane Taggard, *SeattleWomen Newsmagazine*, December 1980.

"A Conspiracy of Friends: How the Northwest School Got Its Start Around Morris Graves's Kitchen Table." *Pacific Northwest*, December 1984, 28–31.

"Bill Cumming, Painter: The Story of a Pretty Good Cartoonist." Interview with Billy King, "Artists Express," Seattle Community College Television broadcast, 2002.

"Radical Art: 'Northwest School' Artist Paints the Human Condition." Interview with Brian Kidd, *Madison Park Times*, August 2004, 1, 5.

PHOTOGRAPHIC CREDITS

Jim Ball, Jim Ball Photo: page 154
Annette Bauman: pages 144, 148
Eduardo Calderón: figs. 9, 15, 17, 31; pl. 4
Bill Cannon: pl. 58
William Cumming: pl. 49
Christopher Dahl: fig. 3
Dean Davis: fig. 20
Frank DeSantis: pl. 13
Paul Foster: pl. 40
David Howe: fig. 42
Ron Karabaich, Old Town Photo: pls. 45, 46
Thomas Kelly: figs. 19, 23, 24, 25, 26, 27, 28, 48; pls. 3, 25, 26, 33, 35, 43; page 155
Paul Macapia: figs. 9, 13; pls. 2, 8
Bob Mattherson: figs. 1, 2, 7, 10, 11, 12, 18; pls. 5, 6, 7
Richard Nicol: figs. 4, 6, 21, 22, 29, 32, 33, 34, 35, 39, 40, 41, 43, 44, 46, 49, 51; pls. 1, 9, 12, 14, 15, 16, 17, 18, 19, 20-24, 28, 29, 30, 32, 34, 36, 37, 38, 39, 41, 42, 44, 47, 48, 51, 52, 53, 54, 55, 56, 57, 59, 61, 62, 63, 64, 65, 66, 67, 68, 69, 70, 71, 72, 73, 74, 75, 76, 77; page 146
David Scherrer: fig. 30; pl. 31

Berry-Hill Galleries, New York: fig. 45
Charles and Emma Frye Art Museum: pages 2, 6; fig. 38
City of Seattle Mayor's Office of Arts & Cultural Affairs: figs. 5, 36
Francine Seders Gallery: fig. 14
Photo-Art: fig. 50
Portland Art Museum: figs. 8, 37
SAFECO Insurance Companies: pl. 60
Tacoma Art Museum: pl. 11
Whatcom Museum of History & Art: pl. 27

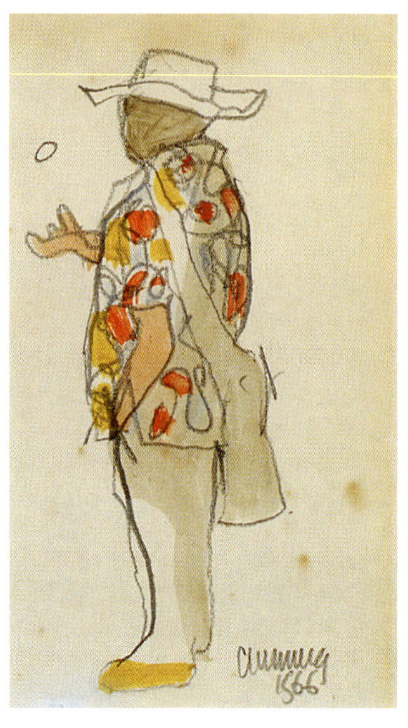